**The Global Business Game:**

# a strategic management and international business simulation

## Player's Manual

**Joseph Wolfe, Ph.D.**
**Experiential Adventures LLC**
Professor Emeritus, University of Tulsa

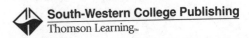

South-Western College Publishing
Thomson Learning

*The Global Business Game: A Strategic Management and International Business Simulation—Player's Manual,* by Joseph Wolfe, Ph.D.

Publisher: Dave Shaut
Executive Editor: John Szilagyi
Media and Technology Editor: Kevin von Gillern
Media Production Editor: Robin Browning
Marketing Manager: Rob Bloom
Production Editor: Kelly Keeler
Manufacturing Coordinator: Dana Schwartz
Production House: Pre-Press Company, Inc.
Printer: West Publishing

Printed in the United States of America
1  2  3  4  5  02  01  00  99

For more information contact South-Western College Publishing, 5101 Madison Road, Cincinnati, Ohio, 45227, or find us on the Internet at http://www.swcollege.com

For permission to use material from this text or product, contact us by
• telephone: 1-800-730-2214
• fax: 1-800-730-2215
• web: http://www.thomsonrights.com

**Library of Congress Cataloguing-in-Publication Data**

Wolfe, Joseph A. (Joseph Allen)
    The global business game: a strategic management and
international business simulation : player's manual / Joseph Wolfe.
        p.   cm.
    Includes bibliographical reference and index.
    ISBN 0-324-00376-5
    1. Management—Study and teaching—Simulation methods.   I. Title.
HD30.4.W65 1999
658.4'0352—dc21
                                                99-17253

This book is printed on acid-free paper

*To my wife, Nancy, who has made possible so many wonderful experiences.*

# Contents

# Table of Exhibits

## 5   Manufacturing Operations   73

## 6   Finance, Financial Markets, and Accounting Operations   89

## 7   Simulation Operations and Playing Procedures   117

# Preface

Globalization and technology are rapidly altering the nature of international business today. The process of developing and making strategic decisions is being continuously changed through the advancement of technology and the sophistication of the global business environment. In the world arena, current economic, political, and technological events play a significant role in how we formulate strategies for both short-and long-term goals.

When we decided to create *The Global Business Game,* we recognized the immense challenges that the fast-paced business world of today presents. Thus, using a flexible platform, we created a simulation that changes as the world changes. In handling currency fluctuations, maneuvering through critical political and and economic incidents, using real economic data, students develop strategies and techniques that model situations they will encounter throughout their business careers. Working with a top software developer and an experienced editorial team, *The Global Business Game* provides a new, unique simulation that takes the lead amongst a new millenium of strategic games.

*The Global Business Game* can be used as a stand-alone product or as core supplement for a course in Strategic Management, Business Policy, or International Management. Ideal for use with any text, the simulation follows the traditional approach to strategy. *The Global Business Game* is also uniquely flexible. Game Administrators are given the tools to decide the number and variety of products, the location of company operations, whether to invoke critical incidents, as well as other data that define the perimeters of play. Unlike other games, *The Global Business Game* offers a Game Administrator's Manual that is simple and complete.

In *The Global Business Game,* students assume management of a firm that produces television sets. The company is now under attack from its competitors and is confronting consumer demands for higher quality products and features. To ensure a unique business experience for each player, the simulation offers the following features:

- **Global Focus.** Competition is based in countries representing the three major trade regions and agreements—the United States, Mexico, Germany, Spain, Taiwan and Thailand.

- **Flexible Business Environment.** The Game Administrator decides the number and variety of products manufactured and sold, as well as the location of company operations. Choices range from a one-country, one-product operation to three products in six countries.

- **Generic Strategies and Grand Strategies.** Students can design and implement a full range of strategies to increase their firm's competitiveness.

- **International Dynamics.** Players experience currency fluctuations, value-added taxes and dividend taxes, technology transfers, joint ventures, cross licensing, differing labor wage rates, and productivity/absenteeism rates, as well as off-shore manufacturing opportunities.

- **Supports Windows® 95/98.** The Game uses standard Windows functionality, including spreadsheet files for use in Excel®.

- **Market Research Studies.** Market research studies on competitors can be purchased in order to plan which markets to enter and to improve competitive advantage.

- **Critical Incidents.** The Game Administrator can invoke a number of critical incidents, which emphasize the "soft" side of the strategic manager's decision-making situation.

- **Reality-based.** Real-world economic data is available by country and by various financial markets on a quarterly basis.

The business game of today is an extremely complex entity and requires a great number of talents and skills to bring it from a concept to something that is alive and usable for management education and development purposes. *The Global Business Game* is the most recent example of how computer-based games will be designed, programmed, and distributed in the future. Because of its complexity, most of which will lie below the page and will not be apparent to the game user, the list of those who should be acknowledged would be formidable and interminable. Thus, for the sake of brevity, and also for honor, I will acknowledge those who have had the most direct impact on the development of *The Global Business Game.*

First and foremost, I acknowledge the help of my wife, Nancy, who has read and re-read the game's written text too many times to mention. She has also served as a game assistant and creative companion in the many uses of various business games overseas, where my beliefs in the universality of the gaming experience were intensified. Within academic circles, I want to acknowledge the energy with which C. Richard Roberts served as my major coauthor on many of my research studies on the validity of business games. Also within the academic realm, J. Bernard Keys has been very important in my associations with other gaming professionals and their academic societies. He has been at the center of the business gaming movement since the early 1970s and was kind enough to recognize and encourage my talents. In a more broad academic context, my efforts with both the Association for Business Games and Experiential Learning and the journal *Simulation & Gaming* have served as outlets for my research, as well as providing informed opinions about the nature of games and the experiential learning process. The last group in the academic realm that must be acknowledged are my many, many students of all types and needs, who helped me learn more about how games should be designed and used.

South-Western College Publishing assembled a very professional and thorough team that was a delight to work with. Katherine Pruitt-Schenck, Development Editor/Project Manager, must be acknowledged for bringing both my cases and business game work to South-Western's attention. It was this act that put this project into motion. Also within South-Western, the efforts of the publishing team headed by John Szilagyi, Executive Editor, together with Kelly Keeler, Production Editor, Robin Browning, Media Production Editor, Kevin von Gillern, Media Technology Editor, and Rob Bloom, Marketing Manager, have made this project a reality.

The next individuals associated with *The Global Business Game* were those assembled by Horizons Interactive. Dave Fullen served as the patient and thoughtful coordinator of the game's user interface and the thousands of lines program code that had to be created. In his role he served as liaison for the myriad of issues that arise when creating such a complex product. Those on his team include Doug Brown, Interface Designer at Horizons Interactive, and programmers Brian Makuch and Joe Keller, at Bitfoundry.

I hope that I have done justice to all of those who have helped in this project, whether mentioned here or known only to me. I have been honored by their efforts and my associations with them, and I trust this business game returns the favor.

Joseph Wolfe
May 1, 1999

# Chapter 1

# The Global Household Audio and Video Equipment Industry

This chapter provides you with a general introduction to the world that has been created by *The Global Business Game*'s (GBG) model. The game itself is very flexible and provides your instructor or Game Administrator with a number of options regarding its complexity. Depending on which learning objectives have been chosen for you, your company may be competing as a manufacturer of 25-inch color television sets for sale in your home country, which might be the United States. Should your Game Administrator wish to give you more strategic options, your company might be allowed to manufacture nationally branded 25-inch and 27-inch sets plus another privately branded 25-inch set for sale by one of the country's large electronics or general-merchandise chains. If your Game Administrator wants to present you with a challenge that has international trade dimensions, you might have the option of building new manufacturing facilities in the Western European countries of Germany and Spain and/or the Asian countries of Taiwan and Thailand. Under these conditions, your company could sell the sets made in those countries throughout the world. Before your game begins, your instructor or Game Administrator will inform you of your particular game's configuration and will provide you with start-up information on how your firm has done in its most recent business quarter.

*The Global Business Game* itself is a simplified model of the structure and details of the television segment of the Household Audio and Video Equipment Industry (SIC 3651200.)* Because the GBG is a teaching simulation, however, it simplifies the real world, for if it exactly captured reality, it would take a lifetime to master! Instead, the game's model captures those elements essential to understanding how globally competitive industries operate and the options and operating methods allowed firms in such industries, and to give you a chance to practice strategic management and to better understand your own strengths and weaknesses as a key decision maker in business. Since many companies and industries now compete at the international level, even the strongest domestic firms are no longer protected from foreign competition. Such factors as fast, inexpensive communications, rising income levels in numerous countries, and the internationalization of consumer tastes and expectations have created world markets for a large array of goods and products. For financial survival, at the minimum, or financial security and growth, at the maximum, companies must mount and withstand competition on the international level, and the GBG has been created to help you become more attuned to this competitive world.

Your company's previous management group in *The Global Business Game* had chosen to compete in a smaller segment of the household audio and video equipment industry. Because this is a global industry, many different-sized companies manufacture and sell their products across their national borders; these products are as diverse as

---

* The *Standard Industrial Classification Manual* describes this industry as "Establishments primarily engaged in manufacturing electronic audio and video equipment for home entertainment (including automotive), such as television sets, radio broadcast receivers, tape players, phonographs, and video recorders and players. This industry also includes establishments primarily engaged in manufacturing public address systems and music distribution apparatus." See *Standard Industrial Classification Manual*, 1987. Springfield, Va.: National Technical Information Service, 1987, p. 228.

juke boxes, microphones, television sets, and remote control devices. Considering your firm's more limited assets, as well as its specialized competencies, it chose a number of years ago to manufacture and sell through wholesale distributors a more limited line of middle-sized home television sets (SIC 3651200)—after having dabbled in small clock radios, record turntables, and audio tape recorders and players.

## Industry Demand and Product Characteristics

The demand for television sets of an individual nation and the world depends on a number of intertwined factors. These factors are both economic and socioeconomic in nature and consist of disposable incomes and literacy levels, the country's degree of electrification, amount of leisure time and how people use it, the relative costs of alternative pastimes and diversions, and the population's size and number of household units.

The set you are making is the result of a series of inventions and discoveries that began in Britain in 1908, when Campbell-Swinton proved that light signals could be transmitted and received by a cathode-ray tube. In 1920 John Logie Baird demonstrated "radio-vision" in London. Four years later he presented his transmitting and receiving system at the Wembley Exhibition. This was a mechanical system using synchronized spinning disks. Britain was also the first country to have regular television service. This was begun in November 1936 by the BBC from a London hilltop.

Although the British were at the vanguard regarding television's basic technological research, it was in the United States that its commercial possibilities and mass-market appeal were the most thoroughly exploited. Applied research was directed by RCA's Director of Electronic Research V. K. Zworykin in the early 1930s. RCA invented the Iconoscope as the part of the camera for capturing the images that were broadcast, and then the Kinescope, for viewing the images that had been received. By the late 1940s, television stations were operating in most of America's largest cities, although viewing hours were restricted.

**Exhibit 1.1   25- and 27-Inch Sets with Remote Selectors**

**25-Inch Set Features:**

Remote control
On-screen multilingual menu
Closed-caption capability
Closed captioning when muted
Stereo capability
Commercial-skip timer
Separate audio program
12-month parts warranty
24-month picture-tube warranty

**27-Inch Set Features:**

Universal remote control
Color-"warmth" adjustment
Automatic volume control
S-video-input jack
Multiple-input jacks
On-screen multilingual menu
Closed-caption capability
Closed captioning when muted
Stereo sound

Ambience sound
Audio-output jacks
Commercial-skip timer
Picture-in-picture
Channel block-out
12-month parts warranty
24-month picture-tube warranty

Whereas many black-and-white television sets were being purchased by American consumers at this time, demonstrations of color television sets were occurring simultaneously. The CBS Network's field sequential system of spinning colored disks initially challenged RCA and its NBC Network for supremacy, but the latter's more complicated but theoretically superior three-color gun system prevailed. Today almost all new television sets are color sets, and all come with a number of convenience features.

The most popular-sized sets in North America are those whose picture tube diagonally measures 25 or 27 inches across the face. These sets lie between the industry's smallest models,19 and 20 inches, and its big-screen models, measuring 31 inches or more. In the United States, the industry's 25-inch TVs are often used as secondary or even tertiary sets in larger bedrooms or dens. The big-screen sets are used in large family rooms. Monophonic 25-inch sets retail in the United States for from $250 to $280, with those featuring stereophonic or "surround" sound retailing for $270 to $350. This class of sets, which is presented in Exhibit 1.1, is limited regarding the number of features and amenities found in them.

In contrast, the industry's 27-inch sets offer very fine pictures, higher quality sound, and a host of useful features. Many provide color-"warmth" adjustments that present flesh tones and interiors in a more favorable light, automatic volume controls that tone down loud advertisements, S-video-input jacks that take advantage of the superior picture quality generated by Hi8 or S-VHS-C camcorders, picture-in-picture, and audio circuitry that emulates surround sound. Exhibit 1.1 cites the typical features found on sets in this size category. These television sets currently retail for $350 to $580 in the United States but receive higher prices in foreign markets due to tariffs and value-added taxes (VATs) often levied on them. They are also retailed through relatively inefficient marketing channels.

Sets of these two sizes produce acceptable pictures and sound as well as featuring remote-control devices. There are substantial differences, however, in the reliability of the various brands found in the marketplace. Many consumers attach great importance to having a set not prone to breakdowns. Exhibit 1.2 presents the five-year frequency of repair records associated with the world's major television brands.

**Exhibit 1.2    Repairs and Serious Problems by Brand**

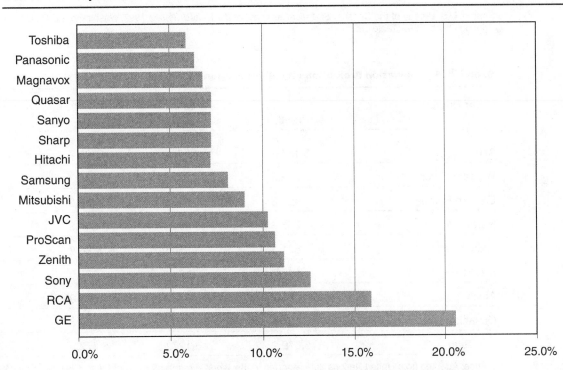

**Reported Repairs and Breakdowns on 25- and 27-Inch Sets**

Source: "Ratings and Recommendations: 27-Inch TV Sets," *Consumer Reports* (March 1998), p. 29.

The demand for these features, and the ability to pay for them, differ between countries. The number of broadcast television channels, let alone the number of cable channels, also varies radically from country to country. Additionally, the television set's use as a home entertainment medium varies depending upon the household's financial circumstances. Various features are also more or less attractive due to differing literacy levels, the availability of repair facilities, and the product's life-cycle stage within each country. Depending on the situation, increased complexity or greater product sophistication could be a product disadvantage. Exhibit 1.3 shows that a high degree of product saturation and market maturity exists in the United States for television sets. The markets of Taiwan, Mexico, and Thailand are relatively unsaturated in this regard.

## World and National Markets

Because the household audio and video equipment industry is global in scope, competitors must systematically monitor many global economic trends and developments. Raw population projections, such as those shown in Exhibit 1.4, indicate that the world's population will increase about 44% in the very long term. This results in a 1.5% average annual increase in the number of people who could potentially watch a television set. The greatest growth will be found in the developing areas of Africa, the Middle East, and Latin America.

**Exhibit 1.3   Television-Set Ownership in the United States**

| Item | 1970 | 1980 | 1992 | 1993 | 1994 | 1995 |
|---|---|---|---|---|---|---|
| Percent of households | 95.3 | 97.9 | 98.3 | 98.3 | 98.3 | 98.3 |
| Sets (hundreds of thousands) | 81.0 | 128.0 | 192.0 | 201.0 | 211.0 | 217.0 |
| Sets per home | 1.4 | 1.7 | 2.1 | 2.2 | 2.2 | 2.3 |
| Color sets (hundreds of thousands) | 21.0 | 63.0 | 91.0 | 92.0 | 93.0 | 94.0 |

Source: U.S. Bureau of the Census, *Statistical Abstract of the United States: 1997*. Washington, D.C.: U.S. Government Printing Office, 1997, Table 888.

**Exhibit 1.4   Population Projections by Major Region (hundreds of thousands)**

| Major Region | 1996 | Years 2000 | 2025 | Long-Term Growth (Percent) |
|---|---|---|---|---|
| Asia | 3,151.1 | 3,375.4 | 4,196.7 | 33.2 |
| Western Europe | 388.3 | 392.1 | 395.7 | 1.9 |
| Eastern Europe | 421.3 | 435.8 | 498.3 | 18.3 |
| North America | 286.8 | 297.7 | 347.3 | 21.1 |
| Latin America | 501.3 | 550.0 | 786.6 | 56.9 |
| Middle East | 148.7 | 168.3 | 270.0 | 81.6 |
| Africa | 753.2 | 877.4 | 1,642.9 | 118.1 |
| Oceania | 28.5 | 30.4 | 39.5 | 38.6 |
| Total | 5,679.2 | 6,127.1 | 8,177.0 | 44.0 |

Source: Adapted from United Nations data reported in the *World Almanac & Book of Facts 1991*. New York: World Almanac Books, 1991, p. 772.

**Exhibit 1.5    Population Projections for Selected Countries (hundreds of thousands)**

| Country | 1996 | Year 2000 | 2010 | Long-Term Growth (Percent) |
|---|---|---|---|---|
| Germany | 83.5 | 85.7 | 88.9 | 6.5 |
| Mexico | 95.8 | 102.9 | 120.1 | 25.4 |
| Spain | 39.2 | 39.6 | 40.4 | 3.1 |
| Taiwan | 21.5 | 22.2 | 24.0 | 28.8 |
| Thailand | 58.9 | 61.1 | 66.1 | 11.6 |
| United States | 265.6 | 275.0 | 298.0 | 12.2 |
| Total | 564.5 | 586.5 | 637.5 | 12.9 |

Source: Derived from data in Annmarie Muth (ed.), *Statistical Abstract of the World*. Detroit: Gale Research, 1997, pp. 354, 623, 874, 920, 937, and 993.

Although the gross estimates for these areas are notable, your company's previous management group has been relatively uninterested in conducting international operations and has focused solely on its home country of the United States. Some in your company, however, are aware of international developments, especially the profits that might be gained through expanded operations encouraged in North America by NAFTA, and in Western Europe and Asia via their respective trading zones of the European Union (EU) and APEC (Asia Pacific Economic Cooperation). Exhibit 1.5 shows the projected population growth rates for these economic zones and for the specific countries possibly available to you in *The Global Business Game*.

Understanding that a nation's growth is a factor to be considered when seeking foreign markets, your company was also interested in the buying power of each nation's population, as well as each nation's current stock of television sets. Exhibit 1.6 displays each nation's television-set ownership in 1997. On a per capita basis, a relatively low level of television-set saturation has been realized in Thailand, whereas Germany is rapidly approaching the saturation point.

To create their best estimates of each nation's buying power regarding the purchase of TV sets and other consumer products, your company collected the raw data displayed in Exhibit 1.7. The results of this analysis are presented in Exhibit 1.8, with the size of the circles indicating each country's relative size within the set of countries considered and Market Intensity indicating each country's relative wealth or past experience as a consumer nation.

Although your Game Administrator may inform you that different conditions will apply to your simulation, when Exhibit 1.8 was created against comparable data from the 1988 period, your prior management group obtained a general feeling about most factors that made various markets more or less attractive investment opportunities.

As part of your company's research into various new markets and manufacturing sites, a portfolio was collected for each country. The following reviews certain macroeconomic features for the six countries that appeared to be likely expansion candidates.

**Exhibit 1.6    Television-Set Ownership, 1997 (thousands)**

| Country | Television Sets |
|---|---|
| United States | 223,295.6 |
| Germany | 46,704.6 |
| Mexico | 15,994.0 |
| Spain | 15,697.7 |
| Taiwan | 7,218.5 |
| Thailand | 6,994.2 |

Source: Derived from ratios presented in the *World Almanac & Book of Facts 1998*. New York: World Almanac Books, 1998, pp. 767, 798-799, 820, 824-825, and 832.

**Exhibit 1.7   Selected Raw Economic Data**

| Economic Factor | Germany | Mexico | Spain | Taiwan | Thailand | United States |
|---|---|---|---|---|---|---|
| Total population[1] | 83.5 | 95.8 | 39.2 | 21.5 | 58.9 | 266.9 |
| % Urban population | 87.0% | 74.0% | 77.0% | 75.0% | 20.0% | 76.0% |
| Private consumption[2] | 1401.1 | 177.5 | 346.3 | 133.6 | 90.2 | 4727.4 |
| Steel consumption[3] | 70.7 | 15.0 | 13.5 | 17.4 | 10.0 | 153.8 |
| Cement consumption[3] | 40.2 | 31.5 | 25.1 | 23.7 | 29.9 | 77.9 |
| Electricity consumption[4] | 495.8 | 145.2 | 154.1 | 121.8 | 77.5 | 3600.0 |
| Telephones[1] | 44.0 | 12.0 | 15.1 | 10.3 | 1.6 | 182.6 |
| Passenger cars[1] | 40.5 | 14.6 | 14.2 | 4.1 | 1.4 | 172.0 |
| Television sets[1] | 44.8 | 13.1 | 15.7 | 6.7 | 3.3 | 215.0 |

[1] In millions.
[2] In billions of US$.
[3] In millions of metric tons.
[4] In billions of kilowatt hours.

Source: Various sources, including *Statistical Yearbook: 1995*, New York: United Nations, 1997; Annmarie Muth (ed.), *Statistical Abstract of the World*, Detroit: Gale Research, 1997; *1997 World Bank Atlas*, Washington, D.C.: World Bank, 1997; and U.S. Bureau of the Census, *Statistical Abstract of the United States: 1997*, Washington, D.C.:, U.S. Government Printing Office, 1997.

**Exhibit 1.8   Size, Growth and Intensity of Prospective Country Markets**

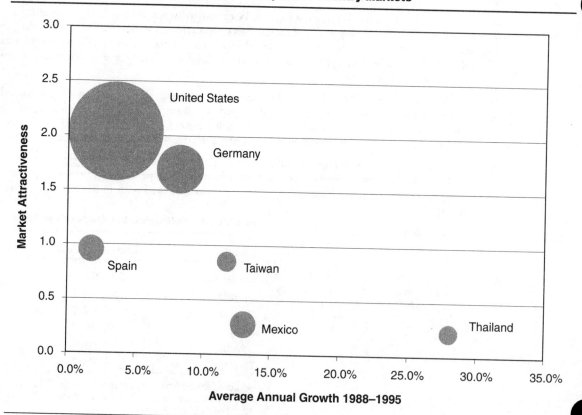

*Germany.* The official reunification of the Federal Republic of Germany (West Germany) with the German Democratic Republic (East Germany) at midnight October 2–3, 1990, created an expanded economic unit of over 77 million people. As the European Community has taken shape, Germany has assumed a central role in its affairs as well as in the value of the new Euro in "Euroland." A low internal inflation rate and elaborate rail, roadway, and telephone infrastructures, along with a pro-business governmental posture, make this country an attractive economic opportunity. Its per capita income, while not as great as that found in the Scandinavian countries, is the highest in Europe after Denmark. Its major industries are steel, ships, vehicles, machinery, coal, and chemicals. About 40 percent of its labor force is engaged in industry and commerce, and 54 percent of its workers are engaged in various service industries. Less positive features are labor rates that are the highest in the world—the equivalent of $31.79 per hour in the late 1990s—a work week simultaneously shortened from 37 to 35 hours plus vacations lasting up to six weeks, and highly participative union relations.

Key statistics for Germany in the late 1990s:
  Major cities—Essen (6.5 million), Frankfurt (3.6 million), Berlin (3.3 million), Cologne (3.0 million), Dusseldorf (3.0 million), Hamburg (1.6 million), and Munich (1.3 million).
  Population density—610 per square mile
  Land mass—349,300 sq. kilometers
  Literacy rate—100%, with ten years of compulsory education
  Newspaper circulation—317 per 1,000 population
  Airports with scheduled flights—28
  Physicians—1 per 298 persons
  Hospital beds—1 per 130 persons
  Infant mortality—6 per 1,000 births

*Spain.* This country has been a favorite manufacturing site for European firms wishing to lower their labor costs. The economy has been growing at a relatively high rate of about 3.4 percent for the past several years, although its unemployment rate is the highest in Western Europe, at around 21.9 percent. Despite this level of unemployment, wages have been rising, and they have been outgaining increases in worker productivity. A certain degree of political unrest lingers on in Spain, as a 1981 coup attempted by right-wing military officers was foiled by King Juan Carlos. Basque extremists have continued their campaign for independence, despite having been granted political autonomy in January 1980. Spain is also seeking the return of Gibraltar from the British, who gained control of the entrance to the Mediterranean Sea in 1704.

Key statistics for Spain in the late 1990s:
  Major cities—Madrid (4.1 million), Barcelona (2.8 million) Valencia (.8 million), Sevilla (.7 million) and Zaragoza (.6 million).
  Population density—200 per square mile
  Land mass—499,400 sq. kilometers
  Literacy rate—97%, with ten years of compulsory education
  Newspaper circulation—104 per 1,000 population
  Airports—12
  Physicians—1 per 246 persons
  Hospital beds—1 per 234 persons
  Infant mortality—6 per 1,000 births

*Mexico.* Despite the discovery of perhaps the world's largest oil reserves in the late 1960s Mexico's economy has reaped little benefit. The country's economic and political history have both been turbulent. Various administrations have attempted to improve the population's welfare through economic and social reforms, but little real progress has been made. Agricultural crops and farm prices have recently come under government control, as have imports and exports. The peso was devalued in the 1980s, and private banks were nationalized to restore monetary security. It has been estimated that an amount almost 40 percent as large as Mexico's official GDP is obtained through illegal or undocumented activities, thus depriving the government of much-needed tax revenues. Despite one of the hemisphere's lowest factory labor rates, at the equivalent of about $1.56 an hour, much unemployment and underemployment exists.

Key statistics for Mexico in the late 1990s:
    Major cities—Mexico City (18.0 million), Guadalajara (3.0 million), and Monterrey (2.7 million).
    Population density—129 per square mile
    Land mass—1,908,700 sq. kilometers
    Literacy rate—90%, with ten years of compulsory education
    Newspaper circulation—113 per 1,000 population
    Airports—83
    Physicians—1 per 613 persons
    Hospital beds—1 per 1,196 persons
    Infant mortality—24 per 1,000 births

*Taiwan.* Now called Chinese Taipei or the Taiwan Province of China, this densely populated country—about the size of New Hampshire and Connecticut combined—manufactures textiles, clothing, electronics, processed foods, chemicals, and plastics. Land reform, U.S. aid and investment, and universal education have helped the country to advance rapidly since its creation by two million Kuomintang supporters in 1949. Its 38-year-old martial law was lifted in 1987, and its relations with the People's Republic of China have become more flexible. Inflationary pressures have relaxed and its economic growth has been relatively unaffected by the Asian meltdown of mid-1998. The pro-business government invested NT$ 83.2 billion in the construction of the 3,643-hectare Changhua off-shore industrial zone, completed in 1998. The country's legislature is attempting to further accelerate economic development by replacing its Statute for the Encouragement of Investment with new, more favorable legislation. Japanese and Australian firms have made the largest investment in Taiwan, with total new foreign investment in 1997 amounting to more than $4.3 billion.

Key statistics for Taiwan in the late 1990s:
    Major cities—Taipei (2.6 million), Kaohsiung (1.4 million), Taichung (.9 million), and Tainan (.7 million).
    Population density—1,550 per square mile
    Land mass—35,745 sq. kilometers
    Literacy rate—94%, with nine years of compulsory education
    Airports—13
    Physicians—1 per 864 persons
    Hospital beds—1 per 204 persons
    Infant mortality—7 per 1,000 births

*Thailand.* The economic collapse of the Pacific Rim's countries was precipitated by this country's devaluation of its currency in July 1997. This has hit Thailand especially hard. Its economy was never very robust, and the corruption that has traditionally existed in high places made it especially difficult for the government to take effective action. Short-term interest rates soured to 21.5% by mid-1998. The prime rate was 15.5% in May 1998, industrial production fell and GDP fell about 4.5% for 1998 with consumer prices falling about 10.2%. It is also experiencing an AIDS outbreak of epidemic dimensions. Because of the economy's downturn, Thailand received $17.2 billion in emergency loans in August 1997 from the International Monetary Fund. In May 1998 Thailand's central bank nationalized seven of the country's ailing finance companies. The financial empires of the country's two most important forces, the military and the Sophonpanich family, who control, respectively, the Thai Military Bank and the Bangkok Bank, are also experiencing distress.

Key statistics for Thailand in the late 1990s:
    Major cities—Bangkok (6.5 million), Nakhon Ratchasima (.2 million), Chiang Mai (.2 million) and
        Hat Yai (.2 million)
    Population density—300 per square mile
    Land mass—510,900 sq. kilometers
    Literacy rate—94%, with nine years of compulsory education
    Newspaper circulation—48 per 1,000 population
    Airports with scheduled flights—25
    Physicians—1 per 4,245 persons
    Hospital beds—1 per 599 persons
    Infant mortality—32.0 per 1,000 births

*United States.*  Once incomparable in most economic activities, this country's businesses have encountered strong competition on their home soil, while finding it difficult to sell many of their products overseas. Despite these problems, the United States is both the world's richest and largest market and one whose government is basically pro business. Its relatively low interest and inflation rates have led to the longest run of GDP growth in its history. Because of its relatively high labor costs, about $18.24 per hour, a number of its major corporations have established off-shore manufacturing operations. Alternatively, a major source of new investment has come from foreign corporations seeking footholds in North American markets. In recent years, the dollar has risen against most European and Asian currencies. It appears it will also be strong against the euro.

Key statistics for the United States in 1997:
> Major cities—New York City (7.4 million), Los Angeles (3.4 million), Chicago
> (3.1 million), Houston (1.7 million), and Philadelphia (1.6 million).
> Population density—72 per square mile
> Land mass—9,159,100 sq. kilometers
> Literacy rate—99%
> Newspaper circulation—228 per 1,000 population
> Airports—834 with scheduled flights
> Physicians—1 per 381 persons
> Hospital beds—1 per 232 persons
> Infant mortality—7 per 1,000 births

## Country Seasonal Demand

Your company has also collected information on past television set sales by nation. In gathering this data, it became clear that television set sales in the consumer goods market varied throughout the year, regardless of each country's underlying macroeconomic elements, and that seasonal variation differed from country to country. In the United States, sets of the size you manufacture have proven to be good Christmas gifts for a child's bedroom. In Germany and Spain, two countries that have many rabid soccer fans, it has been found that television-set sales spike in June, shortly before the World Cup matches begin.

The empirically derived seasonal indicators your management group has created are presented in Exhibit 1.9. These indices, because they are based on long-term, relatively constant factors, will not change over the course of your simulation. They also reflect the fact that distributors stock their warehouses well before retailers stock their shelves with television sets in anticipation of consumer demand.

**Exhibit 1.9   Television-Set Seasonal Indices by Quarter**

| Country | Quarter 1 | Quarter 2 | Quarter 3 | Quarter 4 |
|---------|-----------|-----------|-----------|-----------|
| Germany | 1.17 | 1.08 | .83 | .92 |
| Mexico | 1.21 | 1.11 | .81 | .87 |
| Spain | 1.19 | 1.10 | .79 | .92 |
| Taiwan | .84 | 1.00 | 1.12 | 1.04 |
| Thailand | .94 | 1.02 | 1.03 | 1.01 |
| U.S. | .74 | .82 | 1.31 | 1.13 |

## Competitive Strategies in Global Industries

A global industry can be defined as one where the industry's participants are present in all key international markets, demand for the product is standardized and the product itself is fairly standardized, and a significant portion of the product's components or raw materials are obtained from international sources. Accordingly, the automobile industry is a global industry; this could also be said of the tire industry, the watch and watch-parts industry, and the pharmaceutical industry.

Because of the growing importance of global competitiveness, various authors have attempted to describe the basic strategies that can be employed by companies competing in them. Michael Porter suggests that four competitive strategies exist in global industries—broad-line global competition, global focus, national focus, and protected niche. Another expert, Milton Leontiades, also suggests four different strategies that can be employed—high market share globally, global niche, high market share nationally, and national niche.

While these descriptions seem to capture how many firms compete in their global industries, Allen Morrison has empirically investigated how firms actually compete in these industries. The following competitive strategies have been successfully employed, and they have been labelled as follows:

a. Domestic Product Specialization strategy
b. Exporting, High-Quality Offerings strategy
c. International, Product Innovation strategy
d. Global, Combination strategy

Companies pursuing a Domestic Product Specialization strategy possessed a strong domestic orientation and tended to engage in product specialization. These companies placed a strong emphasis on manufacturing and marketing skill as applied to their domestic market, maintaining a reputation for quality and engaging in product specialization. In carrying out their strategy, the firms promoted innovative manufacturing, emphasized modern plant and equipment, and developed efficient manufacturing processes. Little emphasis was put on international investment. They competed in very few foreign countries and paid little attention to political and international trends and factors.

Companies pursuing an Exporting, High-Quality Offerings strategy exported domestically produced high-quality products and high-quality services. These firms possessed relatively few assets in the foreign countries they served, and they limited their direct investments to a relatively few nations. They also lobbied foreign governments and sought U.S. government aid in entering foreign markets. In implementing this strategy, these firms placed a low emphasis on manufacturing efficiency and product specialization, instead emphasizing having a positive industry reputation. Accordingly, they did not emphasize being price competitive.

Another group of companies employed a strategy of International, Product Innovation. These firms competed in many particular countries with highly innovative products. A high emphasis was placed on having a quality reputation, honing their marketing and manufacturing skills and engaging in a fairly large amount of foreign investment, but only in selected countries. Because of a reputation for innovation, these companies produced high-priced products for specific niches. They also emphasized product specialization.

The last strategy employed by those in global industries was termed by Morrison as a Global, Combination strategy. Companies pursuing this strategy had high levels of international investments, were engaged in the internal affairs of the nations they dealt with, and maintained many subsidiaries or joint ventures throughout the world. Although generally emphasizing manufacturing and marketing prowess, they operationalized the marketing dimension by monitoring market opportunities, managing distribution channels, and developing creative marketing methods.

In determining how your company should compete in *The Global Business Game* in the future, the strategies that have been used in the real world can be used, to some great degree, in the game you are about to play. In choosing which strategy to implement, you should consider a number of factors. Those would be the internal resources possessed by your management team, the physical and financial resources your company has at this time and can make available to itself, and the global opportunities available to all companies in your industry. Exhibit 1.10 summarizes the features associated with the grand strategies that have just been described. Various pre-game exercises presented in Chapter 3, on organizing company operations, should help you to create and implement the corporate and functional-level strategies you may choose for your firm.

**Exhibit 1.10 Strategies in Global Industries**

| Grand Strategy | Features |
| --- | --- |
| Domestic Product Specialization | Basically a domestic producer engaging in product specialization with few foreign sales. Emphasis on manufacturing and marketing skill in their home market and maintaining a quality reputation. Manufacturing emphasis featuring innovative manufacturing, modern plant and equipment, and the development of efficient manufacturing processes. |
| Exporting, High-Quality Offerings | Basically, export of domestically produced high-quality products and high-quality services. The possession of relatively few assets in foreign countries but the lobbying of foreign and domestic governments to help them be competitive. A low emphasis on manufacturing efficiency, price competitiveness, or product specialization; a high emphasis on within-industry reputation. |
| International, Product Innovation | Competition and fairly heavy foreign investment in many selected countries with highly innovative products. A strong emphasis on a high-quality reputation and having marketing and manufacturing skills. Feature high-priced, specialized products made for specific niches. |
| Global, Combination | High levels of international investment, many subsidiaries or joint ventures throughout the world, a great amount of involvement in internal political affairs. General emphasis on manufacturing and marketing prowess, but the marketing dimension dominates through monitoring market opportunities and developing creative marketing methods. |

## Additional Readings

Bartlett, C. (1986) Building and managing the transnational: The new organizational challenge. In M. E. Porter (ed.), *Competition in Global Industries*. Boston: Harvard Business School.

Bartlett, C., and S. Ghoshal. (1987) *Managing across Borders: The Transnational Solution*. Boston: Harvard Business School.

Chandler, A. D. (1986) The evolution of modern global competition. In M. E. Porter (ed.), *Competition in Global Industries*. Boston: Harvard Business School.

Cvar, M. (1984) Competitive strategies in global industries. Ph.D. dissertation, Harvard Business School.

Davidson, W., and P. Haspeslagh. (1982) Shaping a global product organization. *Harvard Business Review* 60: 125–132.

Doz, Y. (1987) International industries: Fragmentation versus globalization. In B. Guile and H. Brooks (eds.), *Technology and Global Industry: Companies and Nations in the World Economy*. Washington, D.C.: National Academy Press.

Flaherty, M. (1986) Coordinating international manufacturing and technology. In M. E. Porter (ed.), *Competition in Global Industries*. Boston: Harvard Business School.

Indicators of market size for 117 countries. (1990) *Business International* 37, no. 30: 245–256.

Leontiades, M. (1986) Going global: Global strategies vs. national strategies. *Long Range Planning* 19: 96–104.

Levitt, T. (1983) The globalization of markets. *Harvard Business Review* 61: 92–102.

Morrison, A. J. (1990) *Strategies in Global Industries: How U. S. Businesses Compete*. New York: Quorum Books, pp. 39–46, 113–121, 133–135.

Porter, M. E. (1980) *Competitive Strategy: Techniques for Analyzing Industries and Competitors*. New York: Free Press.

———. (1986) Changing patterns of international competition. *California Management Review* 28: 9–40.

# Chapter 2

# Company History and Background

The company you will be running was born of the enthusiasms of Gary Elliott, Arthur Moore, David Stevenson, and Casimir (Casey) Sobieski. They had served together in the Signal Corps during World War II but had previously been employed as electronics engineers at RCA's David Sarnoff Laboratories. The work they performed there was the basic research that made television commercially feasible. Because they were avid tinkerers and experimenters with everything that went into that era's electronic gear, they dreamed of starting their own home electronics firm once the war was over.

By early 1948, after mustering out of the Signal Corps, they had accumulated enough private capital to start making products, but ones that did not require large amounts of start-up monies. Although they yearned to get into making television sets, they first turned their attention to making the more easily assembled FM radios and wire recorders that were just being introduced in the United States.

Their first television set was a very small unit introduced in 1954. It was given the brand name MagnaArgus. The MagnaArgus had a 10-inch picture tube with a resulting screen size of $8\frac{5}{8}'' \times 6\frac{1}{4}''$. It retailed for $275. The company's picture tubes were purchased under an RCA licensing agreement with the sets hand assembled in a small leased plant in Erie, Pennsylvania. The set sold well in its regional markets of western New York and northern Ohio, but limited quantities of picture tubes and quality-assurance problems kept the partners from expanding their sales territory.

A number of successor models were produced, and the company had visions of becoming a national brand. As the 1960s wore on, however, your company's founders were unable to broaden the firm's product line of television sets and had to fall back on the production of high-fidelity equipment and FM tuners as a way of stabilizing their earnings. More importantly, a number of domestic television-set manufacturers were being squeezed out of existence, and by the early 1970s foreign manufacturers from the Pacific Rim had entered the industry and were making great headway with their reliable yet moderately priced offerings. Your company's market position and economic fortunes began to deteriorate and its founders decided to go public in 1985 under the corporate name MagnaArgus, Inc. This was done to obtain enough new capital to either grow—or die—by becoming a niche television-set manufacturer.

With its new capital, and an expanded board of directors and shareholder interests to consider, your firm took a number of years to implement its new strategy of focused efforts. Its high-fidelity equipment products were pulled from the market, and new specialty dealers and wholesalers had to be enlisted. Most importantly, its Erie, Pennsylvania, production operations had to be converted to full-time television-set manufacturing, albeit at a very flexible level of operations, given a lack of knowledge of the scale of operations the company could attain as a niche player.

Your firm was often in a precarious situation, but it has survived and has generated modest but unstable profits. Its founders have long since given up active management of the company, and in fact, three of them have died—after transferring their share holdings to their children, who have pursued other interests. Knowing that their children had no interest in running your company, Gary, Arthur, David, and Casey had actively hired and groomed new managers as their replacements. You are now the newest generation of their management team, and they have placed their legacy in your hands.

In anticipation of future, possible global growth, as well as hoping to insure the company's survival, Gary Elliott, as your firm's last active co-founding manager, asked your company's accounting firm to create an accounting system that would handle most eventualities. Your accounting firm complied and prepared mock-ups of the types of reports the new system would produce if all possible company operations were implemented.

Because your company was operating only in your home country of the United States when the mock-ups were created, only the Income Statements, Balance Sheets, and Industry Reports for the United States are described in depth. Should your Game Administrator choose a different home country and additional market areas for your simulation, the Start-Up reports provided at the beginning of play would reflect that change. Your Game Administrator will also inform you before play begins of the number of different television sets you will be able to sell and the markets and countries in which you will be allowed to compete. Appropriate printouts will be provided for these conditions. At this juncture the reports for each additional market area and country in which your company decides to operate are basically the same as your North American report, except that all monetary values would be stated in the relevant country currencies, while your Corporate report summarizes and consolidates the reports generated by each country's operation. The decisions made by the company shown here can be found in its Decision Logs, which appear on pages 15–20.

# Global Industry Report

The pages of this report are received by all companies in your industry. The report displays information commonly known by companies in a real-world industry, and you can assume that the information presented is as accurate as possible.

**GLOBAL INDUSTRY 1 REPORT**—These two lines designate the industry to which your company has been assigned in the simulation. Your Game Administrator may create a number of independently operating industries. Your own company's performance will be judged only against the performance of the other firms competing in your own industry.

**YEAR 1998**—This indicates the simulation's operating year. Your Game Administrator will inform you of the game's starting year and starting quarter, as well as the number of operating years your game will entail.

**QUARTER 4**—This part of this line identifies the simulation's operating quarter. Your Game Administrator will inform you about the number of quarters your simulation will run. Quarter 4 would be the business year's fourth quarter while, for example, YEAR 1999, QUARTER 2 would be the second quarter of the year 1999.

**WAGE RATES**—The average wage, in local currency values, of workers that can be assigned to assembling 25" and 27" sets.

**SHORT-TERM RATE**—The general interest rates found for 90-Day loans in each Market Area's major financial markets of New York City, Frankfurt and Tokyo. This is an indicator of the interest rate a country operation would have to pay for a 90-Day Short Term Loan given the country unit's Credit Rating.

**BOND RATE**—A statement of the general yield rates found for 10-Year Bonds in each Area's major financial markets of New York City, Frankfurt and Tokyo. This is an indicator of the nominal interest rate a country operation would have to pay for a 10-Year Callable Bond given the country unit's Credit Rating. This Bond Rate serves as the basis of your firm's effective interest rate on its 20-Year Bonds.

**STOCK MARKET INDEX**—The stock market indices associated with each market area's financial center. For North America this is the Dow Jones Industrial Average (DJIA), for Western Europe it is the Frankfurt DAX-30, and for Asia it is Tokyo's Nikkei 225. These indices will be updated throughout the simulation and can be found via the Internet or in any of the commonly available financial newspapers such as the *Wall Street Journal*'s Section C.

## Decision Log

Industry __A__    Firm __1__    Quarter __4__    Year _1998_

## Marketing

| Decision | United States | Mexico | Germany | Spain | Taiwan | Thailand |
|---|---|---|---|---|---|---|
| 25" TV List Price | 105.00 | | | | | |
| 25" TV Actual Price | 102.83 | | | | | |
| 27" TV List Price | 123.00 | | | | | |
| 27" TV Actual Price | 122.40 | | | | | |
| 25" TV Contract Bid | 0 | | | | | |
| 27" TV Contract Bid | 0 | | | | | |
| 25" TV Advertising | 4,000 | | | | | |
| 27" TV Advertising | 9,000 | | | | | |
| Sales Offices | 3 | | | | | |
| Distribution Centers | 1 | | | | | |
| Independent Wholesalers | 4 | | | | | |
| Company-Owned Wholesalers | 0 | | | | | |
| Sales Representatives | 6 | | | | | |
| Trainees | 1 | | | | | |
| Sales Rep Base Salary | 7,000 | | | | | |
| 25" TV Commission | 1.50% | | | | | |
| 27" TV Commission | 2.00% | | | | | |
| Sales Rep Training | 5,000 | | | | | |
| Product R&D | 5,000 | | | | | |

## Decision Log

Industry __A__    Firm __1__    Quarter __4__    Year _1998_

### Marketing Logistics

| Decision | United States | Mexico | Germany | Spain | Taiwan | Thailand |
|---|---|---|---|---|---|---|
| 25" TV Distribution from: | 0 | | | | | |
| 25" TV Distribution to: | 0 | | | | | |
| 27" TV Distribution from: | 0 | | | | | |
| 27" TV Distribution to: | 0 | | | | | |
| 25" TV Contract Distribution | 0 | | | | | |
| 27" TV Contract Distribution | 0 | | | | | |
| Surface Shipping | 0 | | | | | |
| Exair Shipping | 0 | | | | | |

### Subassembly Purchases

| Decision | United States | Mexico | Germany | Spain | Taiwan | Thailand |
|---|---|---|---|---|---|---|
| Group 1 Grade A | 2,584 | | | | | |
| Group 1 Grade B | 2,584 | | | | | |
| Group 1 Grade C | 517 | | | | | |
| Group 2 Grade A | 1,974 | | | | | |
| Group 2 Grade B | 1,974 | | | | | |
| Group 2 Grade C | 395 | | | | | |

## Decision Log

Industry  _A_      Firm  _1_      Quarter  _4_      Year  _1998_

## Production and Operations Management

| Decision | United States | Mexico | Germany | Spain | Taiwan | Thailand |
|---|---|---|---|---|---|---|
| Shift 1 25" TVs | 23,800 | | | | | |
| Shift 2 25" TVs | 23,800 | | | | | |
| Shift 1 27" TVs | 46,100 | | | | | |
| Shift 2 27" TVs | 46,100 | | | | | |
| Line Supervisors | 2 | | | | | |
| Shift 1 25" TV Workers | 57 | | | | | |
| Shift 2 25" TV Workers | 56 | | | | | |
| Shift 1 27" TV Workers | 54 | | | | | |
| Shift 2 27" TV Workers | 56 | | | | | |
| Automaton Technicians | 3 | | | | | |
| Line Worker Training | 4,000 | | | | | |
| Automaton Technician Training | 4,000 | | | | | |
| Quality Control Training | 13,000 | | | | | |
| QC Sampling Program | A | | | | | |

## Decision Log

Industry __A__    Firm __1__    Quarter __4__    Year _1998_

## Financial Management

| Decision | United States | Mexico | Germany | Spain | Taiwan | Thailand |
|---|---|---|---|---|---|---|
| Stock Issue | 0 | | | | | |
| Stock Purchase | 0 | | | | | |
| Stock Dividend | 0 | | | | | |
| Short-Term Investment | 0 | | | | | |
| Short-Term Loan | 0 | | | | | |
| Bond Issue | 0 | | | | | |
| Bond Call | 0 | | | | | |
| Cash Distribution to: | 0 | | | | | |
| Cash Distribution from: | 0 | | | | | |
| To Retained Earnings | 0 | | | | | |

## Decision Log

Industry __A__     Firm __1__     Quarter __4__     Year _1998_

### Plant Capacity and Plant Maintenance

| Decision | United States | Mexico | Germany | Spain | Taiwan | Thailand |
|---|---|---|---|---|---|---|
| Base Capacity | 0 | | | | | |
| Automaton Type 1 | 0 | | | | | |
| Automaton Type 2 | 0 | | | | | |
| Line Maintenance | 4,000 | | | | | |
| Auto 1 Maintenance | 110 | | | | | |
| Auto 2 Maintenance | 250 | | | | | |

### Marketing Research Request

| Question | Charge | Choice |
|---|---|---|
| 1 | $1,500 | |
| 2 | $1,500 | |
| 3 | $500 | |
| 4 | $500 | |
| 5 | $1,000 | |
| 6 | $2,000 | |
| 7 | $2,000 | |
| 8 | $750 | |
| 9 | $250 | |
| 10 | $250 | |
| 11 | $300 | |
| 12 | $300 | |
| Total | | |

### Critical Incidence Response

| Incident | Response |
|---|---|
| | |
| | |
| | |

## Intrafirm Automaton Transfers

| From: | U.S. | Mexico | Germany | Spain | Taiwan | Thailand |
|---|---|---|---|---|---|---|
| **United States** | | | | | | |
| Auto 1 | XX | | | | | |
| Auto 2 | XX | | | | | |
| **Mexico** | | | | | | |
| Auto 1 | | XX | | | | |
| Auto 2 | | XX | | | | |
| **Germany** | | | | | | |
| Auto 1 | | | XX | | | |
| Auto 2 | | | XX | | | |
| **Spain** | | | | | | |
| Auto 1 | | | | XX | | |
| Auto 2 | | | | XX | | |
| **Taiwan** | | | | | | |
| Auto 1 | | | | | XX | |
| Auto 2 | | | | | XX | |
| **Thailand** | | | | | | |
| Auto 1 | | | | | | XX |
| Auto 2 | | | | | | XX |

# Global Industry A Report
Year 1998 Quarter 4

| U.S. | |
|---|---|
| Wage Rates: | |
| 25" TV | 17.56 |
| 27" TV | 17.74 |
| Short-Term Rate | 4.73% |
| Bond Rate | 7.95% |
| Stock Market Index | 10537.05 |
| GDP Q4 1998 | 100.00 |
| GDP Q1 1999 | 100.00 |
| GDP Q4 1999 | 100.23 |

| Subassemblies | Grade A | Grade B | Grade C |
|---|---|---|---|
| Group 1 | 168.96 | 128.80 | 115.00 |
| Group 2 | 579.31 | 463.45 | 403.00 |

| Bulletins |
|---|
| The Home Electronics King retail chain is soliciting private-label bids for its Kingston brand of television sets for delivery next quarter. The winning bidder will supply the following with a Quality Index at or above 7.76: |

| | |
|---|---|
| 25" TVs | 1,654 |
| 27" TVs | 3,073 |

# Global Industry A Report
Year 1998 Quarter 4

## Currency Cross Rates

| | U.S. | EU | Thailand | Taiwan | Spain | Mexico | Germany |
|---|---|---|---|---|---|---|---|
| Dollar | 1.0000 | 0.9334 | 39.9200 | 31.7500 | 155.3200 | 9.4650 | 1.8258 |
| Euro | 1.0714 | 1.0000 | 42.7684 | 34.0154 | 166.4024 | 10.1403 | 1.9561 |
| Baht | 0.0251 | 0.0234 | 1.0000 | 0.7953 | 3.8908 | 0.2371 | 0.0457 |
| NTDollar | 0.0315 | 0.0294 | 1.2573 | 1.0000 | 4.8920 | 0.2981 | 0.0575 |
| Peseta | 0.0064 | 0.0060 | 0.2570 | 0.2044 | 1.0000 | 0.0609 | 0.0118 |
| Peso | 0.1057 | 0.0986 | 4.2176 | 3.3545 | 16.4099 | 1.0000 | 0.1929 |
| D-Mark | 0.5477 | 0.5112 | 21.8644 | 17.3896 | 85.0696 | 5.1840 | 1.0000 |

# Global Industry A Report
Year 1998 Quarter 4

## Firm Summaries

### Firm 1 - MagnaArgus Corporation

| US$ U.S. | |
| --- | --- |
| 25" TV: | |
| List Price | 105.00 |
| Actual Price | 102.83 |
| 27" TV: | |
| List Price | 123.00 |
| Actual Price | 122.40 |
| Contract Bid | |
| 25" TV | 0.00 |
| 27" TV | 0.00 |
| Sales Offices | 3 |
| Distribution Centers | 1 |
| C-Wholesaler | 0 |
| I-Wholesaler | 4 |
| Salesreps | 5 |

### Firm 2 - Global Megapolis, Corp.

| US$ U.S. | |
| --- | --- |
| 25" TV: | |
| List Price | 105.00 |
| Actual Price | 102.83 |
| 27" TV: | |
| List Price | 123.00 |
| Actual Price | 122.40 |
| Contract Bid | |
| 25" TV | 0.00 |
| 27" TV | 0.00 |
| Sales Offices | 3 |
| Distribution Centers | 1 |
| C-Wholesaler | 0 |
| I-Wholesaler | 4 |
| Salesreps | 6 |

# Global Industry A Report
Year 1998 Quarter 4

## Consolidated Performance Indicators

| Firm | US$ Profit | ROA | E.P.S. | ROE | US$ Stock Price | Perform. Index |
| --- | --- | --- | --- | --- | --- | --- |
| Firm 1 - MagnaArgus Corporation | 120,281 | 1.35% | 0.048 | 1.30% | 14.49 | 1.00 |
| Firm 2 - Global Megapolis, Corp. | 120,281 | 1.35% | 0.048 | 1.30% | 14.49 | 1.00 |
| Firm 3 - Home Electronics, Inc. | 120,281 | 1.35% | 0.048 | 1.30% | 14.49 | 1.00 |
| Firm 4 - Voltavision Company | 120,281 | 1.35% | 0.048 | 1.30% | 14.49 | 1.00 |

GDP YEAR/QUARTER—Each relevant country's quarterly Gross Domestic Product is reported as an index number based on the year 1988 for the current year and operating quarter and its predicted value for the following quarter and four quarters hence by year. The values presented here reflect either real-world data or numbers created by your Game Administrator to reflect comparative growth rates between the economies being simulated.

SUBASSEMBLIES—The lot price of the Subassemblies needed for the manufacture of each television set, FOB Hong Kong by Group and Grade. These prices may vary throughout the simulation's run.

BULLETIN—A listing of various events or announcements associated with your simulation. Your Game Administrator may present Critical Incidents for you to solve and Bids and Offers for used automatons, and retailers' requests for bids on Privately Labelled sets will be found here. Periodic announcements of new product patents obtained, fines and penalties assessed, and factory openings and expansions will also be found on this Bulletin Board.

CURRENCY CROSS RATES—Displays the currency exchange rates in effect during the decision quarter. These rates may change from quarter to quarter.

GLOBAL INDUSTRY A REPORT—This information is presented to all firms in your industry. Your industry will begin with between three and nine companies competing with one another.

25" TV LIST PRICE—Each company's list price to wholesalers for its 25" television sets in the countries listed.

25" TV ACTUAL PRICE—A fairly accurate estimate of the actual market price wholesalers paid for 25" sets in the previous quarter. This price reflects trade discounts and price incentives employed by each firm to induce greater sales of their 25" television sets in the countries listed.

27" TV LIST PRICE—The company's list price to wholesalers for its 27" television sets in the countries listed.

27" TV ACTUAL PRICE—A somewhat accurate estimate of the actual price wholesalers paid for the designated product in the previous quarter. This price reflects trade discounts and price incentives used to further stimulate sales of its 27" television sets in the countries listed.

25" TV CONTRACT BID—A fairly accurate estimate of the unit price charged for 25" sets as either a product for private-label purposes or for contract sales to another firm. If both private-label contracts and manufacturing-contract sales were made, this is the weighted price of those two sales.

27" TV CONTRACT BID—A fairly accurate estimate of the unit price charged for 27" television sets as either a product for private-label purposes or for contract sales to another firm. If both private-label contracts and manufacturing-contract sales were made, this is the weighted price of those two sales.

SALES OFFICES—The quarter's total lease and administrative expenses for all Sales Offices in operation. This expense does not include any salaries and commissions earned by Sales Representatives but covers any hiring, firing, moving expenses associated with the sales staff.

DISTRIBUTION CENTERS—The number of Regional Distribution Centers in operation by country.

C-WHOLESALER—The number of Company-Owned Wholesalers in operation by country.

I-WHOLESALER—The number of Independent Wholesalers being employed by country.

SALESREPS—The number of Sales Representatives used by the company within its Sales Offices in each country.

CONSOLIDATED PERFORMANCE INDICATORS—A report on the economic performance of all companies in your industry at the Consolidated or Corporate level. The measures used are common criteria of overall organizational effectiveness. Your Game Administrator may use any or all these indicators. If the indicators shown here are employed, they may be weighted at the Game Administrator's discretion, and you will be informed of the weighting scheme being employed.

PROFIT—The company's total Earnings or Profit for the quarter.

ROA—The company's Rate of Return on Assets for the quarter. This is the firm's Earnings for the quarter divided by the firm's Assets for the quarter.

E.P.S.— The company's Earnings Per Share for the quarter. This is the firm's Owners' Equity divided by the number of shares outstanding at the quarter's end.

ROE—The company's Rate-of-Return on Owners' Equity for the quarter. This is the firm's Earnings for the quarter divided by the quarter's ending Owners' Equity (Paid-In Capital plus Retained Earnings).

STOCK PRICE—The firm's Stock Price at the quarter's end.

PERFORMANCE INDEX—The weighted ranked average of the quarter's performance indicators as chosen by your Game Administrator.

## Market/Country Area Reports

The next set of reports you receive contain material that is unique and confidential to your own company's operations. Assuming your Home Country is the United States, you would receive Balance Sheets, Income Statements, and Operating Reports only for North American Operations, and then only for United States operations, but not for Mexico, which operates within NAFTA. If your company is allowed to enter any of the other market areas available in the simulation, such as APEC or EU, you would receive similar reports for the particular market areas and countries involved.

**NORTH AMERICAN CONSOLIDATED INCOME STATEMENT**—A line identifying the market area's operations. Identical sheets are supplied for the APEC and EU market areas. Because the United States is your Home Country in this example, the results obtained in other countries and market areas "consolidate" to North American operations.

**FIRM 1 MAGNA ARGUS CORPORATION**—Your company's Firm number and name. Your Game Administrator will assign you a company number, but you will create your firm's name before the game's start-up quarter, which is described in Chapter 7.

**YEAR 1998 QUARTER 4**—A line indicating year simulation's operating year and quarter.

**GROSS REVENUES**—All revenues associated with the sale of your company's television sets. If the country in which the sale was made levies a value-added tax (VAT) or imposes tariff on the firm's products, these taxes are included in the firm's Gross Revenues. This amount includes currently generated Sales as well as Back Orders filled from the previous operating quarter. It is possible that your Sales Representatives will write more orders than can be supplied from either your company's current production and/or Finished Goods inventories on products transferred in. Should this occur, your firm allocates its available units according to the following priorities. The first priority will be product Contract sales to other firms in your industry. The second priority will be Contract sales obtained for private-brand purposes. The third priority will be the filling of old Back Orders, unless you have lowered your firm's actual price for that product. If the actual price has been lowered, the Back Orders for that product will be cancelled at the original price, but will be shipped and billed at the new, actual price. The next priority will be the shipment of goods generated by new sales in the current quarter. Should the total of all these operations entail a shortfall, that shortfall will the next quarter's Back Orders.

**VALUE-ADDED TAX**—Any value-added taxes (VATs) the firm collects for the government must be rebated each quarter. The VAT is a tax the value you have added through the manufacturing process to the raw materials your company has purchased. In the simulation this is a tax on Net Revenue minus the value of all subassemblies found in the quarter's Cost of Goods Sold. Any relevant tariffs are added to the firm's Cost of Goods Sold at the combined country and economic zone tariff rates.

**NET SALES**—An algebraic sum. This constitutes all revenues associated with your company's main form of activity.

**OTHER INCOME**—Nonoperating revenue sources available to your company.

**CAPITAL SALES GAINS/LOSSES**—Any gains or losses on the sale of Automatons above or below their book value at the time of their sale.

**INVESTMENT INCOME**—Income earned on 90-Day Short Term Investments.

**LICENSES**—Income earned on Patent Licenses granted to other firms.

# NAFTA Consolidated Income Statement
Year 1998 Quarter 4

## Firm 1 - MagnaArgus Corporation

|  | US$ Consolidated | US$ U.S. |
|---|---|---|
| **Revenues:** | | |
| Gross Revenues | 6,737,522 | 6,737,522 |
| Value-Added Tax | 0 | 0 |
| Net Sales | 6,737,522 | 6,737,522 |
| | | |
| Other Income: | | |
| Capital Sales Gains/Losses | 0 | 0 |
| Investment Income | 0 | 0 |
| Licenses | 0 | 0 |
| Non-Operating Income | 0 | 0 |
| **Total Revenue** | 6,737,522 | 6,737,522 |
| | | |
| **Expenses:** | | |
| Cost of Goods Sold | 5,033,426 | 5,033,426 |
| Advertising | 13,000 | 13,000 |
| General Administration | 167,379 | 167,379 |
| Sales Offices | 430,000 | 430,000 |
| Distribution Centers | 194,259 | 194,259 |
| Wholesale Operations | 44,000 | 44,000 |
| Sales Force Salaries | 165,572 | 165,572 |
| Trainees | 9,100 | 9,100 |
| Training and Development | 13,000 | 13,000 |
| Inventory Charges | 171,432 | 171,432 |
| Shipping | 138,542 | 138,542 |
| License Fees | 0 | 0 |
| Research and Development | 5,000 | 5,000 |
| Quality Control | 51,256 | 51,256 |
| Depreciation | 69,750 | 69,750 |
| Maintenance | 4,860 | 4,860 |
| Interest Charges: | | |
| Overdrafts | 0 | 0 |
| Short-Term Loan | 0 | 0 |
| Bonds | 0 | 0 |
| Miscellaneous | 0 | 0 |
| **Total Expenses** | 6,510,576 | 6,510,576 |
| | | |
| Income Before Taxes | 226,946 | 226,946 |
| Income Tax | 106,664 | 106,664 |
| Dividend Tax | 0 | 0 |
| **Net Income** | 120,281 | 120,281 |

NON-OPERATING INCOME—The algebraic sum of the four previous items. This constitutes income from activities incidental to your company's main manufacturing and sales activities.

TOTAL INCOME—The sum of all previous items.

COST OF GOODS SOLD—The unit manufacturing costs of all products sold during the quarter plus any applicable tariffs. This is basically the unit costs for television sets you produced yourself or obtained from other company-owned units through transfers in or Contract manufacturing performed for you by other firms in the industry. For sales that have been through intracompany transfers, your unit cost is the transfer price used to make the transfer, which included shipping costs and administrative overhead. For intercompany transfers in or manufacturing Contract sales, your unit cost is the transfer price agreed upon by both parties, with the seller paying the shipping costs involved.

ADVERTISING—The unit's total Advertising budget.

GENERAL ADMINISTRATION—The unit's total expenses for top Executive compensation, a liason executive to coordinate the activities of each country market in operation, factory Superintendancy, line Supervision and severance pay for any discharged Supervisors, the plant's size based on the available labor hours and new plant construction/expansion and equipment purchases and transfers.

SALES OFFICES—The quarter's total lease and administrative expenses for all Sales Offices in operation. This amount does not include the salaries and commissions earned by Sales Representatives attached to each Sales Office but includes the salaries and moving expenses of all personnel and the training and development costs of all non-Trainee sales staff.

DISTRIBUTION CENTERS—All expenses associated with Distribution Center operations. This amount includes the costs of warranty work performed at each Center, administrative overhead, and lease payments, but not unit inventory and handling charges. If an area does not have a Distribution Center and all goods are shipped directly from the Market/Country's factory, warranty work is both performed and charged at the plant level.

WHOLESALE OPERATIONS—The quarter's total expenses for all company-owned wholesale operations.

SALES FORCE SALARIES—Salaries and Commissions to all Sales Representatives on the unit's payroll. Sales reps who quit the company leave on the quarter's last day and collect all monies owed them at that time.

TRAINEES—Salaries for all personnel in training in your firm's Sales office(s).

TRAINING AND DEVELOPMENT—Your unit's Training and Development budget for the quarter. This account combines the individual budgets you have appropriated for training programs for those who work in your factories as either assembly-line workers or automaton Technicians and experienced Sales Representatives.

INVENTORY CHARGES—Inventory carrying and Handling charges on the number of Subassemblies and Finished Goods held in inventory on the previous operating quarter's last day. Inventory charges are not incurred on Contract sales by your firm to other firms in your industry or for any sets you make for Private-Label retailers.

SHIPPING—Shipping charges on products obtained for inventory through intercompany manufacturing Contract sales, Subassemblies received from your components consolidator in Hong Kong, and products shipped from your factories to your Distribution Centers. The shipping costs associated with the purchase of new automatons are considered to be part of the acquisition costs of adding or building new plant capacity and are capitalized and subsequently depreciated. The same accounting procedures apply to the interfirm and intrafirm sale or transfer of used automatons. Contract and Private-Label sales are shipped FOB your factory, and these units do not go through any of your Distribution Centers, if you have them.

LICENSE FEES—Payments made by your firm to other companies for the use of their Patented Features.

RESEARCH AND DEVELOPMENT—Your unit's Research and Development budget for the quarter.

QUALITY CONTROL—Your unit's Quality Control budget for the quarter.

DEPRECIATION—The quarter's total Depreciation charges on fixed Plant and Equipment. A 20-year depreciation schedule applies to Plant and Equipment, with a 10-year depreciation schedule earmarked for automatons. This is a noncash expense.

MAINTENANCE—Your unit's Maintenance budget for the quarter. This amount is the total of individual budgets for general factory maintenance, line maintenance, and maintenance by automaton type.

INTEREST CHARGES—This section gathers the interest charges on all the forms of debt your firm has used during the quarter.

OVERDRAFTS—Overdrafts associated with Interest expenses forced on your company's Corporate operations due to cash shortfalls in any of your operating units. Because your Corporate-level operations are ultimately responsible and accountable for the solvency of all Market/Country Area operations, all cash shortfalls must be covered at your company's Corporate level. Should country area operations place your Corporation into technical bankruptcy, an Overdraft is issued.

SHORT-TERM LOAN—The interest expenses associated with your operating unit's 90-Day Loan.

BONDS—The interest charge on the face value and nominal interest rate on all your company's outstanding Bonds. Should the operating unit call all or a portion of its outstanding Bond debt, the portion called will appear as an expense in this account, with the portion of the Unamortized Bond Discount being called charged against current Earnings.

MISCELLANEOUS—This includes three items: the cost of the Merlin Group's Marketing Research Studies; fines, penalties, or credits issued by the Game Administrator; and assorted costs associated with Critical Incident responses.

TOTAL EXPENSES—The sum of all Expenses listed.

INCOME BEFORE TAXES—Total Revenues less total expenses for the quarter.

TAXABLE INCOME— Income before taxes.

INCOME TAX—Federal and local taxes collected on all operating units. For nondomestic country unit operations that levy Dividend Taxes, an additional line appears covering these taxes on Retained Earnings that are repatriated to the firm's Home Country. Taxes are collected on a quarterly basis. If income is negative, the negative amount will be counted for tax-credit purposes and offsets on positive earnings for three years or 12 quarters.

DIVIDEND TAX—Any taxes levied by foreign governments on Retained Earnings repatriated to the company's Home Country. These taxes have already been paid at the Country/Market level by the time they are consolidated at the Headquarters level.

NET INCOME—Your operating unit's earnings after all taxes and expenses have been paid.

**NORTH AMERICAN CONSOLIDATED BALANCE SHEET**—A line identifying the market area's operations. Identical sheets are supplied for the APEC and EU market areas.

FIRM 1 MAGNAARGUS CORPORATION—A line identifying the company number as well as the unique, new name you have created for your company as part of the game start-up process.

CASH—All cash assets held by the Area operation and currently available for cash-flow purposes during the next quarter.

ACCOUNTS RECEIVABLE—Monies owed your firm by your independent wholesale customers. This amount is collected and will be available to your firm the following quarter. Through a tight credit policy and the required use of performance bonds, all accounts are paid in full within 90 days of the following business quarter.

TAX CREDIT—Any tax credits earned by Country Units. These are applied automatically by the simulation at the Country Unit level to off-set later earnings that would normally be taxed. In the firm's Home Country Balance Sheet this account is replaced by "Due From Country Unit(s)". This account accumulates all cash advances that have been made to any Country Unit(s).

SHORT-TERM INVESTMENTS—The total value of the investment your company has made in its respective local 90-day money markets. This amount returns to the Cash Account on the first day of the next operating quarter, with the interest earned on the investments also going to the firm's Cash Account.

SUBASSEMBLIES—The market value of all Grades and Groups of Subassemblies available for production in the next quarter based on their purchase price during the quarter of acquisition.

FINISHED GOODS INVENTORIES—The value of all products held in inventory at the quarter's end after all sales and product transfers have been conducted. This figure is the weighted average of the per unit costs of all contributors to this pool of products.

# NAFTA Consolidated Balance Sheet
Year 1998 Quarter 4

## Firm 1 - MagnaArgus Corporation

| | US$ Consolidated | US$ U.S. | |
|---|---|---|---|
| **Assets:** | | | |
| Cash | 798,425 | 798,425 | |
| Accounts Receivable | 1,347,504 | 1,347,504 | |
| Tax Credit | 0 | 0 | |
| Short-Term Investments | 0 | 0 | |
| Due From Country Unit(s) | XXX | 0 | |
| Inventories: | | | |
| Subassemblies | 3,327,898 | 3,327,898 | |
| Finished Goods | 0 | 0 | |
| Goods in Transit | 0 | 0 | |
| Total Current Assets | 5,473,827 | 5,473,827 | |
| Capital in Progress | 0 | 0 | |
| Plant and Equipment | 4,545,000 | 4,545,000 | |
| Less Depreciation | 1,138,500 | 1,138,500 | |
| Total Fixed Assets | 3,406,500 | 3,406,500 | |
| **Total Assets** | 8,880,327 | 8,880,327 | |
| **Liabilities and Owner's Equity:** | | | |
| Accounts Payable | 1,090,842 | 1,090,842 | |
| Overdraft | 0 | 0 | |
| Due to Home Country | XXX | XXX | |
| Short-Term Loan | 0 | 0 | |
| Total Current Liabilities | 1,090,842 | 1,090,842 | |
| Bonds | 0 | 0 | |
| Total Liabilities | 1,090,842 | 1,090,842 | |
| Stockholder's Equity: | | | |
| Common Stock | 2,500,000 | 2,500,000 | |
| Paid-In Capital | 1,475,823 | 1,475,823 | |
| Current Earnings | 120,281 | 120,281 | |
| Retained Earnings/Deficit | 3,693,381 | 3,693,381 | |
| Exchange Gains/Losses | 0 | 0 | |
| Total Stockholder's Equity | 7,789,485 | 7,789,485 | |
| **Total Liabilities and Owner's Equity** | 8,880,327 | 8,880,327 | |

GOODS IN TRANSIT—The administered or transfer "price" value of all Intrafirm goods being shipped by Surface, given that it takes a full quarter for them to arrive at their destination.

CAPITAL IN PROGRESS—The total value of any Plant Construction being conducted by the firm within the hemisphere and the Net Book Value of any new or used automatons being purchased from your machine-tool supplier or other companies in your industry. This Capital In Progress begins to depreciate in the first quarter that it is operational.

PLANT AND EQUIPMENT—The original value of all new plant and equipment purchased, the market value of used Automated Workstations purchased from other firms, and the remaining Book Value on used automatons Transferred In to your Market Area's operations. Once built and installed, all Plant and Equipment is subject to a 20-year straight-line depreciation rate of 1/20th per year or 1/80th per quarter on its original value except for automatons, which depreciate on a 10-year schedule at the rate of 1/10th per year or 1/40th per quarter.

LESS DEPRECIATION—The total amount of Depreciation that has occurred on all assets owned by the operating unit since their purchase date.

ACCOUNTS PAYABLE—The value of monies payable during the next operating quarter. Consists of portions of the operating quarter's factory labor costs, executive, General Administration, and plant Supervision salaries, advance purchases of Subassemblies and Tax Credits.

OVERDRAFT—An emergency loan automatically granted by the simulation to cover any total-company cash shortages. In a Country Unit's Balance Sheet, this account is replaced by "Due to Home Country." This loan will be automatically paid off by the simulation through its own cash-flow operations, but must be taken into consideration when making your next quarter's cash projections.

SHORT TERM LOAN—A 90-Day loan requested by your company. This loan will be automatically paid off in the simulation's following quarter, although it can be rolled over quarter after quarter.

BONDS—The original face value of all 10-Year Bonds floated by your operating unit.

STOCKHOLDER'S EQUITY—The sum of all the monies owed to the company's shareholders. At the Home Country level, this account is augmented by "Exchange Gains/Losses."

COMMON STOCK—The par value of all shares outstanding. The value shown in the parentheses states your company's number of shares outstanding. This account is inoperative at the Country Unit level.

PAID-IN CAPITAL—The total value of all stock issues selling above or below par. This account is inoperative at the Country Unit level.

CURRENT EARNINGS—Your operating unit's profits or losses for the quarter.

RETAINED EARNINGS/DEFICIT—The sum of all previous "Earnings from Operations."

EXCHANGE GAINS/LOSSES—An algebraic sum of currency gains and losses associated with translating Country Unit results into Home Country unit results.

TOTAL RETAINED EARNINGS—The algebraic sum of all items in this account transferred to and held by your Corporation's Consolidated Balance Sheet for stock declaration or earnings retention purposes. Because stock can only be issued at your Home Country site, the line covering PAID-IN CAPITAL appears only on your Consolidated Balance Sheet.

## Market/Country Operations Reports

The next set of reports is unique to your operations. Depending on the number of market areas and products available to you, a number of Market/Country Area reports are generated by the simulation. In these reports the data is usually reported in units of products, although at various times interest-rate percentages, indices, and ratings are reported.

OPERATIONS REPORT—An indication of the type of report being presented.

YEAR 1998 QUARTER 4— The Year and Quarter of operations being reported.

FIRM 1 MAGNAARGUS CORPORATION—The firm being reported.

CREDIT RATING—The Credit Rating associated with each country operation. This rating is highly dependent on the firm's current liquidity, its total debt/equity ratio and its times-interest-earned coverage. This rating ranges from AAA to C, with an AAA rating representing a firm entitled to the unit country's Prime Rate for short-term loans and the Home Country's federal government 10-year bond rate plus 1.0 percentage point. A C rating indicates a firm that has fallen into technical insolvency during the current quarter.

BOND RATE—The nominal or face rate applicable to 10-year bonds by each country operation. This rate is greatly influenced by the firm's liquidity, its debt-management skills, as indicated by its Credit Rating, and its amount of Owners' Equity, given its total Long-Term debt. The effective rate, or the actual interest rate, charged for any Bond issue is the result of the interaction between the firm's liquidity and equity value and the yield rates prevailing in the Market/Country Area's major money market. In this case the money-market area is New York City.

INTEREST RATE—The interest rate for a 90-Day Loan in the firm's Home Country money market, given the unit's Credit Rating.

UNIT SALES—A breakdown of the actual units sold through all channels available.

25" TV SALES—The number of 25-inch television sets sold in each country through both C-WHOLESALERS (company-owned Wholesalers) or I-WHOLESALERS (independent Wholesalers).

27" TV SALES—The number of 27-inch television sets sold in each country through your company's channels of C-WHOLESALERS and I-WHOLESALERS.

CONTRACT SALES—The number of Contract units sold by your company by set size and country. These can be contracted units manufactured for other firms in your industry or private-label sales by retailers.

MARKET SHARE—Your company's proportion of total units sold by Product and Market/Country Area. This statistic does not include Contract sales made in each country.

BACKORDERS—The number of units Back Ordered for delivery in the next quarter. The delivery of these units takes precedence over the delivery of newly generated sales but is of a lower priority than shipments to other country units or contract sales.

PRODUCTION—The number of units your company has scheduled for production by product and shift. Two shifts are available, with Overtime operations available as a 25% extension of each plant's second shift.

PLANT SUPERVISORS—The number of Supervisors assigned to each factory in each country's manufacturing operation.

ACTUAL WORKERS—The number of factory workers who actually appear for work by shift and by products scheduled for each shift. The total number of workers who actually appear is a function of each country labor force's natural culturally-based inclinations or "work ethic" for the type of work and wages provided by your firm, their health and the number of legal holidays that are observed.

HOURS DELIVERED—The number of worker labor hours that were actually delivered by shift and products. This amount is circumscribed by the availability of raw materials for products scheduled for production, the amount of training and supervision workers have received in previous quarters, equipment-maintenance budgets, and your work crew's "work ethic." It is on this amount of hours, given the prevailing wage rates in your Market/Country area, that your factory's wage bill will be calculated.

WARRANTY WORK—The number of units upon which warranty work was performed by your firm's Distribution Centers and/or Factories. The amount of warranty work executed is a function of the Quality Control programs conducted during the quarter.

GOODS IN TRANSIT—The number of units in shipment by product to any non-Home Country operation via Surface transportation. These goods take one quarter to arrive at their destination point. While In Transit they remain on the Sending unit's Balance Sheet. Upon their arrival the following quarter, the receiving unit's Finished Goods Inventory is updated by the shipped-in amount. Its Finished Goods Inventory account on its Balance Sheet will reflect the entire value of the shipment, whereas its Cash Account will be debited by this same value. The sending unit's Cash Account will be credited with the transfer price, and its Finished Goods Inventory account will be debited by the same amount. Because Private-Label sales can only be made to domestic retailers, shipments to them are not by air express. Contract sales, because they are negotiated far in advance, are shipped only by Surface transportation and will always appear as Goods in Transit for one quarter.

FINISHED GOODS INVENTORY—The total number of products held in temporary storage in your factories or Distribution Centers. All Private-Label TVs of acceptable quality are shipped directly to the contracting retailer and therefore do not enter your firm's Finished Goods Inventory. If your firm's Private-Label sets are not acceptable to the party who contracted them, *they* will appear as Finished Goods, to be reworked at the appropriate reworking charge.

UNIT COST—The average unit cost of your company's two products and any Private-Label TVs you have made. The cost reported here is the weighted average of older units in inventory and those units possibly added in the current quarter.

QUALITY INDEX—An indication of the physical quality of the products produced in the operating quarter. This index ranges from 1.0 to 10.0, with a "1.0" indicating products of very low quality, a "5.0" indicating an average level of quality, and a "10.0" associated with products of the highest quality. For successful Contract/ Private Branding sales, the product's Quality Index must meet at least the quality grade contracted. For products made under license to other firms in your industry, you must produce your units at or above the Quality Index level specified in the contract. If this level is not attained during the contract's production quarter, the contract order is cancelled by the contracting firm and the sets are returned to your Finished Goods Inventory for reworking. The charge for the rework performed is assessed at 15% of the direct costs of your firm's most recent production quarter for the set size involved in the Contract.

SUBASSEMBLY INVENTORY—The number of Subassemblies available for next quarter's production by Subassembly Group and their Grades. Two Groups of Subassemblies are required to complete a television set and these Subassemblies can be purchased in three different quality Grades.

PLANT CONFIGURATION—The mixture of assembly-line-attended production methods, as possibly augmented by Automated Workstations (automatons) of two levels of self-control and technical complexity. This mixture determines the engineering-based productivity of your firms' factories. The amount of production hours generated by the combination of workers and automatons is reported as total Labor Hours, which can be distributed between your products, given their assembly-labor-hour requirements. Base Capacity is reported in the total number of workers that can man each eight-hour shift. Automatons are reported in the number of AUTO1s and AUTO2s installed in each factory.

NEW CAPACITY IN PROGRESS—The incremental changes being made in your plant-operating capabilities through either capacity expansions, new plant construction, or automaton acquisitions.

PRODUCT DISTRIBUTION FROM/TO—A statement of the products actually shipped from and to various country units in the decision quarter. The number of units actually shipped may not equal the amounts you planned due to a number of factors, such as running out of raw-material Subassemblies, not scheduling enough line workers, or having equipment breakdowns.

SHIPPING METHOD—A restatement of your firm's decisions on how to ship products within and between countries. Regular Surface nondomestic shipments take one quarter for delivery and are also reported as "Goods in Transit." All within-area shipments are delivered to Distribution Centers during the same quarter for sale. Express Air (ExAir) shipping allows the receipt of all nondomestic products to other countries in the same quarter. Your company can use a mixture of both transportation methods between country units during the same quarter.

AUTOMATON DISTRIBUTION—A restatement of how your company distributed Intracompany and intercompany transfers of automatons by automaton type and destination. The values produced here must agree with the units stated in any Automaton Sale and Transfer Agreement forms your firm submitted for the quarter. If an agreement was not recognized by the simulation or was not approved by the Game Administrator, no values will appear on this report. This indicates the transaction was voided.

MAINTENANCE EFFECT—An index of the suitability of Maintenance Budgets expended. Values above 1.00 indicate excessive maintenance monies with values below 1.00 indicate inadequate maintenance budgets and one that can cause equipment breakdowns and higher line worker absentee rates.

CASH—A statement of how you transferred cash between companies.

# Operations Report
Year 1998 Quarter 4

## Firm 1 - MagnaArgus Corporation

| | U.S. |
|---|---|
| Credit Rating | AAA |
| Bond Rate | 8.95% |
| Short-Term Rate | 4.73% |
| 25" TV Sales: | |
| C-Wholesaler | 0 |
| I-Wholesaler | 24079 |
| 27" TV Sales: | |
| C-Wholesaler | 0 |
| I-Wholesaler | 34816 |
| Contract Sales: | |
| 25" TV | 0 |
| 27" TV | 0 |
| Market Share: | |
| 25" TV | 25.0% |
| 27" TV | 25.5% |
| Backorders: | |
| 25" TV | 1537 |
| 27" TV | 5723 |
| Production: | |
| Shift 1 25" TV | 12568 |
| Shift 2 27" TV | 15724 |
| Shift 2 25" TV | 11633 |
| Shift 2 27" TV | 15661 |
| Overtime 25" TV | 0 |
| Overtime 27" TV | 3606 |
| Plant Supervisors | 2 |
| Workers: | |
| Shift 1 25" TV | 51 |
| Shift 1 27" TV | 48 |
| Shift 2 25" TV | 50 |
| Shift 2 27" TV | 50 |
| Hours Delivered: | |
| Shift 1 25" TV | 22622.4 |
| Shift 1 27" TV | 31448.0 |
| Shift 2 25" TV | 20939.4 |
| Shift 2 27" TV | 31322.0 |
| Overtime 25" TV | 0.0 |
| Overtime 27" TV | 7212.0 |
| Warranty Work: | |
| 25" TV | 1445 |
| 27" TV | 2089 |
| Goods In Transit: | |
| 25" TV | 0 |
| 27" TV | 0 |
| Contract 25" TV | 0 |
| Contract 27" TV | 0 |

Finished Goods Inventory:
    25" TV                              0
    27" TV                              0
Unit Cost:
    25" TV                         85.986
    27" TV                         84.378
Quality Index:
    25" TV                           7.37
    27" TV                           7.37
    Contract                         0.00
Subassembly Inventory:
    Group 1 Grade A               285723
    Group 1 Grade B               285722
    Group 1 Grade C                57166
    Group 2 Grade A               214856
    Group 2 Grade B               214857
    Group 2 Grade C                42420
Plant Configuration:
    Base Capacity                    140
    Automaton 1 Machines               2
    Automaton 2 Machines               1
    Labor Hours                    76505
New Capacity In Progress:
    Base Capacity                      0
    Automaton 1 Machines               0
    Automaton 2 Machines               0
Product Distribution From:
    25" TV                             0
    27" TV                             0
    Contract                           0
Product Distribution To:
    25" TV                             0
    27" TV                             0
    Contract                           0
Shipping Method:
    Surface                        29447
    Express Air                        0
Automaton Distribution:
    Automaton 1 Machines               0
    Automaton 2 Machines               0
Maintenance Effect                   1.54
Cash:
    From                               0
    To                                 0
Retained Earnings From                 0

**Firm Operation Notes**

United States - Firm 1 had 1 Sales Representative(s) quit at the end of the quarter.

RETAINED EARNINGS FROM—A statement of how you asked your company's offshore operations to remit their own Retained Earnings to your Home Country's Retained Earnings account. Because of Dividend Taxes levied in each foreign country, the amount of Retained Earnings ultimately arriving at Headquarters will be less than the stated amount.

## Your Next Steps

You have now been presented with the basic types of outputs *The Global Business Game* produces. In the next chapter of your Player's Manual you will find suggestions as to how to organize your company and your activities so you will be as successful as possible and will learn as much as practical. Additionally, just as this chapter has dealt with the game's *outputs,* the next chapter will begin to deal with your *inputs* to the game. These entail the decision-making forms through which you will summarize the many smaller decisions you will have to make. Chapter 4, which covers the simulation's marketing and marketing-logistics operations, and Chapter 6, which covers the game's financial and accounting operations, will present you with various standard decision-making aids that have been found useful to those who play management games. In those chapters you will find sales forecasting work sheets, cash-flow work sheets, and *Pro Forma* income statements and balance sheets.

# CHAPTER 3

# Organizing Company Operations

As members of your company's new management team, you may or may not know each other very well. Your Game Administrator may have randomly assigned you to your decision-making group. You may have been allowed to choose your own teammates. Or, some combination of methods may have been employed for "balance" —or otherwise to create what your Game Administrator thinks makes for an ideal management team for *The Global Business Game.* Whatever method was used for setting up teams, your group will have to organize itself as a social group, then as a learning group, and finally as a management group that has to take over a fairly complex company in a highly competitive industry.

A wide range of behaviors and attitudes present themselves when the typical business game begins. Some players want to jump right in, confidently espousing a number of big ideas they have for running the company. Others are more conservative and adopt a wait-and-see attitude to avoid making major mistakes. Between these two extremes lie a number of self-denials and defense mechanisms which, while real and significant, must be resolved if your team is to be effective.

This chapter is designed to help your team to be as intelligent and deliberate as possible, given the ambiguities of the simulated marketplace. A number of exercises have been created for your use. Your Game Administrator or instructor may assign some of these as homework or may use them in class. In addition or instead, your Game Administrator may use other exercises to help you obtain the high cohesion associated with successful teams and companies. Whatever the course of action taken, the saying "Well begun is half done" is correct. If you prepare your team well for this gaming experience, you will have forestalled many problems that would otherwise be likely to occur later. Take the time now to engage in the material found in this chapter, and you will ultimately have a much more solid team in *The Global Business Game.*

## Creating an Effective Management Team

Those engaged in any group decision-making exercise or situation must solve two issues if the group is to be effective. Those two issues are its *social* problem and its *task* problem. The social problem deals with work-group relations, including peer relations, social hierarchy, leadership roles, and what is acceptable and unacceptable behavior. It basically involves how the group's members get along with each other, and embraces those small social matters that make people want to spend time with each other for the sheer fun of it.

The other problem is the group's task problem. This involves understanding the concepts and skills required to facilitate an understanding of the group's tasks while assembling or developing the skills and ideas necessary for accomplishing results. Some decision-making teams emphasize the tasks confronting them but neglect to service the group's social needs. Sometimes they just hope the social aspects do not get in their way. Other decision-making groups have a great time being together, but often sacrifice optimal economic or task-performance results for social performance or their own sense of personal well-being.

Because both problems must be solved if you are going to have a socially stable and economically effective management team in *The Global Business Game,* your group will find it worthwhile to engage in the social and task-oriented exercises found in this manual. These types of exercises, as simple as they appear, are useful for both game-playing and real-world executive decision-making groups. Take the time now to go "through the ropes" before the game begins and you'll start off on a stronger footing regarding the goals and objectives possessed by each member of your team. You will also gain a better understanding of the goals and objectives your company has decided to pursue, using your time together efficiently and also satisfying your own learning needs.

## Personal-Goal and Group Norm-Setting Exercise

This is an information-sharing exercise where you are asked to specifically present to others the outcomes you expect from this gaming experience. This includes what you bring to the situation and what you expect from your teammates. You may discover that there are strong similarities between what everybody wants, the talents they have, and their expectations. You may also discover whether your team has a redundancy of talent and whether its talents complement and enhance each other.

Alternatively, through using this exercise you may discover that there are strong and conflicting differences in expectations between your group's members. You may discover that some want more from the situation than you want, or that some are heavily committed to other activities and cannot dedicate many hours to the simulation. You may also discover that your team is unbalanced in its technical skills and interests, for example, having a large number of people who like finance and none who like operations management or who feel comfortable with the marketplace's ambiguities. If your team is to be an optimally effective management and learning group, the nature of these differences must be understood, and accommodations have to be made by everyone.

The Personal-Goal and Group Norm-Setting Exercise should be conducted before you begin playing *The Global Business Game.* Briefly meet when your group has been first formed to determine when and where you will conduct this exercise. At this briefing session, scan the exercise's tasks and procedures so everyone knows the advance preparation that is needed if the exercise is to proceed smoothly and productively.

## Executive Evaluation Form

If your management group conducted the Personal-Goal and Group Norm-Setting Exercise, you probably discovered there were a number of individual business-related traits, attitudes, and skills that your group considered desirable during the simulation's run. Real-world firms try to reward the behaviors they desire through elaborate reward and employee-evaluation systems. You are encouraged to employ this same method when you play *The Global Business Game.* You cannot dole out real money, but you can let others on your team know how their performance is perceived. If they are deficient, you can help them to be better performers in this learning situation.

# Personal-Goal and Group Norm-Setting Exercise

## Introduction

The decision-making group you have joined for *The Global Business Game* may be made up of people you know, people you *think* you know, and some who are complete strangers. It is important to know the skills and motivations your teammates have and what they expect from you if you are to have an effective learning experience. Your group must also learn and accept certain group norms about how things are done as you run your simulated company. The purpose of this exercise is to bring into the open everybody's expectations, to appreciate the talents, skills, and motivations possessed by everyone on your team, and to reach an understanding regarding your learning group's operating rules.

## Outcomes

After completing this exercise you should be aware of:

1. What each member of your management team expects from the simulation experience.

2. The array of talents and skills your management team possesses.

3. A mutually agreed-upon plan or guide for conducting future decision-making sessions.

## Pre-Exercise Preparation

Prepare the following three lists before meeting as a group, covering what you want to learn from this game experience, what you bring to the exercise, and what you expect from others on your decision-making team.

| What I Expect for Myself | What I Bring to My Decision-Making Team | What I Expect of My Teammates |
|---|---|---|
| 1. _____ | 1. _____ | 1. _____ |
| 2. _____ | 2. _____ | 2. _____ |
| 3. _____ | 3. _____ | 3. _____ |
| 4. _____ | 4. _____ | 4. _____ |
| 5. _____ | 5. _____ | 5. _____ |
| 6. _____ | 6. _____ | 6. _____ |

After completing your lists, be prepared to discuss them at a teammate group meeting about what you expect from the experience itself and what you expect of your teammates.

## Group Meeting Materials and Supplies

Blackboard and chalk or flip chart with felt-tip markers. Room with moveable seating.

## Group Meeting Procedure

### Step 1

Group shares its individual lists of "What I Expect for Myself." Arrange the expectations in two columns on the blackboard or flip chart with one for the expectations that are the same for all in the group and the other column for any expectations that are held by only one person.

### Step 2

Group shares its respective lists of "What I Bring to My Decision-Making Team." Arrange on the same blackboard or flip chart these talents in one column, noting those talents that have more than one citation.

*Continued*

## Personal-Goal and Group Norm-Setting Exercise, *continued*

### Step 3

Group shares its individual lists of "What I Expect of My Teammates." Arrange these expectations in one column on the blackboard or flip chart, noting those expectations mentioned more than once.

### Step 4

Discuss by chart any large discrepancies existing between the group's general expectations for themselves, what they expect from each other, and what skills, talents, and enthusiasms they bring to the gaming experience.

### Step 5

For each large discrepancy, work out accommodations or reconciliations that are mutually agreeable to the group. If an accord cannot be reached, or an impasse exists within your group, report this result to your Game Administrator for a possible team-intervention effort.

### Step 6

Complete the following chart for guiding your company's initial decision-making sessions.

| | |
|---|---|
| **Decision-making day** | |
| **Decision-making time** | |
| **Meeting place** | |

Source: This exercise is adapted from Peter P. Dawson, *Fundamentals of Organizational Behavior: An Experiential Approach.* Englewood Cliffs, N.J.: Prentice-Hall, 1985, pp. 27–28.

On pages 40 and 41 you will find two blank copies of a suggested Executive Evaluation Form. Multiple copies may be made so that each team member can individually each other member privately. These individual, privately administered evaluations should then be averaged to provide each player with a summary evaluation of his/her performance. Whether you use this form or create one of your own, make sure the behaviors you evaluate are directly related to those your group believes are tied to organizational performance. Accordingly, the following summarizes the enlightened management rules that should guide your evaluation process:

1. Use evaluation criteria that are directly related to both organizational performance and the group's performance.

2. Recognize that not all criteria are equally important even though all may be desirable. Weight the criteria based on your group's beliefs on how important each one is for the accomplishment of your company's success in the game.

3. Conduct two rounds of executive evaluation during the course of the game. This provides all members feedback on how they are performing and gives those who are lacking in some categories an opportunity to improve their performance. It is suggested that you administer the Executive Evaluation Form at the simulation's midpoint and at its endgame.

4. When providing both positive and negative feedback to your teammates, use specific examples of the behaviors they demonstrated that were desirable or undesirable.

5. If a teammate has been underperforming based on criteria established by the group, provide the teammate with an opportunity to create a plan to bring his/her performance up to at least an "Acceptable" level. The group should monitor the individual's progress and provide interim feedback on the progress that has been made before the group's second round of executive evaluation.

# Mission Statement and Organizational Purpose

Today's large-scale real-world organizations find themselves competing in many markets with a wide number of products and employing thousands of workers. Although these activities have allowed them to be more competitive, they have also often caused them to lose their sense of identity and purpose as they become more complex and more distanced from their origins and founding executives. The cure for this problem in recent years has been the creation of company mission statements, spelling out the firm's purpose, what makes it special, and how it believes it should conduct its business.

Just as mission statements are beneficial to real-world firms, the creation of one for your company in *The Global Business Game* will also be useful. When your group first gets together, a number of strategic choices will have to be made about your company's operations. By creating a mission statement your group will be forced to come to grips with such organizationally defining questions as what you want your company to be, what products you will sell, in how many markets you will sell them, and what production and distribution systems your company will use.

The Mission-Statement Exercise (on page 42) will help you create a useful mission statement for your firm. The exercise uses five major sections that address individually those areas that define the nature of the business enterprise in both its physical and abstract forms. Research has found that the most effective mission statements address the areas covered in this exercise. These areas are the company's scale and scope of operations, the nature of the products or services produced, the production method employed, the prime beneficiaries of the firm's activities, and the values the company embraces or wishes to encourage.

Your company should perform the exercise before the simulation begins, ending with your writing a short but well-understood statement of your company's mission, its reason for being. In going through your exercise and completing your Mission Statement, you may ultimately choose to be a relatively small and efficient company and one that produces only 25" sets for sale in the United States. You may, on the other hand, decide to have a wide scope of activities by producing 25" and 27" sets for sale on your own account, sold to Private Label retailers and sold to other manufacturers in your industry. This would be done in as many markets as possible.

Regarding your firm's production method, you may build and use labor-intensive plants in low labor-cost areas. You could also choose to build highly automated plants close to the world's major markets for television sets. When deciding who your company is really working for, you may determine that the prime beneficiary of your efforts should be share holders, who want income from their investment. In that event, you would insure that modest yet dependable dividends were declared every quarter. The values your company espouses may be creativity and spirited entrepreneurship. Alternatively, you may embrace fiscal responsibility and corporate stewardship as the values for your firm to support and reward.

# Executive Evaluation Form

Rate each member of your management team, except yourself, on their performance in *The Global Business Game,* using the following scale and point values:

1 = Clearly excellent, a strong force for high group performance

2 = Above expectations, more than adequate performance

3 = Acceptable, adequate performance

4 = Below expectations, barely adequate performance

5 = Unacceptable, behavior damages group effectiveness

Use the criterion weights agreed upon by your group in the "Weight" column. The sum of these weights must equal 100 or 1.00. Obtain a weighted average for each player. In the "Notes" section, cite specific instances of desirable or undesirable behaviors. When finished with your evaluation, submit it to a person on your team designated for this purpose. Make sure your Executive Evaluation Form is unidentified.

| Criterion | Weight | Players' Names and Ratings | | | | |
|---|---|---|---|---|---|---|
| | .__ | | | | | |
| | .__ | | | | | |
| | .__ | | | | | |
| | .__ | | | | | |
| | .__ | | | | | |
| | .__ | | | | | |
| | .__ | | | | | |
| Summary Evaluation | 1.00 | | | | | |

Notes:

_____

_____

_____

_____

_____

_____

# Executive Evaluation Form

Rate each member of your management team, except yourself, on their performance in *The Global Business Game,* using the following scale and point values:

1 = Clearly excellent, a strong force for high group performance

2 = Above expectations, more than adequate performance

3 = Acceptable, adequate performance

4 = Below expectations, barely adequate performance

5 = Unacceptable, behavior damages group effectiveness

Use the criterion weights agreed upon by your group in the "Weight" column. The sum of these weights must equal 100 or 1.00. Obtain a weighted average for each player. In the "Notes" section, cite specific instances of desirable or undesirable behaviors. When finished with your evaluation, submit it to a person on your team designated for this purpose. Make sure your Executive Evaluation Form is unidentified.

| Criterion | Weight | Players' Names and Ratings | | | | |
|---|---|---|---|---|---|---|
|  | .___ |  |  |  |  |  |
|  | .___ |  |  |  |  |  |
|  | .___ |  |  |  |  |  |
|  | .___ |  |  |  |  |  |
|  | .___ |  |  |  |  |  |
|  | .___ |  |  |  |  |  |
|  | .___ |  |  |  |  |  |
| Summary Evaluation | 1.00 |  |  |  |  |  |

Notes:

_____

_____

_____

_____

_____

_____

_____

# Mission-Statement Exercise

## Introduction

Mission statements are useful devices for helping a company to focus its activities and represent itself to the public. These statements should cover those activity areas that shape what the organization is and what it does. It is important for your company's new management team to understand the nature of its activities and to a have a strong sense of identity. This exercise will force your company to generally define what it is, as well as bringing about a commonly agreed upon understanding of what you are as a company.

## Outcomes

After completing this exercise you will

1. Know what you think makes your company distinctive.
2. Know the components of the ideal Mission Statement.
3. Know how the components of an ideal Mission Statement are applied to your company.
4. Have a Mission Statement for your company.

## Group-Meeting Materials and Supplies

Blackboard and chalk or flip chart with felt-tip markers. Room with moveable seating.

## Group-Meeting Procedure

### Step 1

Complete together as a group the following form by completing the incomplete sentence that introduces each component of the mission statement.

### Step 2

Based on the Mission Statement sentences you generated on the form, bring them together in the Mission Statement box. You now have your company's Mission Statement.

# Mission-Statement Components Form

Complete the following sentences:

**Our Company's Scope and Scale of Operations Will Be:**

_____

_____

_____

**Our Products or Services Will Be:**

_____

_____

_____

**We Will Produce Our Products and Services By:**

_____

_____

_____

**Our Company Exists Primarily for the Benefit of:**

_____

_____

_____

**We Will Engage in All Our Activities by Embracing the Values of:**

_____

_____

_____

**Mission-Statement Box**

_____

_____

_____

_____

# Possible Organizational Forms

The strategic-management literature has posited a relationship between the firm's strategy and the structure used to carry out that strategy. Debate exists on the causal relationship between the two, however, as well as the locus of the forces that cause the firm to change either its strategy or its structure.

Despite this debate, your company in *The Global Business Game* should determine at least how you will structure your decision-making meetings, as well as the roles or duties you want each of your teammates to perform. Large, formal organizations rely on organizational forms that are based on functions, divisions, or strategic business units. Most business-game teams are more pragmatic and use simple, *ad hoc* structures. The most important element in all this is that your decision-making sessions must be planful, focused, and driven by a desire to succeed.

As much as your team in *The Global Business Game* does not need the clutter of a formal organizational structure, it *does* need a sense of order, responsibility, and accountability. One way to accomplish this is by creating position descriptions or lists of duties to be performed by each player on your team. When you create these position descriptions you might consider the various ways real-world organizations set up both position descriptions and the actual positions or specializations of labor they feel are needed in their companies.

Depending on how your Game Administrator has structured *The Global Business Game* for play, different sets of positions will be more appropriate than others. If your game is relatively constrained—say, for only one product being sold just in the United States—it would be most appropriate to build your firm's position descriptions around the basic business functions being performed. This is known as the Functional Structure or Activity Grouping form. Here, if you were a four-person team, you might have one player handle your firm's marketing, another act as the Operations Manager of your factory, another handling finances, and another doing the firm's bookkeeping and accounting.

If your Game Administrator has made your simulation more complex by increasing the variety of television sets you can produce, still limiting the number of markets within which you can sell those sets, you may decide to use position descriptions based on those found in organizations that departmentalize themselves by product. This would be the Output Grouping form. If your Game Administrator has created a gaming situation where you can sell a limited range of products in many markets, you might use the position descriptions found in firms that group their activities by customer and country. This organizational form uses User/Customer Groups.

The most complex organizational forms, and ones that generate position descriptions appropriate for a version of *The Global Business Game* where a very wide range of products can be made and sold in all six country markets, are those termed Multifocused forms. These forms are associated with Matrix Organizations and the Hybrid organizational structure. Exhibit 3.1 illustrates the possible use of each of the forms that have just been described.

# Position Descriptions

With these organizational forms in mind, you can now create position descriptions, position titles, and lists of the duties of each member of your team. If your simulation has been designed to be relatively simple and you are a four-member team, the likely position titles might be (1) Chief Executive Office or President, (2) V-P Marketing, (3) V-P Finance/Accounting, and (4) V-P Manufacturing or Operations Management, all within the Functional form. If your Game Administrator has chosen to have you play a relatively complex version of *The Global Business Game,* and has put six or seven executives on each management team, you might create titles and job descriptions appropriate for the Hybrid form.

The forms on pages 46 and 47 will help you formalize the titles and job duties associated with whatever form you feel is appropriate for your company's competitive situation. Once you have accomplished this task, you might tie the duties associated with these positions to the Executive Evaluation Forms you may have created. By doing this step, you can make any midgame and endgame performance evaluations of your "executives" even more specific, thereby taking further steps to ensure that everyone on your management team pulls their weight. With this step, you also make sure that everyone is recognized for their efforts.

**Exhibit 3.1   Possible Organizational Forms for Position Descriptions**

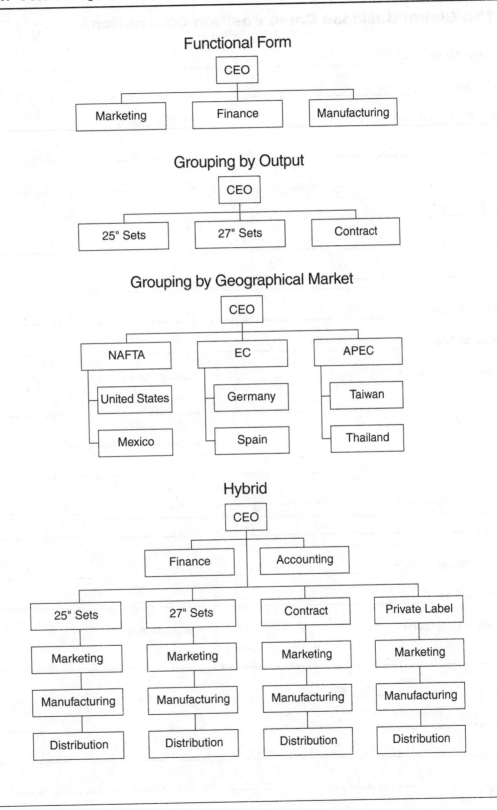

# The Global Business Game Position Descriptions

Player Name _____

Position Title _____

Position Description                          Position Duties

_____                    _____

_____                    _____

_____                    _____

_____                    _____

_____                    _____

Player Name _____

Position Title _____

Position Description                          Position Duties

_____                    _____

_____                    _____

_____                    _____

_____                    _____

_____                    _____

Player Name _____

Position Title _____

Position Description                          Position Duties

_____                    _____

_____                    _____

_____                    _____

_____                    _____

_____                    _____

# The Global Business Game Position Descriptions

Player Name _____

Position Title _____

Position Description

_____

_____

_____

_____

_____

Position Duties

_____

_____

_____

_____

_____

Player Name _____

Position Title _____

Position Description

_____

_____

_____

_____

_____

Position Duties

_____

_____

_____

_____

_____

Player Name _____

Position Title _____

Position Description

_____

_____

_____

_____

_____

Position Duties

_____

_____

_____

_____

_____

# Opportunities and Threats

If your firm is to be successful in *The Global Business Game,* your management group must get a feeling for the nature of the business environment in which it competes. One popular method for understanding the business environment's general characteristics is to conduct an Opportunities and Threats analysis. By convention, an Opportunity is any factor external to the firm that may help it to achieve the results it desires. Conversely, Threats are external factors that may frustrate or defeat the firm's attempts to achieve its desired outcomes.

These factors lie in what have variously been termed the firm's macroeconomic, remote, or general environment. This environment, in turn, is comprised of a number of segments or sectors for the purposes of conducting a finer-grained analysis of the firm's situation*. The most commonly cited sectors or segments and their elements are the following:

1. Demographic—The market's population size, age structure, geographic distribution, education levels, ethnic mix and income distribution.

2. Economic—The market's overall wealth or GDP, per capita wealth, inflation rate, interest rate patterns, growth, trade and budget deficits or surpluses and business and personal savings rates.

3. Political/Legal—The market's political stability, governmental attitudes towards business, antitrust, taxation, unemployment and labor training laws, protectionist and deregulation policies and educational support and philosophies.

4. Sociocultural—Workforce diversity, environmental concerns, life-style choices, female labor force participation, quality of life and quality of work life, career expectations and product liability and product safety concerns.

5. Technological—Rate of product and process innovations, funding for basic and applied research and communications infrastructure.

6. Global—Existence of global markets, cultural and institutional diversity, emerging markets, absolute and comparative advantage of nations, capital fluidity, trading blocks, international law and trade governance.

At the business game's beginning, it is likely that all companies will start off in equal positions. Thus, all firms are facing the same macroeconomic environment. The only differences between the companies will lie in the quality of the decisions each management group makes. This quality, in turn, is based on the amount of "sweat and brain power" each team brings to the game.

Because all teams are facing the same environment, how you perceive it is very important. Does your group see danger lurking in every corner? Does it appear to you that nothing can fail and that the world is full of opportunities? Or do you see a mixture of "goods" and "bads" in the macroenvironment your firm faces?

The Opportunities and Threats Exercise on the following pages will help your management team externalize its beliefs about the macroeconomic environment. Most of the information needed for you to fill in the macroeconomic characteristics of each country's market in the simulation can be found in Chapter 1 of this manual. Carefully review the particulars of each country in your world and national markets and transfer them to the countries found in the Perceived Opportunities and Threats Form. As examples of how you might work through this exercise, your group may decide that Thailand's Political/Legal sector is more a Threat than an Opportunity, due to the instability of its ruling family and military groups. You may also decide that Germany's high per capita wealth and technological prowess is a real Opportunity, and that Mexico's proximity to the United States, combined with its low labor rates, is another Opportunity. What is most important here is how your group perceives the situation and ultimately what you will do with the Threats and Opportunities you are facing.

---

*This presentation generally follows that of Michael A. Hitt, R. Duane Ireland, and Robert E. Hoskisson, *Strategic Management: Competitiveness and Globalization.*  Minneapolis/St. Paul: West Publishing Company, 1997, pp. 43, 47–56.

## Opportunities and Threats Exercise

### Introduction

Analyzing the firm's Opportunities and Threats as management perceives them is an important step in determining the strategic actions that might be taken. This is especially important for firms operating in diverse worldwide markets such as yours in *The Global Business Game.* This exercise will cause your management group to realize, and reach a common understanding of, the Opportunities and Threats that delimit your company's general environment and have a long-term influence on the successes associated with your responses to that environment.

### Outcomes

After completing this exercise you will:

1. Have defined what your management group thinks are the business Opportunities available to any company in the simulation by major country markets.

2. Have defined what your management group thinks are the business Threats facing any company in the simulation by major country markets.

### Group Meeting Materials and Supplies

Blackboard and chalk or flip chart with felt-tip markers. A room with moveable seating.

### Group Meeting Procedure

Complete as a group the following form.

# Perceived Opportunities and Threats Form

Fill in, for each country market available to you in *The Global Business Game,* the Opportunities and Threats faced by every firm.

## Opportunities

| Sector | United States | Mexico |
|---|---|---|
| Demographic | | |
| Economic | | |
| Sociocultural | | |
| Political/Legal | | |
| Technological | | |
| Global | | |

## Threats

| Sector | United States | Mexico |
|---|---|---|
| Demographic | | |
| Economic | | |
| Sociocultural | | |
| Political/Legal | | |
| Technological | | |
| Global | | |

## Opportunities

| Sector | Germany | Spain |
|---|---|---|
| Demographic | | |
| Economic | | |
| Sociocultural | | |
| Political/Legal | | |
| Technological | | |
| Global | | |

## Threats

| Sector | Germany | Spain |
|---|---|---|
| Demographic | | |
| Economic | | |
| Sociocultural | | |
| Political/Legal | | |
| Technological | | |
| Global | | |

## Opportunities

| Sector | Taiwan | Thailand |
| --- | --- | --- |
| Demographic | | |
| Economic | | |
| Sociocultural | | |
| Political/Legal | | |
| Technological | | |
| Global | | |

## Threats

| Sector | Taiwan | Thailand |
| --- | --- | --- |
| Demographic | | |
| Economic | | |
| Sociocultural | | |
| Political/Legal | | |
| Technological | | |
| Global | | |

# Strategic Objectives and the Strategic Planning Hierarchy

As the managers of your company, your ultimate task is to insure its long-term strength and viability. To do this, some basic decisions have to be made that have long-term consequences in this regard. Such decisions are *strategic* as they dramatically change the organization's ability to compete and to control its destiny. After these strategic decisions have been made and resources have been committed to their accomplishment, your firm will make a number of short-term decisions within the parameters established by your strategic decisions. These short-term decisions are *tactical* decisions: basically, moves within a previously determined field of play.

From this presentation you can see that a sequence or hierarchy of strategy exists. This hierarchy entails (1) the choice of strategy the firm will pursue, (2) the establishment of strategic objectives that must be obtained if the strategy is to be accomplished (which in turn indicates whether the strategy that is being implemented is working), (3) a set of support policies used in the firm's functional areas to simplify decision making by establishing general decision rules, and (4) standard operating procedures that dictate how daily, recurring operations will be handled. If all this is done correctly, the firm's strategy will be correctly implemented and controlled.

This is an extremely important and a very logical process. The Strategy Hierarchy Exercise can help your company implement and control whatever strategy or strategies it chooses to pursue. In this exercise you are asked to create a statement of your firm's strategy and then to generate a number of quantified objectives that must be accomplished if the strategy's implementation is to be effectively monitored. From this starting point you are then asked to create (1) a number of policies that should guide the decisions of those in charge of the firm's functional areas and (2) two operating procedures that must be adhered to when making decisions in each of the functional areas.

From this presentation you can see that a sequence or hierarchy of strategy exists. This hierarchy entails (1) the choice of the strategy the firm will pursue, (2) the establishment of strategic objectives that must be obtained if the strategy is to be accomplished, (3) a set of support policies used in the firm's functional areas to simplify decision making by establishing general desision rules, and (4) standard operating procedures that dictate how daily, recurring operations will be handled. If all this is done correctly, the firm's strategy will be correctly implemented and controlled.

Over the next three pages, the Strategy Hierarchy Exercise will help your company implement and control whatever strategy or strategies it chooses to pursue. In this exercise you are asked to create a statement of your firm's strategy and then to generate a number of quantified objectives that must be accomplished if the strategy's implementation is to be effectively monitored. From this starting point, you are then asked to create (1) a number of policies that should guide the decisions of those in charge of the firm's functional areas and (2) two operating procedures that must be adhered to when making decisions in each of the functional areas.

# Strategy Hierarchy Exercise

## Introduction

Any firm in a dynamic or changing business environment must make strategic decisions. These decisions affect the long-term health of the firm. Assuming the firm has made the correct choice of strategy, the next task is to implement that strategy and to make sure the strategy's implications permeate every organizational level and functional area. Thus a strategy hierarchy exists from the organization's top to bottom, and it entails a logical sequence of subordinate decisions and actions. The completion of this exercise will exemplify the strategy hierarchy associated with a firm's Grand Strategy of Market Development.

## Outcomes

After completing this exercise you should be aware of:

1. The nature of the strategy hierarchy.

2. The array and the nature of the subordinate decisions which flow down the strategy hierarchy.

3. How to create a strategy hierarchy for your own firm given its own choice of Grand or Generic Strategy.

## Group Meeting Materials and Supplies

Blackboard and chalk or flip chart with felt-tip markers. A room with moveable seating.

## Group Meeting Procedure

For the Grand Strategy of Market Development chosen by the firm in the exercise, fill in for each hierarchical level on the Strategy Hierarchy Worksheet the actions, written statements, and guidelines the firm should create by functional area for the successful implementation of such a strategy.

### Step 1

State in a simple, one-sentence form the firm's strategy.

### Step 2

State a set of Strategic Objectives that are quantifiable and measurable that must be accomplished within certain time periods if the strategy is to be fully realized and successfully implemented. The accomplishment or failure to accomplish these objectives should indicate to top management whether the firm has succeeded or failed at realizing the results of the Market Development strategy it has chosen.

### Step 3

Create for each of the firm's major functional areas—marketing, finance, and manufacturing—a set of policies that support the implementation of the Market Development Strategy chosen by the firm.

### Step 4

Create for each of the firm's major functional areas a set of Standard Operating Procedures the staff of each functional area *must* follow in carrying out their duties in support of the firm's Grand Strategy of Market Development.

# Strategy Hierarchy Worksheet

The firm in our exercise wants to grow in sales and has chosen a Grand Strategy of Market Development as the way this will be accomplished. Thus, it will not develop new products but will instead create or enter new markets with the products it is currently producing.

## Strategy Statement

Place here a simple statement of the Grand Strategy the company intends to pursue.

_____

_____

## Strategic Objectives

Place here a number of quantified goals or objectives, tied to specific time periods, that would indicate to you whether the chosen Grand Strategy is being accomplished.

1. _____

   _____

2. _____

   _____

3. _____

   _____

4. _____

   _____

## Functional Area Policies

Place here policies each functional area should pursue. These policies should directly support the long-term implementation of the firm's Grand Strategy of Market Development.

| Marketing | Finance | Manufacturing |
|-----------|---------|---------------|
| _____ | _____ | _____ |
| _____ | _____ | _____ |
| _____ | _____ | _____ |
| _____ | _____ | _____ |

## Functional Area Standard Operating Procedures

Place here two (2) standard operating procedures that those in charge of each particular functional area should follow on a round-by-round basis within the guidelines established by the functional area's policies.

**Marketing**

1. _____

_____

_____

_____

_____

_____

2. _____

_____

_____

_____

_____

_____

**Finance**

1. _____

_____

_____

_____

_____

_____

2. _____

_____

_____

_____

_____

_____

**Manufacturing**

1. _____

_____

_____

_____

_____

_____

2. _____

_____

_____

_____

_____

_____

# Recording Your Decisions

It has been found that the more successful firms in both business games and real-world firms are "planful" and orderly in their decision-making processes. A number of quarterly Decision Logs can be found in this manual's Appendix A. The entries in these logs summarize, and neatly tie together, the disparate decisions you have made by country market for each of your firm's functional areas.

As you go through your group's decision-making process, enter your decisions in pencil (you will be changing entries many times before you decide on the final ones) in the log you have designated for the current quarter. At the end of your decision-making session, you should review *as a group* all the entries you have made in your log to insure they are the decision entries you want to have implemented. Chapter 7 will detail how the decisions you make for your company in the simulation are entered for computer processing. This process is essentially one of transferring entries from the quarter's Decision Log to the appropriate screens on your computer's monitor.

# Critical Incidents

Over the course of the simulation your Game Administrator may want to use some of the Critical Incidents in Global Industries. These incidents bring a number of additional dimensions to your game and involve a number of the intangibles of managerial decision making. These incidents are found in Appendix E of this manual and can be invoked at any time by the Game Administrator. If a critical incident is in effect for a particular quarter, an appropriate announcement will be made via either the game's Bulletin Board or some other method preferred by your instructor or Game Administrator.

Four responses are available to your company for each incident. The incidents themselves introduce you to a situation as a "mini case" that requires a decision on your part. In reviewing the choices available, you may feel that none are adequate, or, conversely, that each alternative possesses merit. Discuss among your management group the pros and cons of each alternative, however, and choose the one you think is best, based on your knowledge of both the situation posed in the Critical Incident and enlightened real-world responses to the same situation. The choices you make for the incidents will directly and indirectly affect your firm's profitability. These effects will be strongest in the simulation's current decision-making quarter and will be completely dissipated within one year of the choice's occurrence.

# A Well-Organized Team

By this chapter's end you have been exposed to the behavioral side of computer-based business games. If you performed the exercises in this chapter, everyone on your team should have a fairly good idea about how your company should manage its decision-making sessions and the talents and enthusiasms of each of your teammates, and a sense of purpose and direction. On this basis, your group has started to become a tight-knit, cohesive, and purposeful unit, able to go on to its next challenges, which deal with understanding the mechanics of running your simulated company. The next three chapters of this manual deal with the mechanics and details of your firm's marketing, production, finance, and accounting operations.

### Additional Readings

Anthony, William P., and Pamela L. Perrewe. (1986) *Human Resource Management.* New York: Dryden Press.

Berelson, Bernard, and Gary A. Steiner. (1964) *Human Behavior, An Inventory of Scientific Findings.* New York: Harcourt Brace Jovanovich, pp. 325–327, 332, 352.

David, Fred. (1989) How companies define their mission. *Long-Range Planning* 22: 90–97.

Fisher, Cynthia, Lyle F. Schoenfeldt, and James B. Shaw. (1999) *Human Resource Management.* Boston: Houghton Mifflin.

Hammond, John S., Ralph L. Keeney, and Howard Raiffa. (1998) *Smart Choices: A Practical Guide to Making Better Decisions.* Boston: Harvard Business School Press.

Harrison, Frank. (1999) *The Managerial Decision-Making Process.* Boston: Houghton Mifflin.

Katzenbach, Jon R. (ed.). (1998) *The Work of Teams.* Boston: Harvard Business School Press.

Levine, Stewart. (1998) *Getting to Resolution: Turning Conflict into Collaboration.* San Francisco: Berrett-Koehler Publishers.

Martocchio, Joseph. (1998) *Strategic Compensation Management.* Englewood Cliffs, N.J.: Prentice-Hall.

Pearce, John A., II, and Fred David. (1987) Corporate mission statements: The bottom line. *Academy of Management Executive* 1: 109–116.

Ulrich, Dave. (1998) *Delivering Results: A New Mandate for Human Resource Professionals.* Boston: Harvard Business School Press.

Wines, L. (1996) Compensation plans that support strategy. *Journal of Business Strategy* 17, no. 4: 17–20.

## Chapter 4

# Marketing and Marketing Logistics

Your company's major revenue source comes from selling the television sets delivered through your Distribution Centers. You can manufacture these sets yourself or you can get them through contract sales from other firms in your industry. These television sets, regardless of how they are obtained, are then distributed through wholesaling operations that you either own or use in cooperation with independent wholesalers who sell related home-electronics items. Shipments to these wholesalers are recorded as "Sales" from your company's Distribution Centers or factories. If you make any television sets for a retailer's private labeling program, those units will be shipped FOB directly to the retailer's distribution center from the factory producing them. Your TV sets, along with those of your rivals, are then retailed, where they meet the real challenges of the marketplace.

This scenario traces the simple movement of goods from factory to wholesaler to retailer shown in Exhibit 4.1. To be a successful marketer, however, you must thoroughly understand the details of the markets you have entered or may enter in the future, as well as understand how to handle the logistics of supplying your wholesalers and Distribution Centers with the products you want to sell. This chapter provides you with details regarding the markets and market segments in which you can compete, the logistics of national and international product distribution, how preferential demand for your television sets can be accomplished, and how you can obtain proprietary information about your markets and marketing efforts.

**Exhibit 4.1   Marketing Channels and Channel Participants**

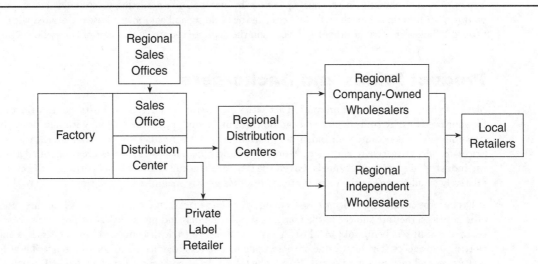

# Demand Creation

The factors affecting the general demand for television sets and the seasonal demand factor associated with each country market has already been presented in Chapter 1. Although your firm has little influence on each marketing area's macroeconomic and socioeconomic factors, it *can* influence the derived demand for its branded television sets in a number of ways. This can be done through (1) changes and improvements in product quality and features, (2) the relative size of your quarterly advertising budgets, (3) the amount of service you provide your Wholesalers through the number of Distribution Centers and Sales Offices you have, (4) the total number of Wholesalers handling your products, and (5) the number of Sales Representatives you have and the types of sales-incentive programs you use to motivate them.

Product quality and product features pertain to the physical properties of your products. These physical changes are obtained through (1) Research and Development expenditures, (2) the quality of the Subassemblies you used in each television set you make, (3) the level of quality control you obtain through your company's Quality Control budgets, and (4) the reliabilities of the two types of automatons your company uses in its manufacturing process. While these efforts physically differentiate your products, they can also be differentiated in a psychological sense. This is done through the prices you charge for your TVs, the strength of your sales promotions, and the distribution channel support you apply.

Sales-promotion efforts entail the relative size of the advertising programs you conduct in your various geographic markets for each product sold by TV-set size, the magnitude of your sales forces, and your sales force's quality and enthusiasm. Sales force quality is determined by the amount of money you spend on its Training and Development, and its enthusiasm or zeal is largely determined by the amount of incentives you use to encourage the staff to pursue sales.

The effectiveness of your advertising program is determined by a number of factors both within and outside your company's control. The controllable factor is the size of your advertising budget on a product-by-product basis. The factors you cannot control are the sizes of your competitors' advertising budgets and each nation's ability to read and respond to your print advertisements. This latter factor is indicated by each country's literacy and newspaper readership rates, presented in the national profiles in Chapter 1.

Channel support entails your advertising programs, which tend to pull your products through the distribution channel, and the amount of service and delivery promptness you provide them through the number of Distribution Centers you operate. The number of Sales Representatives you employ out of Sales Offices in each geographic market tends to push your products through each country's distribution channel. When adding new Sales Offices to those already in operation, your simulation will open the new office in the country's next-largest city-related market. If you add more offices later, the simulation moves to the next larger city-market. Accordingly, in the United States, your first Sales Office would be in New York City, its next office would be in Los Angeles, and the next would be in Chicago, as this is the size order of America's cities—indicated in Chapter 1's national profiles.

You can also control marketing channel operations by owning and conducting your own wholesale operations. If you do this, your firm must bear the risks and costs of the building and equipment leases associated with these Company-Owned Wholesalers. On the other hand, you gain the dedicated efforts of this part of your wholesaling function.

# Product Prices and Backorders

Many of your company's sales promotion activities are attempts to lessen the impact of raw prices on the demand for your products. To some degree you can do this but product prices are still very important to your ultimate consumers. This is because your independent wholesalers want to stock the sets that are the easiest to sell and low prices are very attractive to end-users. More importantly, manufacturer's prices are multiplied as they go through the industry's distribution channels. Given the standard markups each channel participant expects to take, a relatively small change in the manufacturer's prices is greatly magnified by the time it gets to the retail level.

It has become standard practice to use Catalogue or "List Prices" in your industry. While these are each firm's official prices, they are subject to the market's supply and demand pressures. Thus they are never the actual prices charged for the sets being sold. All List Prices are subject to trade discounts, volume incentives and unit-based slotting allowances. The total value of these trade incentives are reflected in the differences between each firm's List Prices and each product's Actual Price. The Global Industry Report lists each firm's List Prices for the quarter. Actual Prices are also reported but this information has taken one quarter to collect and report accurately. Thus the "Actual Price" listed in the Global Industry Report is for the previous quarter's sales by company.

Each firm's Sales Representatives are paid their Commissions on List Prices rather than Actual Prices. This is because each product's final prices is not under the direct control of your Salesreps although you are encouraging them to conclude all sales as close to your list Price as possible.

If your Salesreps write orders for more units than can be supplied by your firm that quarter, a Backorder condition will occur. This filling of the Backorders receives a priority treatment in the following quarter with these Backorders taking a higher delivery priority than that given to the quarter's new orders. If your firm lowers a product's Actual Price between quarters, Backorders are filled at the lower price. The Commission paid on these sales, still, will be on the List Price that initially created the sale.

## Product Segments

Within each Country/Market area, depending on the game's complexity, you may sell both models of your television sets except within your Home Country where you can also dedicate some of your factory's capacity to the manufacture of sets for private or store-brand sales. Each of your nationally branded sets can be targeted for the industry's various price and quality segments through the (1) quality-control measures taken by your company, (2) degree of reliability fostered by the amount of automaticity you employed in your manufacturing processes, and (3) quality mix of the Subassembly grades found in each television set. For private-brand sales, announcements of bids requests will appear quarterly on the simulation's Bulletin Board. To win the bid for the quarter, your firm must be the lowest bidder while producing at or above the product Quality Grade Index announced in the retailer's request.

Regarding your company's branded products, it appears to your customers that the industry's best sets are made from the finest materials available. The product's finish has a custom-made appearance, and the product experiences very few failures or warranty repairs and therefore is considered very reliable. In the simulation products in this league, use the highest grade subassemblies, using highly automated and closely supervised manufacturing process. Products in this category have consistently earned "Best Quality" ratings or Quality Indices in the 7.00 to 10.00 range in various consumer magazines, such as *Consumer Reports*.

Of average quality are television sets with Quality Indices ranging from 4.00 to 6.99. These products are very reliable but have fewer features that could malfunction, use good subassemblies that are less sophisticated, and employ a finished appearance that is pleasing but not highly crafted. The lowest-grade products have Quality Indices below 4.00. These sets have often earned "Best Value" ratings in various consumers' digests and electronics magazines, although some break down under long-term use. In the United States, these would be products for the mass market or discount stores. Other retailers often use these products as promotional items or as promotional traffic builders. These sets have relatively few convenience features and have shorter life expectancies.

Your firm's retailers have traditionally given you much support. This is because your products have had generally high-quality levels. Those companies in your industry that manufacture sets of lower quality have had difficulty getting retailers to stock their products once their customers started complaining about them. Exhibit 4.2 summarizes the characteristics of the product grades found for the television sets you can manufacture and/or sell.

When selling your sets in the different countries found in *The Global Business Game,* you will find that, as in the real world, each country is in a different life-cycle stage of its acceptance of these products. Thus these products are used for somewhat different purposes in each nation. You can capitalize on these usage differences by differentiating the quality, features, and prices of your offerings from country to country. For example, in the United States the proportion of customers buying new, basic-featured 25" sets may be comparatively low. In Thailand such a set may be considered very desirable. For the more fully featured 27" sets, the demand for these multiple features may be higher in Germany than in the United States, due to the former country's greater interest in highly technical products. Alternatively, the typical German home is smaller sized, so a very reliable 25" set might be more desirable than a larger, less reliable 27" set.

Although it may be a good idea to target your offerings for certain market segments, the frequent switching from segment to segment on your company's part can lead to customer confusion. Some firms have found it best to stay in a particular price/feature/quality segment for several periods before attempting to upgrade or downgrade their television sets to match a segment's particular needs.

**Exhibit 4.2    Product Grades and Market Segments**

| Quality Index | Market Segment | Feature Characteristics |
|---|---|---|
| 9.00–10.00 | Select, high-price segment | Highest-grade materials; custom-crafted appearance; very reliable under heavy use; electronics salon retailer service and "cutting edge" product features and conveniences |
| 5.00–8.99 | Moderate-price segment; department store quality | Good-grade materials; pleasing appearance; very reliable under moderate use; many convenience features |
| 0.00–4.99 | Low-price segment; promotional and discount store quality | Basic-grade materials; plain appearance; basic convenience features; minimal retailer service support |

**Exhibit 4.3    Distribution Center and Sales Office Start-Up and Shut-Down Costs (in local currencies)**

| Country | Distribution Center | | Sales Office | |
|---|---|---|---|---|
| | Start-Up | Shut-Down | Start-Up | Shut-Down |
| Germany | 66,000 | 82,000 | 45,500 | 34,000 |
| Mexico | 297,000 | 360,000 | 14,200 | 10,600 |
| Spain | 518,000 | 640,000 | 193,600 | 144,200 |
| Taiwan | 1,140,000 | 1,400,000 | 56,500 | 42,300 |
| Thailand | 1,300,000 | 1,610,000 | 64,800 | 48,600 |
| United States | 45,000 | 56,000 | 20,000 | 15,000 |

# Distribution Centers and Sales Offices

In distributing your products, each factory initially operates as its own warehouse and sales office. Accordingly, if your company has a factory in a particular country, your firm automatically possesses one Distribution Center and one Sales Office. Should you wish to distribute products in a country where you do not have a factory, or you wish to have better coverage of a particular country market, your firm can lease warehousing space and Sales Offices according to the schedule in Exhibit 4.3.

If your firm wants to improve the service level it provides its wholesalers and therefore obtain long-term goodwill and customer reorders, additional Sales Offices, which may or may not be attached to any company-owned wholesalers you may have, can be leased to accomplish these ends. Over the simulation's duration you can increase or decrease the number of Sales Offices operated within each country, as well as your number of Distribution Centers. The lease-cancellation penalty is the same regardless of the remaining number of quarters left on the lease being cancelled.

When choosing the number of Sales Offices you operate, as well as the number of Sales Representatives you want to assign to them, it would be wise to consider the geographic expanses and population densities involved in the countries within which you conduct business. You can assume that diminishing marginal returns on additional Sales Offices, Distribution Centers, and Sales Representatives will begin immediately after the leasing of your first additional Sales Office, Distribution Center, Sales Representative and Company-Owned Wholesaler. This is because your company has chosen a marketing policy of initially establishing itself in each country's most populous city and then moving sequentially to the next smaller population area with its additions.

With more Distribution Centers, your firm obtains faster delivery times to its wholesalers within its particular geographic area as well as minimizing the shipping charges retailers must pay when getting your television sets from your Distribution Centers. This higher level of accessibility improves the service level you provide your wholesalers. And you can expect wholesalers to be more loyal to those companies that provide them with better service.

When determining the shipping charges your firm encounters during the business quarter to get your television sets to Distribution Centers, remember that your factory counts as one Distribution Center. Thus this factory-related Distribution Center does not require a shipping charge as it simply ships products held temporarily in storage as they come off the assembly line. Shipping charges are incurred for getting goods to all your other domestic Centers. These charges are spread equally over the number of Distribution Centers you have in operation, minus one for the factory's Distribution operation. The following example demonstrates an activity that results in a $691,666 shipping charge appearing on an American-based country operation's Income Statement.

415,000 Units shipped within the United States
5 Distribution Centers
1 Factory distribution operation
69,167 Units shipped per distribution operation (415,000/6)
345,833 Units shipped to Distribution Centers
69,167 Units distributed by factory distribution operation
US$691,666 Shipping charges incurred (345,833 × $2.00)

## Shipping Methods

Under normal conditions you will probably be making all your shipments by regular Surface transportation to your Distribution Centers. This is an inexpensive and relatively reliable method for domestic operations. For overseas sales, however, it is very slow. For operations between the United States and Germany, for instance, between loading your TVs on rail cars in Erie, Pa., and delivering them to your port in Newark, N.J., then shipping them across the Atlantic Ocean to the German port of Hamburg for rail shipping within Germany itself, a number of months will have elapsed. Because all sales, except those which are made either under Contract or for Private-Label purposes, are made through your firm's Distribution Centers, all orders must be filled from these Centers. Accordingly, your Centers must be fully stocked at the beginning of the quarter, or experience enough inboard shipments during the quarter to allow them to make all their sales, thereby avoiding Backorders and causing possible customer dissatisfaction. You can assume, unless Express Air Shipping methods are employed, that all shipments within a country can be completed during the quarter and that shipments between countries on continents take one quarter to complete.

Through careful planning, you can save your firm money by only using regular Surface shipping. There may be occasions, however, when you have misplanned, have experienced greater sales during the previous quarter than anticipated, or merely would like to speed up your firm's inventory cycle. If this is the case, you can service any of your Distribution Centers by using Express Air (ExAir) Shipments.

As listed in Exhibit 4.4, the ExAir rate is about three times higher than the Surface rate. Your firm, however, may feel this higher cost is compensated for because you will not have dissatisfied retailers seeking other wholesale suppliers in future quarters. When making your quarter's decision, you must allocate each factory's production shipments by the number of units that are to be shipped through Surface transportation and Air Express.

### Exhibit 4.4   Unit Shipping Rates (in U.S. dollars)

| Geographic Market | Shipping Method | |
| --- | --- | --- |
|  | Surface | ExAir |
| Within North America | $ 2.00 | $ 6.20 |
| North America to Europe | 9.00 | 27.90 |
| North America to Asia | 12.00 | 36.00 |
| Within Europe | $ 2.50 | $ 7.48 |
| Europe to North America | 10.00 | 30.50 |
| Europe to Asia | 15.50 | 48.70 |
| Within Asia | $ 4.50 | $ 13.50 |
| Asia to North America | $18.50 | 52.75 |
| Asia to Europe | 18.00 | 53.80 |

## Inventory-Handling Charges

Your company's products are very durable and so they are not subject to deterioration under normal warehousing conditions. Because of this the direct inventory charges for your finished goods are fairly low on a per unit basis. Handling charges, however, are fairly high for your company's television sets because of their fragile components. The handling charges for your 27" set are slightly higher than for your 25" sets, as your larger sets are more complex and have more parts that can be broken. No handling and inventory charges are due on Contract or Private-Label sets as these are shipped directly to the recipient's own facilities.

The inventory and product-handling costs involved are presented in Exhibit 4.5. They will appear as part of the Inventory Charges on your company's Income Statement and are incurred on all units produced during the quarter, because all units are ultimately handled and inventoried at some level within your firm's physical distribution system.

**Exhibit 4.5   Inventory and Handling Charges by Product (in local currencies)**

| Country | | Product 25-inch | Product 27-inch |
|---|---|---|---|
| Germany: | Inventory | 1.70 | 1.85 |
| | Handling | 2.73 | 2.96 |
| Mexico: | Inventory | .50 | .56 |
| | Handling | .85 | .90 |
| Spain: | Inventory | 7.00 | 7.65 |
| | Handling | 11.30 | 12.25 |
| Taiwan: | Inventory | 6.25 | 6.75 |
| | Handling | 10.00 | 10.85 |
| Thailand: | Inventory | 2.40 | 2.60 |
| | Handling | 3.83 | 4.15 |
| United States: | Inventory | .75 | .80 |
| | Handling | 1.20 | 1.30 |

# Distribution Center and Sales Office Expenses

The administrative charges and general overhead and operational expenses associated with each Distribution Center and its Sales Office have a fairly fixed cost regardless whether the Centers operate out of your factories or are leased. Because of this fixed-cost nature, there are certain economies of scale that can be realized in your company's logistics function. Exhibit 4.6 itemizes the charges linked to each country and its operation. These charges include lease payments, heat, light and utilities, and front-office salaries.

# Independent Wholesale Operations

Your company, as is the industry's norm, has used independent Wholesalers to service its customers. These Wholesalers handle a large number of products from other manufacturers, but none of these products competes directly with yours. In this regard each Wholesaler is totally dedicated to taking orders for your television sets from its retail customers, as well as engaging in a modest amount of its own wholesale advertising.

Because they are independent Wholesalers with years of experience in the electronic-appliance business, they require minimal attention from your company's Sales Representatives. Thus the costs of servicing or supporting each independent Wholesaler is rather low, as shown by country in Exhibit 4.7. An additional benefit in using independent Wholesalers lies in the fact that they lighten the load on your Sales Representatives and allow them to work more directly with retailers to promote the sale of your products.

**Exhibit 4.6 Quarterly Distribution Center and Sales Office Overhead Costs (in local currencies)**

| Country | Operation | |
| --- | --- | --- |
| | Distribution Center | Sales Office |
| Germany | 254,700 | 196,100 |
| Spain | 517,000 | 310,200 |
| Mexico | 78,000 | 60,300 |
| Taiwan | 940,600 | 718,000 |
| Thailand | 342,200 | 278,000 |
| United States | 110,000 | 86,000 |

**Exhibit 4.7 Independent Wholesaler Servicing Costs (in local currencies)**

| Country | Cost |
| --- | --- |
| Germany | 19,800 |
| Spain | 37,200 |
| Mexico | 23,650 |
| Taiwan | 70,400 |
| Thailand | 24,600 |
| United States | 11,000 |

# Company-Owned Wholesale Operations

In your industry the use of independent Wholesalers has been the practice for many years. This situation, however, has begun to change. With the arrival of Super Stores, Category Killer and Big Box retail operations, the bargaining power between these types of retailers and their wholesalers has shifted. With small, local wholesaling operations under threat, a number of home-electronics manufacturers have begun to create their own wholesale operations as well as countervailing the power of these larger retailers.

By creating a number of your own Wholesalers you obtain their full-time dedication to your products while retaining for them the standard 40.0 percent markup on merchandise cost the independent wholesalers have needed in the past to cover their own costs of doing business. Moreover, each independent Wholesaler sells a wide range of products and their attentions are naturally divided. Also their natural loyalties are to themselves rather than to *your* company.

By creating your own Wholesalers, however, your company has to bear the fixed-cost risks associated with leasing arrangements and certain semi-variable shipping and associated personnel costs. Independent Wholesalers are almost free, as they require minimal attention by your company—although you must provide them with the markups they need so they can make a reasonable profit.

Should you wish to create a number of your own wholesaling operations, with each one possessing its own Sales Office, your company would be subject to the schedule presented in Exhibit 4.8. This covers the quarterly salaries of personnel associated with each operation, the initial start-up costs, overhead and lease costs, and any shut-down costs should you want to cease a wholesaling operation and eliminate its quarterly salaries. The salaries presented in Exhibit 4.8 do not include those of the Sales Representatives assigned to the market territory's Sales Offices.

**Exhibit 4.8   Company-Owned Wholesaling Operations Costs (in local currencies)**

| Item | United States | Mexico | Germany | Spain | Taiwan | Thailand |
|------|--------------|--------|---------|-------|--------|----------|
| Start-up | 35,000 | 24,700 | 80,000 | 33,000 | 300,000 | 114,000 |
| Shut-down | 52,500 | 37,000 | 12,000 | 49,500 | 450,000 | 171,000 |
| Quarterly lease | 3,000 | 24,400 | 54,000 | 46,200 | 105,500 | 117,000 |
| Salaries | 60,000 | 42,500 | 136,700 | 58,100 | 514,000 | 194,600 |

The amount of business each Company-Owned Wholesaler does is based on the mix of Independent and Company-Owned Wholesalers your firm uses. It is assumed you would place your own Wholesalers in each country market's most important local markets, using Independent Wholesalers to fill out your country's coverage.

On this basis your first Company-Owned Wholesaler would contribute the most to your country's sales volume, with each succeeding Company-Owned Wholesaler contributing less and less to total sales. When deciding on the optimum mix between Independent and Company-Owned Wholesale operations, remember that your company's total sales is partially determined by the total number of Wholesalers you have selling your products.

When calculating the margins your company receives on television sets sold by your own Wholesalers, you can assume that your revenue on each sale would be your manufacturer's Actual Price plus the standard 40.0 percent Wholesaler's markup on cost. As an example, assume that the Actual Price to Independent Wholesalers of your 25" sets is $105 per unit. That Wholesaler would mark the sets up to $147.00 for sale to retailers. If those sets were sold to the same retailers by your Company-Owned Wholesaler, the Independent Wholesaler's markup would be your own. In this case, this amounts to $42 a unit. This markup recovery, however, is not free. You must now bear the costs of running and shipping to a Wholesale operation, also spending much more to get an equal amount of geographic coverage of your country's market.

## Intra-Company Transfers

Your company can produce products in one area or country and sell them in another area. You can also ship finished goods between countries for distribution from your Regional Distribution Centers. In the past, your firm has set its intracompany transfer price by marking up its unit production costs by 10.0 percent. The simulation will maintain this policy by adding a factor of 1.10 to any sending unit's direct manufacturing costs on a per set basis. This markup covers the producing factory's overhead expenses, with the receiving Country/Market absorbing the product's transportation costs.

When making intracompany shipments, the sending country's factory ships the products to Distribution Centers in the designated off-shore country before it makes product shipments to its own domestic Distribution Center(s). Therefore off-shore transfers have a priority over shipments to domestic Distribution Center(s) and the filling of any Backorders obtained in the previous quarter. When shipments are made, the sending factory's inventory valuation is decreased by the standard transfer price, and its cash account is increased by the same amount. The receiving country's inventory valuation is increased by this same transfer price, and its cash account is decreased by this valuation plus the associated shipping charges that are borne by the receiving Country unit. These shipping charges will also appear on the receiving country's Income Statement for the quarter.

All monetary transactions are done at the exchange rates existing between countries during the quarter the transfers occur except for transfers of products between Spain and Germany whose rates are fixed under the new, euro-based monetary system. When making shipments to a country's Distribution Center either from your company's factories or to other Distribution Centers, you can assume that your products will be optimally disbursed among all Centers operating within each industry.

## Sales Force Size

As your firm enters new sales territories, or you experience personnel turnovers, you will have to take steps to maintain or increase the number of Sales Representatives you have in the field. You can do this through two methods. One method is to train new people for sales openings that may eventually occur. The second method is to hire experienced Sales Representatives away from other firms.

It is important that you maintain a steady, experienced and well-trained sales force. The best method you have for doing this is to pay it a competitive salary. When you do this Salesreps do not seek employment with other firms. Despite any outstanding salaries you may pay, however, it is quite likely you will always experience Salesrep "quits." This is because they want to move to other cities, move to other companies just to change the scenery, or because of career moves made by their spouses. Your objective then, is to guard against a higher number of quits than is normal for firm's with sales staffs of your size.

If your company wants to increase its sales force, the least-expensive way to do this is to plan ahead and train new hires in your Sales Offices. Whey they are in training your Trainees are paid the salaries that apply them in Exhibit 4.9a by county. All Trainees must be held in their training programs for at least one quarter. Thereafter they can be moved into the field at the costs shown in the same exhibit. Once in the field they earn the same Base Salaries and subject to the same Commission schedules that apply to the rest of your sales staff.

Training new people in advance of your current needs is a relatively low-cost option. You may wish, however, to move more quickly. This is done by hiring experienced Sales Representatives. If you do this your company uses the services of a personnel search firm. You pay its recruiting fee, as well as the moving expenses incurred by each newly-hired Salesrep, in the quarter they join your company.

Given the market's fluctuations it is entirely possible you may place too many people in the field, or have put too many in training. To make a downward adjustment in your sales staff, you can dismiss or fire them from their positions. There are no costs attached to firing Trainees as they have not yet attained a "career" status in your company. The firing of veteran Sales Representatives is another matter. Out of feelings of appreciation for their past efforts, your firm's policy has been to provide each dismissed Salesrep with a severance package that combines money with outplacement services. The costs associated with the implementation of this policy in each country are also presented in Exhibit 4.9a.

When you submit your sales force decisions each quarter, the simulation will comply with any requests you make. Thus if your sales force initially had ten Salesreps in the United States and your entry for the Decision Quarter was eight Salesreps, the simulation would assume you wanted to fire two Sales Representatives. This action would be taken and a charge of $12,000 would be added to your Sales Office expenses for the quarter. The dismissal of Trainees also operates the same fashion. If you were training three Salesreps in the previous quarter and your entry for this quarter was one Trainee with none being moved into the field, the simulation would remove two Trainees from your company's Sales Office training program.

The simulation will also operate in an intelligent fashion regarding the use of the sales personnel available. Because of language barriers, however, Salesreps cannot be moved between countries. As an example of how the simulation handles the deployment of Sales Representatives, if your past quarter's Salesreps equaled eleven in Germany, and you wanted to have three representatives added to the German sales force while already having two Trainees in your Sales Offices, the simulation would automatically move the two Trainees into the field while hiring one experienced Salesrep off the street. The associated charges of Dm50,280 would be added to your country unit's Sales Force expense for the Decision Quarter.

# Sales Representatives and Sales-Incentive Programs

The quality of your company's selling force is important at the local Sales Office level. This quality level is related to the size of your company's Training and Development budget within each country and the number of Sales Representatives you have. Within each country, a minimal base salary appears to be appropriate given local wage and salary rates. To this base salary your company may want to apply a per unit commission on each of your company's branded sets. On your firm's decision form, this per unit commission is stated as a percent of the firm's List Price for each size of television set you are selling. No commissions are paid on Contract sales as they are negotiated by a separate office in your Home Country's headquarters.

Your sales force's quality is also a function of its turnover rate. As your sales force's turnover increases, its overall effectiveness is diminished. This is because customer relationships are broken and new Sales Representatives must establish their credentials with Wholesalers. As the simulation progresses you will be informed of the loss of Sales Representatives through messages found in your Company Report. Experienced

Sales Representatives are immediately paid the Base Salary you have established in the countries in which they were hired and assigned.

# Import Tariffs, Trading Communities, and Trading Zones

Various countries, either by themselves or jointly through such trading communities as NAFTA, EU, or APEC, have used tariff policies over the years. These policies are intended to stimulate trade within particular areas, provide revenues for the governments affected, and/or protect domestic manufacturers and their workers' jobs from foreign competition. Through tariff actions a country makes foreign products more expensive for domestic consumption, thereby making the domestically produced product comparatively less expensive—regardless of its intrinsic quality or value. Tariff actions, however, often cause foreign governments to impose retaliatory tariffs.

Some of these aspects of tariff policy can be seen in the rate schedules shown in Exhibits 4.9 and 4.10. Exhibit 4.9 displays the tariff rates set by each trading zone. For the purposes of this business game it is assumed that NAFTA, EU, and APEC are in full effect, but in a simplified fashion. Within-zone tariffs are very low or nonexistent, but fairly restrictive tariffs have been applied to all products entering from countries outside each trading zone. These trading-zone tariffs are added to each country's own tariff, if one exists. Exhibit 4.10 shows the tariff rates each country has established for itself against the television sets made in other countries both inside and outside their own trading zones.

**Exhibit 4.9a   Sales Force Hiring, Firing and Deployment Costs (In local currencies)**

| Cost | U.S. | Mexico | Germany | Spain | Thailand | Taiwan |
|---|---|---|---|---|---|---|
| Trainee Salary | 9,100 | 5,850 | 24,800 | 87,000 | 72,300 | 71,601 |
| Trainee Moving | 3,000 | 1,200 | 8,680 | 13,000 | 10,200 | 8,874 |
| Salesrep Hiring | 11,000 | 4,680 | 19,900 | 52,200 | 120,202 | 104,576 |
| Salesrep Firing | 6,000 | 1,100 | 24,800 | 43,500 | 71,300 | 62,031 |
| Salesrep Moving | 4,500 | 1,800 | 13,020 | 19,500 | 15,300 | 13,311 |

**Exhibit 4.9b   Trading Zone Tariff Rates**

| Sending Trading Zone | Receiving Zone | | |
|---|---|---|---|
| | EU | APEC | NAFTA |
| EU | 0.0% | 7.0% | 3.0% |
| APEC | 5.0% | 0.0% | 3.0% |
| NAFTA | 4.0% | 7.0% | 0.0% |

**Exhibit 4.10   Country Tariff Rates**

| Sending Country | Receiving Country | | | | | |
|---|---|---|---|---|---|---|
| | Germany | Mexico | Spain | Taiwan | Thailand | United States |
| Germany | 0.0% | 2.0% | 0.0% | 1.0% | 4.6% | 4.7% |
| Mexico | 0.0% | 0.0% | 5.3% | 0.0% | 0.0% | 0.0% |
| Spain | 0.0% | 4.0% | 0.0% | 8.0% | 1.0% | 1.7% |
| Taiwan | 3.0% | 1.0% | 7.0% | 0.0% | 0.3% | 0.5% |
| Thailand | 4.6% | 0.0% | 3.0% | 0.3% | 0.0% | 6.0% |
| United States | 1.6% | 0.0% | 1.6% | 1.6% | 1.6% | 0.0% |

As an example of how tariffs operate, if an American firm wanted to sell its television sets to customers in Taiwan, it would have to pay a 7.0 percent trading-zone tariff and a 4.0 percent country tariff, for a total tariff charge of 11.0 percent on the product's direct manufacturing costs or its cost-of-goods sold. As a general rule, the United States has been relatively open to foreign competition, whereas many Asian countries have been relatively closed to outside competition. The tariff rates shown in Exhibits 4.9 and 4.10 will be in effect at the beginning of your simulation, but changes in the world's political and economic situation during the simulation may cause various countries to alter their tariff policies.

Should your firm engage in any intrafirm product transfers, the tariffs shown in Exhibits 4.9 and 4.10 will be assessed on the transfer price that was established and will be charged to the receiving country unit. It is assumed that the country's tariff charge is passed on to consumers through the nation's distribution channels, thereby putting foreign-made products at a competitive price disadvantage.

## Research and Development

Although the television industry is in its mature stage, new developments are always occurring in electronics technology. Thus it would be a good idea to engage in a steady program of research. As your firm engages in these efforts, it might even make a discovery that results in an improvement, or a modest innovation that is patentable and has commercial value. This patent, when applied to your television sets, either enhances the set's picture quality or its sound system, or provides a new, highly desirable convenience feature. Thus your firm will obtain a modest competitive advantage, which applies automatically to all TV sets you produce. The strength of this advantage will be greatest during the first quarter of its use, although residual strength will last for almost a year. After about one year, your innovation is effectively duplicated by others in your industry.

When your R&D monies have produced a patentable innovation, you will receive written notification of this fact as part of your firm's quarterly results. Products improved by this innovation will go on sale in the following quarter. Any existing goods in the current quarter's Finished Goods inventory will be retrofitted with the patented feature as part of your company's existing R&D budget.

Getting a patented product improvement requires a number of quarters of R&D projects. Your company should first determine an R&D budget policy and then engage in a steady implementation of that policy. Only through steady budgets will your firm obtain a patentable feature. There is no limit to the number of patents your firm can receive, as any number of research projects can be in operation simultaneously within your firm.

## Patents and Cross-Licensing Agreements

Your firm can also purchase from another firm one of its patented features and can offer your most-recent patented feature to other companies in your industry. To accomplish either of these actions, you must notify the Game Administrator that you have a patented feature you would like to buy or sell at what price. Your Game Administrator will cause the simulation to place an announcement of your offer on the Global Industry Report's Bulletin Board.

To complete the purchase or sale of a patented feature, both parties must use the "Patent Licensing Sale and Patent Transfer Agreement" form found in Appendix F of your *Player's Guide*. This form must be used for each patent-licensing sale or transfer. It must be (1) properly signed and approved by the Game Administrator, (2) signed by both parties to the transaction, and (3) submitted with your decision set for the quarter in which the transaction is to occur. The competitive-advantage time frame cited for the firm that created the patented innovation will immediately accrue to the firm obtaining the patent for its own use.

## Intercompany Contracts and Joint-Licensing Ventures

In addition to being able to transfer your company's patents or buy patents from others, you can engage in joint-licensing ventures. In conducting these ventures, a firm contracts to provide another firm an agreed-upon number of units of product at a negotiated price and quality level. The contracted units are automatically shipped to the purchaser's Distribution Center at the shipping rate applicable to the geographic area within which the units were fabricated.

The sets contracted for will be shipped only if the product Quality Level specified in the contract is matched or exceeded by the contractee. Acceptable contracted units take priority over shipments and sales the selling company could obtain from its own Distribution Center. If the contracted TVs do not meet the Quality Level specified in the contract, they will not be shipped; instead they become part of the contractee's Finished Goods Inventory for sale the next period.

The process by which your firm obtains such a joint-venture partner is initiated by submitting the Product Sale and Transfer Agreement form found in Appendix H of your *Player's Guide.* When you submit this form to your Game Administrator, your company will be listed on the Industry Report's Bids and Offers Posting the following quarter. Should you obtain a potential joint-venture partner, the product, quality grade, and contract length of that venture should be certified and accepted by the Game Administrator and both joint-venture parties. After receiving the properly signed instruments, your Game Administrator will cause the contract to be implemented for the quarter specified in the joint-venture contract.

# Market Research

Your firm can elect to conduct market research as an aid to better understanding how your industry's markets operate. Although you would probably never be able to answer every question you might have about the markets in this game before making future decisions, a modest amount of market research can be conducted for you by The Merlin Group, Ltd. This group is a fairly new market-research firm headquartered in San Jose, California. The types of research studies The Merlin Group will conduct for you, along with their fees, are presented in Exhibit 4.11. Information is available on the unit sales results of your competitors by country, the relative size of each market segment by country, and the perceived quality levels of the products you are facing in the different geographic markets. The Merlin Group's output is in hard-copy form, but it also has a clipboard service that allows you to access the raw data files it used to compile your research report. The files can be automatically transported to Excel by clicking on the clipboard found in "Reports, Merlin Group Reports."

The Merlin Group has quoted its standard rates in American dollars because it is a California-based research firm. It also must receive its payments in American dollars. To obtain its services, your company should pick the items it wants to have researched by selecting the appropriate question number(s) from those listed in your Decision Log's Marketing Research Request form, found in Appendix A of this manual. Merlin's fees will automatically be charged to your current quarter's Consolidated Miscellaneous Expense account.

**Exhibit 4.11   The Merlin Group, Ltd., Research and Rate Schedule**

| Question Number | Charge | Information Provided |
|---|---|---|
| 1 | $1,500 | All company 25" set unit sales by country. |
| 2 | $1,500 | All company 27" set unit sales by country. |
| 3 | $ 500 | Near-term forecast of 25" set unit sales by country. |
| 4 | $ 500 | Near-term forecast of 27" set unit sales by country. |
| 5 | $1,000 | Near-term forecast of unit demand for 25" and 27" Private-label sets. |
| 6 | $2,000 | All 25" set Quality Indices by company and country. |
| 7 | $2,000 | All 27" set Quality Indices by company and country. |
| 8 | $ 750 | Sales Representative Base Salaries by company and country. |
| 9 | $ 250 | All 25" set Advertising budgets by company and country. |
| 10 | $ 250 | All 27" set Advertising budgets by company and country. |
| 11 | $ 300 | Estimated R&D budgets by company and country. |
| 12 | $ 300 | Estimated QC budgets by company and country. |

## Private Label Bids

One of your Home Country's major home electronics chains has run a private branding program of its own for a number of years. The "Kingston" brand has been very successful for the Home Electronics King chain and it has been very competitive with the privately-labeled television sets and home appliances sold by Sears, Wards and K-Mart.

Your game's Global Industry Report Bulletin Board will periodically list bids requests made by the Home Electronics King chain. It will cite the number of sets they want for delivery the next quarter as well as the Quality Grade desired. If your firm wishes to bid for this business it must complete the Private Brand Bid form found in Appendix I. Home Electronics King operates only in your Home Country market and the chain itself pays for all shipping and handling charges associated with the bid. All sets are shipped from your factory and completely bypass any Distribution Centers or wholesalers you use in your normal distribution channel.

The winning bid will go to the firm in your industry with the lowest price and manufactures sets for the contract that meet or exceed the Quality Grade specified in the bid request. If your firm has the lowest price, but fails to deliver either the number of sets demanded or the requisite grade contracted, your winning bid is cancelled and all units intended for Home Electronics King are returned to your firm's Finished Goods inventory. These cancelled sets cannot be re-worked or retro-fitted to improve their quality grade level.

## The Marketing/Production Interface

Your company has now familiarized itself with how products are sold, distributed, and marketed in *The Global Business Game.* Your next task is to learn how to produce as economically and as reliably as possible all the products your Sales Representatives can sell, given the demand you have created for your products through your sales-promotion efforts. It will be very difficult for you to obtain a perfect match between what can be sold and what can be produced and distributed, but you should try to come as close as possible to this ideal.

For your factory or factories to run as smoothly as possible, your firm's marketers must produce fairly accurate sales forecasts while also delivering customers. Information obtained from Merlin may be useful in providing plant management with sales estimates so they can determine how much factory capacity will be needed in the long term and how much should be produced in the short term, given temporary capacity constraints. At this time it might be wise to develop forecasting methods that will help you to coordinate these efforts. Regardless of what you do in this regard, plant operations and marketing go hand in hand, and you must insure that this will be a prosperous collaboration.

### ADDITIONAL READINGS

Czinkota, M. (ed.). (1982) *Export Management.*  New York: Praeger.

Doz, Y., and C. Prahalad. (1980) How MNCs cope with host government demands. *Harvard Business Review* (March/April): 149–160.

Fayerweather, J. (1981) *International Business Strategy and Administration.*  Cambridge, Mass.: Harper & Row.

Ghemawat, P., M. Porter, and R. Rawlinson. (1986) Patterns of international coalition activity. In M. Porter (ed.), *Competition in Global Industries.*  Boston: Harvard Business School.

Hood, N., and S. Young. (1979) *The Economics of Multinational Enterprise.*  New York: Longman.

Lall, S. (1973) Transfer-pricing by multinational manufacturing firms. *Oxford Bulletin of Economics and Statistics* (August): 173–195.

Root, F. (1987) *Entry Strategies for International Markets.*  Lexington, Mass.: Lexington Books.

Shilling, P. (1982) How to make a global joint venture work. *Harvard Business Review* (May/June): 120–127.

Teece, D. (1986) Transactions cost economics and the multinational enterprise. *Journal of Economic Behavior and Organization* 7: 21–45.

# Chapter 5

# Manufacturing Operations

Your company's manufacturing function lies at the core of your operations because your company produces television sets for sale to the consumer market. In Chapter 4, which dealt with marketing and marketing logistics, the emphasis was on selling products and making sure they were the right products at the right price at the right time. This was a market-based or externally derived view of how a firm succeeds in the long term. In this chapter, the focus is an internal one, and the stress is on making those television sets that have sold well in the past as efficiently as possible and delivering them for distribution in adequate quantities.

Based on your company founders' design expertise and their engineering bias, your firm has attempted to obtain a strategic advantage by designing TV sets that have creative circuitry and assembling them under strict quality-control standards. Rather than designing and manufacturing a television set's basic components or subassemblies, your company has put its resources into the creative application of Subassemblies made by others. Given the television industry's relative maturity, which has generated a number of parts suppliers with excess capacity, and the high cost of setting up and running a subassembly factory, your firm has decided to let others produce what are near commodities within the electronics industry.

All your company's current manufacturing operations are conducted in your Home Country of the United States in a wholly owned facility in Erie, Pennsylvania. The site has excellent rail-line and express-highway connections, with additional land space readily available for plant expansions, if desired. The local labor supply is adequate for both your current and future needs, but your firm is subject to the relatively high labor rates charged in this highly industrialized and highly unionized part of the United States. As a hedge against these high labor rates, your company has recently purchased three automated assemblers, or automatons. These automatons are highly productive: they operate at relatively high quality-control levels and require little maintenance and supervision. More importantly, they do not require wages and fringe benefits to make them produce. These automatons also increase a plant's base productivity without requiring additional space.

Despite the attractiveness of your Erie, Pennsylvania site, it is also a long way from most of your major city markets in the United States. It is even further away from your firm's potential overseas markets. Given the global and changing nature of your industry, a number of overseas manufacturing locations may be available to you if your Game Administrator has structured your game in that fashion. If that option is not available to you, wage/cost pressures alone on your Pennsylvania plant may require you to change how you assemble your television sets. Considering either foreign or domestic perspectives, your company may have to make a number of important decisions in this regard.

## The Production Process

Your company uses a standard method for manufacturing its sets. This is the traditional line-attended assembly-line, through-put method used in high-volume, mass-assembly factories found throughout the world. Exhibit 5.1 shows how your plant has been configured, and this is the one you have inherited from your company's previous management group, unless your Game Administrator or instructor has changed your company's starting position.

**Exhibit 5.1   General Factory Operations**

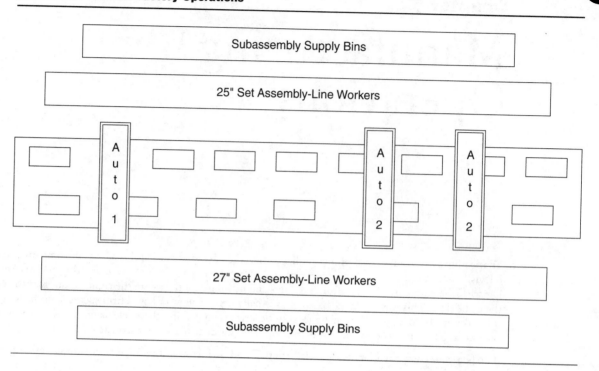

Under this manufacturing system, you have workers who perform their tasks within designated work stations. One side of the assembly line works on 25-inch sets coming down its side of the flat assembly belt. If your company also makes 27-inch sets, the 27-inch sets come down the belt's other side. If you devote your plant exclusively to either one of these two basic sets, the spaces on each side of the assembly line would be occupied by appropriately trained personnel.

Your workers apply components to the television chassis coming down the line from two groups of Subassemblies taken from supply bins placed behind them. The Subassemblies involve each set's audio and visual circuits as well as each unit's cabinetry. Exhibit 5.1 indicates that 25-inch sets are more easily assembled than are 27-inch sets, as they are more closely spaced on the belt. These 25-inch TVs are easier to handle, as the sets have fewer components placed inside the chassis, which gives the workers more room to work with.

Three automatons are currently straddling your assembly belt. This indicates that your facility is operating at a relatively low level of automaticity, as it is employing only one Auto1 and two Auto2s. These mechanical workers, or robots, operate in a humanlike fashion by sensing, through the use of bar codes and transponders, the components that must be installed in the TV chassis when it arrives at its station. As a manufacturing technology, automatons possess an amount of intelligence, require no supervision, and perform minimal maintenance operations and quality-control tests on themselves and their work. In many instances they have replaced many of the operations performed by workers on traditional, hand-tended assembly lines.

More automatons can be added to your line, given your line's base capacity. This *basic capacity* is determined by the *line's length*. Automatons can be placed anywhere along the line, as your Auto1s and Auto2s can be programmed to perform a wide range of functions. When you are adding automatons to your assembly line, you are basically packing your given-sized line with more productive workers, thereby increasing your factory's output without changing its absolute, physical size.

As more automatons are used in your assembly process, fewer and fewer direct laborers are required to make the same number of television sets. The number of technicians needed to reprogram your automatons, however, necessarily increases. Exhibit 5.2 indicates the characteristics of these automatons and the number of higher-paid technicians needed to service them, and Exhibit 5.3 displays the hourly automaton technician pay scales for each country in local currencies and U.S. dollars, assuming the exchange rates shown in The Global Industry Report on page 99. These wage rates may change over time, given the different inflationary pressures existing in each country and the internal labor market for automaton technicians.

One Technician can handle the needs of four Auto1s, but one Technician can comfortably handle only three Auto2s. The Auto1s and Auto2s are progressively more flexible, with Auto2s having a higher quality-control standard and operating rate than Auto1s. When an automaton of either type is placed on an assembly line, it fills the space of two human work stations, one on each side of the line.

As a plant manager or production scheduler, your task is to use your factory's labor-hour capacity to make television sets for shipment to Distribution Centers, whether those labor hours are created by human labor or the artificial labor of automatons. Exhibit 5.4 shows the total number of labor hours it takes to make each of the two set sizes you can manufacture. Given your current plant's base capacity, its length allows 140 workers to be equally split on each side of the assembly line per shift. Without automatons, your factory could produce approximately 622 25-inch television sets each working day, or 3,111 per week. You could make 560 27-inch sets per shift per day. If you were to run two full shifts, your output would effectively double. Under your company's Over-time option, which can run as a 25.0 percent extension of your plant's second shift, your total output could be 1,400 25-inch sets or 1,260 27-inch sets a day. This assumes that all workers scheduled for work actually appear for work.

**Exhibit 5.2  Automaton 8-hour Productivity and Required Technical Support**

| Automaton Type | Hours Generated | Technicians Needed |
|---|---|---|
| Auto1 | 32 | .25 |
| Auto2 | 41 | .30 |

**Exhibit 5.3  Automaton Technician Hourly Wages**

| Country | Local | U.S. Dollars |
|---|---|---|
| United States | US$23.32 | $23.32 |
| Mexico | Mex$16.52 | 1.88 |
| Germany | DM53.13 | 30.01 |
| Spain | Pta 2,204.88 | 14.66 |
| Taiwan | NT$199.78 | 5.90 |
| Thailand | B7,6l6.33 | 1.94 |

**Exhibit 5.4  Labor-Hour Requirements by Product**

| Set Type | Hours |
|---|---|
| 25-inch | 1.8 |
| 27-inch | 2.0 |

Your current plant, however, has three automatons. Although the space required for your automatons eliminates six laborers, the automatons increase the net productivity of your factory. As currently configured, your plant uses 134 workers, two Auto1 and one Auto2. This configuration could theoretically generate 1,186 labor hours per shift, which would work out to 658 25-inch TVs or 593 27-inch sets if your plant were fully staffed.

## Worker Scheduling, Vacations, and Absenteeism

Before each quarter begins, your company must request the total number of workers it wants on the factory's payroll. This is done by assigning workers by shifts to products. Your 27-inch set workers receive an average hourly wage that is higher than that earned by your 25-inch set workers, due to their greater experience and seniority. When scheduling your plant's operations, 27-inch set workers can assemble both their own sets and the simpler 25-inch sets. Workers on 25-inch sets, due to their lack of experience and skill, cannot effectively work on 27-inch sets. Should you desire more sets than can be made by your combination of automatons and 25-inch set workers, you can run 25-inch sets down the 27-inch side of your assembly belt. This action, however, sacrifices production of 27-inch sets.

The prevailing base wage rates for The Global Business Game's six countries by set size are presented in Exhibit 5.5. The rates stated here are in local currencies and may change during the course of the simulation due to wage-rate fluctuations. The prevailing factory wage rates for the countries in the business game will be regularly posted as part of your simulation's quarterly Global Industry Reports. Based on these wage rates, and assuming that no automatons have been installed, a firm making a 25-inch television set in the United States would carry a unit labor charge of $31.61.

Because different hourly wages exist throughout the world, many manufacturers have established offshore plants. Due to Germany's high hourly wages, many manufacturers have chosen not to produce their products in that country. Many German firms themselves have sought lower-cost production sites, with a favorite European site being Spain. Using the currency rates found in the sample Global Industry Report, Exhibit 5.6 reports the base labor costs that would apply to your 27-inch TVs if they were made in the countries shown.

While your company must schedule the number of workers it wants per product before the following quarter's run, the actual number of hours delivered may be lower than scheduled. This may be because of lost hours due to vacations, sick days, and absenteeism, or to running out of Subassemblies, which would cause your plant to temporarily shut down. Vacations and authorized sick days are part of your company's wage and salary benefits plan, but absenteeism is more a function of your work crew's work ethic. Company benefits vary from country to country, as does the work ethic.

In the more disciplined and economically advanced countries of Germany and the United States, you can expect that very few workers will be unofficially absent from work. The absenteeism rate in the less developed countries of Mexico and Thailand, however, may amount to as much as 15.0% of the labor hours requested or scheduled.

Another factor that can cause worker absenteeism is the amount of Maintenance work you budget for your factory. Equipment begins to break down and becomes dangerous to use when your Maintenance Budget is deficient. Under these conditions, workers who either take pride in their work or have concerns for their personal safety, seek employment elsewhere and are often missing from work. In the countries of United States, Germany, and Taiwan, this Maintenance factor is especially important. Regardless of the number of workers who actually report for work, your company must pay the wage bill on the number of workers requested, not the bill for the actual number of labor hours delivered.

These work ethic elements, along with each country's vacation and sick-day regulations, should be factored in to your scheduling practices. Exhibit 5.7 summarizes the prevailing vacation and sick-day practices and behaviors your company faces. As shown, the average vacation for the types of workers your company needs in the United States lasts four weeks, and each worker also takes about five sick days a year. Absenteeism runs about 1.7 days a year. In Germany, the average vacation is six weeks long, and 12 sick days are authorized and usually taken. Absenteeism, however, is very low.

As an example of this factoring in process, if you wanted to have an average of 65 workers in an American plant, you would need 70 workers on the payroll to cover all the vacations that would be taken. Looking at

**Exhibit 5.5    Base-Period Hourly Wage Rates by Factory Task Assignment (in local currencies)**

| Country | Product | |
|---|---|---|
| | 25-inch | 27-inch |
| United States | US$17.56 | US$17.74 |
| Mexico | Mex$11.25 | Mex$11.60 |
| Germany | DM46.84 | DM47.80 |
| Spain | Pta1,674.50 | Pta1,715.00 |
| Taiwan | NT$158.27 | NT$162.81 |
| Thailand | B137.75 | B141.71 |

**Exhibit 5.6    Labor Charges for 27-Inch Sets for Selected Countries**

| Country | Currency | |
|---|---|---|
| | Local | U.S. Dollars |
| Mexico | Mex $23.20 | $2.64 |
| Germany | DM95.60 | $53.99 |
| Spain | Pta3,430.00 | $22.81 |
| Taiwan | NT$325.62 | $9.62 |

**Exhibit 5.7    Vacations, Sick Days, and Absenteeism by Country**

| Country | Vacations (Weeks) | Sick Days (Days) | Absenteeism (Days) |
|---|---|---|---|
| United States | 4 | 5 | 1.7 |
| Mexico | 3 | 3 | 5.4 |
| Germany | 6 | 12 | .2 |
| Spain | 4 | 4 | 2.0 |
| Taiwan | 3 | 8 | .7 |
| Thailand | 2 | 4 | 14.0 |

the German experience, after considering the average number of sick days that would be taken per year, which amounts to 2.4 weeks, you would need to have about three surplus workers on hand to cover for those calling in sick. This surplus amount does not consider the number of additional workers needed to cover Germany's average six-week vacation.

# Television Set Components and Subassemblies

The television sets you manufacture require two general groups of Subassemblies. Both groups must be installed in each set to produce a complete unit. Exhibit 5.8 presents the number of Subassemblies required by the two set sizes you can manufacture, classified by their major groupings. Your 27-inch sets, being the more complex of the two, require the greater number of Subassemblies from both Groups.

**Exhibit 5.8  Product Subassembly Requirements**

| Group | 25-Inch | 27-Inch |
|---|---|---|
| 1 | 8 | 9 |
| 2 | 6 | 7 |

# Subassembly Inventories

Your company has a practice of purchasing its Subassembly raw materials via long-time supplier relationships developed in the very active Hong Kong market for electronic parts. In this center of activity, consolidators gather parts from Pacific Rim producers for large-lot shipments to manufacturers throughout the world. Thus, the prices they quote are FOB Hong Kong in US$, and they are bought and shipped in lots of 100 by Grade and Group.

If you wanted to order 522,347 units of a certain type and grade of Subassembly, you would need to order 5,224 lots to obtain enough units. Make sure when you make your quarterly decision you enter the number of *lots* you want to purchase and not the actual number of Subassembly units you desire. Although your Subassemblies are readily available, their timely delivery is subject to the vagaries of overseas shipping.

For your plant to run full-time, it must have a complete supply of Subassemblies, available in inventory before the quarter begins. If your plant runs out of Subassemblies during the quarter, it will operate as long as it can by drawing down the supply of Subassemblies available and applying them in equal proportions over the units you want manufactured. Once the Subassemblies have been exhausted your plant will shut down and all workers will be furloughed at full pay for the remaining business quarter. Due to the long shipping distances involved and your supply dealers' commitments to other customers, there is no possibility, that your firm could obtain emergency shipments of any additional raw materials needed for a quarter's production run. Thus your company should estimate as accurately as possible its Subassembly requirements in advance.

Exhibit 5.9 lists your simulation's current Subassembly lot prices. These prices have been quoted for the simulation's base period and are subject to change because of inflationary pressures in the producing countries and the supply and demand for the use of the same raw materials in other home and commercial electronic products. Any changes in the lot prices for Subassemblies will be posted as part of the simulation's Global Industry Report.

The shipping charges you must pay per lot to obtain these subassemblies are shown in Exhibit 5.10. These charges include handling, insurance costs, and port-of-entry processing fees. Although lots in different Subassembly Groups weigh about the same, Group 2's greater value and bulkier protective packaging cause them to be more expensive to ship.

**Exhibit 5.9  Subassembly Lot Prices by Grade and Group (in base period US$)**

| Grade | Group 1 | Group 2 |
|---|---|---|
| A | $168.96 | $579.31 |
| B | 128.80 | 463.45 |
| C | 115.00 | 403.00 |

**Exhibit 5.10  Lot Shipping Rates from Hong Kong**

| Destination | Shipping Rate Group 1 | Group 2 |
|---|---|---|
| North America | $ 7.57 | $ 8.43 |
| Western Europe | 13.48 | 15.30 |
| Asia | 6.88 | 7.10 |

## Subassembly Inventory Charges

Your Subassemblies are stored in their original 100-unit lot containers, which minimizes theft, damage, and in-house handling costs. All Subassemblies are also stored in high-security areas within each factory's warehouse as these parts are easily stolen and have a relatively high unit value, given their small size. Thus the cost of storing Subassemblies is more a function of their monetary value and the need to have them on hand to keep assembly lines operating, rather than of their weight or bulk.

The majority of your Subassembly storage costs lie in the insurance coverage required. This coverage, plus the extra warehousemen needed to staff the secured area, amounts to 1.7% of the value of all Subassemblies on hand at the end of the previous business quarter.

## Subassembly Quality Grades

Three quality grades are associated with the two groups of Subassemblies used in your television sets. The Quality Indices associated with these grades are displayed in Exhibit 5.11. These Subassembly grades are processed with equal efficiency by your firm's manufacturing processes. Your inventories are drawn down during the quarter's run in the proportion they are available at the beginning of the quarter, if you have a mix of grades in inventory. By mixing the grades of raw materials used in your TVs, you can have a major impact on their quality levels.

Other factors, however, also affect the physical quality of your products. These are the (1) precision of your Auto1s and Auto2s, (2) amount of Training and Development monies you have budgeted for factory operations, and (3) your plant's Quality Control budget, which screens out defective TV sets before they leave your plant. Considering only the effect of raw-material grades on product quality, however, if you wanted to obtain a Quality Index of 10.0 for a certain run of television sets, you would have to use only Grade A Subassemblies in your manufacturing process.

**Exhibit 5.11   Subassembly Grades and Quality Indices**

| Grade | Quality Index |
|-------|---------------|
| A | 10.0 |
| B | 7.5 |
| C | 5.0 |

As an example, assuming you wanted to make 11,500 25-inch sets, the following start-of-quarter supply of raw materials would produce a group of new 25-inch TVs having a 7.27 Quality Index rating.

| Group | Grade A | Grade B | Grade C |
|-------|---------|---------|---------|
| 1 | 33,557 | 22,098 | 39,338 |
| 2 | 20,412 | 22,704 | 28,884 |

As a check on your mathematics, and your knowledge of your firm's manufacturing processes, this particular run of 11,500 25-inch TVs would leave you with the following ending supply of raw materials by grade and group:

| Group | Grade A | Grade B | Grade C |
|-------|---------|---------|---------|
| 1 | 1,057 | 696 | 1,239 |
| 2 | 851 | 946 | 1,204 |

As a further check on your mathematics, the unit cost of each of your 25-inch sets would be $70.91, using the unit labor charges previously calculated for a set this size.

| | |
|---|---|
| Unit labor cost | $31.61 |
| Subassembly landed costs: | |
| Group 1, Grade Average | 10.98 |
| Group 2, Grade Average | 28.32 |
| Total | $70.91 |

## Straight-Time, Second-Shift Operations, and Overtime

When making your company's production decisions, you must determine which products you want to schedule for production and on what shift(s) they should be produced. You can run partial shifts, or a two-shift operation, or can use Overtime as a 25% extension of your plant's Second Shift. The simulation will automatically assign the number of workers available from the labor pool you have requested for the quarter. You do not have to hire additional workers for any Overtime operations, as the second shift's workers are held over for the hours needed to complete the production run you order.

In scheduling workers, you can assume that productivity is not constant between shifts. Traditionally your plant managers have found that the second shift is about 4.0 percent less productive than the first shift. When Overtime has been scheduled, your managers have noticed an even sharper decrease in productivity, amounting to about 9.0 percent less than the second shift's productivity.

When your factory runs a second shift, a 4.5 percent labor premium is involved. The Overtime hourly labor rate is 1.5 times the second shift's hourly labor rate. Because Overtime is run as an extension of your second shift, the Overtime labor rate is combined with the shift's 4.5 percent labor premium. Using the base labor hour rates presented in Exhibit 5.5, the hourly rates shown in Exhibit 5-12 would be incurred for various shift options in an American factory.

**Exhibit 5.12    United States Assembly-Line Hourly Rates by Shift**

| Shift | Worker Assignment | |
|---|---|---|
| | 25-Inch sets | 27-Inch sets |
| First | $17.56 | $17.74 |
| Second | 18.35 | 18.54 |
| Overtime | 27.53 | 27.81 |

## General Administration and Factory Overhead

Your company's General Administration expenses are a function of a set of both fixed and semi-fixed expenses. The fixed component is the executive salaries you and your management group receive on a quarterly basis. Although your Game Administrator may change this amount, this executive compensation would normally be $50,000 per quarter.

Your company's semi-fixed General Administration expenses entail the costs of your plant's Automaton Technicians, a Factory Superintendant for each factory in operation, a Country Market Liaison executive for each country market in operation, all Assembly Line Supervisors, clerical staff, the capacity of your factory(ies) as measured by base capacity labor hours, and the supervision of any plant construction and equipment transfers or removals. These charges apply to your Erie, Pennsylvania, plant. They also hold for any offshore operations, but in equivalent local currency values and wage rates:

| | |
|---|---|
| Country Market Liaison | $25,000.00/Country |
| Factory Superintendant | $19,000.00/Factory |
| Assembly Line Supervision | $17,000.00/Supervisor |
| Automaton Technicians | $23.32/hour/Technician |
| Factory size | $200.00/Base Labor Hour Capacity |
| Plant construction supervision | 10.0% of Construction Value |
| Equipment transfer/removal supervision | 15.0% of Equipment Book Value |

## Work in Process

A nonsignificant number of units will be left unfinished at the end of each quarter because of the high speed at which your assembly line operates. Thus, your firm will have no Work in Process, and you can assume that all operations and production runs have been cleaned up at each quarter's end.

# Finished Goods Inventories

During your company's operating quarter you will have created a number of units for distribution. All units left over from current production and product transfer-ins from other country and company operations, after making all sales, are gathered into a Finished Goods Inventory account. The Finished Goods inventory valuation of these products is the weighted average of the mix of all products found in your inventories, regardless of their source or the originator's initial cost.

To obtain sales, your company must transfer its products from its factories to its Distribution Center(s). This action is not automatic. If you do not place your products in your Distribution Center(s), they will merely sit in temporary storage at your factories awaiting your disposition. While sitting as Finished Goods on your factory floor, inventory charges are not assessed, as this is temporary in-house storage.

# Warranty Work

Your factory will inevitably produce a modest number of defective television sets. This is due to variances in automaton operating characteristics, the amount of Supervisory and Training and Development attention given to your workers, and the size of your company's Maintenance budget. Defects are quickly discovered by those who buy your sets. When this occurs, they return their defective sets to the retail store from which they made their purchase. If the set is returned while it is under its one-year parts warranty, the retail dealer, in turn, returns the set to the nearest country Distribution Center for warranty repairs. When this happens, the Center absorbs the repair costs in local currency values.

Standard warranty charges are made for each returned set: $20.00 for 25-inch sets and $26.50 for 27-inch sets returned in the United States. Warranty charges in offshore Distribution Centers are in equivalent local currency values. No warranty charges are assessed on Contract sets, as the retailer private-branding your sets performs the warranty work.

# Product Quality

It was pointed out in Chapter 4 on marketing and marketing logistics, that your company can differentiate its products both psychologically and physically. It is here, at the factory operating level, that you implement any strategies you may have for your company regarding product quality and product differentiation.

This chapter's section on Subassembly Quality Grades indicated a major way product quality levels are determined—through the quality mix of the components used in making your sets. Another method is via the mix of automatons you use, due to the tolerance or precision levels associated with each Auto1 and auto2. A third method entails the creation and staffing of factorywide Training and Development programs. These programs enhance your personnel's capabilities and flexibility by training workers in new job techniques and in re-educating the Technicians who program your automatons. The last way you can improve product quality is through the number of Supervisors you employ per factory. Having a greater number of Supervisors helps workers perform at optimal levels because such enlightened management techniques as Quality Circles can be used and closer supervision can be applied to the work as the sets are being assembled.

# Automaton Precision

Just as your automatons produce different amounts of product by set size, they also differ in their ability to produce defect-free products. Exhibit 5.13 shows that your Auto1s and Auto2s have accuracy rates that range from 94.0 percent to 98.5 percent with per-type automaton variances ranging from ±1.2 percent to ±2.5 percent. Depending on the automaton mix in your factories, the products will be directly affected by these empirically derived machine performance ranges, given the quality grade of Subassemblies used in the production process.

The interaction between Subassembly grades and automaton accuracy on television-set quality can be seen in the example presented in Exhibit 5.14. In this example, only Auto1s and Auto2s are used in the production process to eliminate the contaminating effects of human labor efficiencies, Training and Development monies, and Supervision of product quality. If a plant used only Autos1s in the production process, the inventory pool of raw materials shown would result in 25-inch and 27-inch sets with Quality Ratings of 6.85 and 6.93, respectively. If the plant had only Auto2s on its assembly line, the sets would have Quality Ratings of 7.14 and 7.22.

**Exhibit 5.13   Automaton Precision Levels and Variance Rates**

| Automaton | Accuracy | Variance |
|---|---|---|
| Auto1 | 94.5% | ±2.5% |
| Auto2 | 98.5% | ±1.2% |

# Work-Crew Training and Development

Another way you can maintain or improve the quality of your television sets is to actively engage in Training and Development efforts. These efforts are applied to your assembly-line workers and your Automaton Technicians. A small, semi-fixed amount for continued work-crew training is necessary for the efficient operation of your assembly operations. If your basic plant size and the number of assembly workers you have tending the line are increased, you should increase the size of this budget. Alternatively, as the proportion of your assembly operations being accomplished by automatons increases, your assembly-line worker Training and Development budget could be decreased, and the amount you spend on Automaton Technician training could be increased.

In the past your firm has spent the equivalent of about US$5,000 per quarter on its American assembly-line workers, regardless of the number of Automatons installed. Additionally, your company has budgeted another US$5,000 per quarter for Automaton Technician training. When your company's Training and Development

**Exhibit 5.14    The Physical Control of Product Quality**

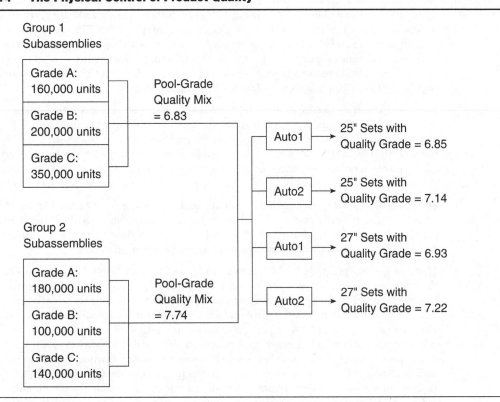

effort falls below a minimum level, product quality falls and the number of products returned for warranty work increases, due to shoddy workmanship and disguised assembly errors.

## Assembly Line Supervision

The number of Supervisors needed to oversee each factory's assembly line is related to the total number of labor hours that must be controlled or supervised, tempered by the plant's level of automaton. If your assembly line's operations are more labor intensive, the level of supervision must be higher and therefore more Supervisors must be on the payroll. If two shifts are used, your number of Supervisors would naturally have to double.

For more highly automated plants, the optimal number of Line Supervisors can be lower. In the past your company has employed one Line Supervisor for every twenty assembly-line workers and one additional Line Supervisor for every ten Automaton Technicians. When your factory operates its second shift or engages in Overtime operations, no premium salary payments are made to your Line Supervisors. A proper ratio of Supervisors to work crews must be maintained to insure optimum productivity. If your level of Line Supervision is below the minimum, product quality will fall and returns and warranty charges will probably increase.

Assembly-Line Supervision is treated as part of your company's General Administration expense. Each Line Supervisor earns a salary comparable to the prevailing rate in the factory's country and is about 1.4 times the salary earned by Automaton Technicians. If your company discharges any Line Supervisors during a quarter, a one-time General Administration charge of US$13,750 occurs. This charge covers severance pay and job-search counseling.

## Quality Control Budget

In the past your company has relied on self-inspection and the precision of its automatons to insure that you were making TV sets with adequate quality levels. Because of the greater importance of quality in product performance, however, your company has recently installed a Quality-Control program. You have hired a Quality-Control Supervisor making the equivalent of US$10,000 per quarter and have given this person the authority to request additional monies for various new Quality-Control programs. These programs entail drawing product samples from the assembly line for quality-assurance tests, with larger budgets allowing for more thorough testing. If you want to spend less than the current US$10,000 for Quality Control, you can do so. With less money spent in this area, you lose the services of a full-time Quality-Control Supervisor but instead use one on a part-time basis, depending on the salary level you have budgeted.

Because your current Quality-Control program is very new, your previous management team had not drawn any conclusions regarding the value of this effort. In theory, however, the Quality-Control Budget should increase the perceived quality of your television sets, as any off-grade sets coming down your assembly line are immediately taken off the line and thus are kept from the public. If very few of your defective products ever entered the marketplace your company's managers felt, surveys—such as the ones conducted by *Consumer Reports* and presented in Exhibit 1.3—would generate superior quality perceptions, on a par with those of Toshiba and Panasonic.

Your company's Quality-Control Supervisor currently holds monthly Quality Circle meetings, but more importantly, statistically controlled studies of product samples can be used to predict and control the number of products returned for Warranty work. The quality or rigor of these sampling studies is determined by the size of the sample the Quality-Control Supervisor draws from current production.

Three sample-size programs have been designed by your Quality-Control Supervisor. These programs, along with their costs and the quality-control standard that is expected to be achieved, are presented in Exhibit 5.15. For Quality-Control Program A, a .05 percent sample of all units produced at the designated factory would be drawn, with the guarantee that about 6.0 percent of the products that are actually defective would be released for sales. This program adds US$13,000 to your company's Quality-Control budget. If you wanted to insure that even fewer defective products reached the market, you could employ Quality-Control Program C. In this case 98.5 percent of all products reaching the marketplace would be perfect, resulting in a quality level far superior to that achieved by Toshiba. These quality control programs use destructive tests to examine the quality of the product samples drawn. Because these tests make them unusable for sale they are deducted from the total number of units available for sale and their total value at the plant's manufacturing cost is transferred to the quality control program's budget.

# Plant and Equipment Maintenance

As your plants are used over time, and the rate at which they are used intensifies, maintenance problems can increase. Wear and tear is normal and can be expected. If your plant does not use many automatons, your Maintenance budget naturally must be higher, as automatons maintain themselves and thereby your plant's overall Maintenance needs are lower. Nonetheless, windows get broken, roofs need repair, and assembly-belt drives and bearings need periodic replacement.

Your firm should budget its Maintenance monies based on each factory's rate of use, as measured by (1) the number of labor hours actually delivered, including all shifts and Overtime, and (2) the proportion of those hours delivered by automatons. Exhibit 5.16 lists the recommended Maintenance monies that should be allocated to each of your types of automatons. For plant Maintenance in general, in each past quarter your company has been spending about US$20.00 per worker scheduled. If your Maintenance budgets fall significantly below the recommended amounts, the number of labor hours available in subsequent quarters will fall, due to the presence of equipment that has completely broken down. If this case occurs, you can recover this lost capacity only by purchasing new base capacity.

**Exhibit 5.15  Quality-Control Inspection Programs**

| Sample-Size Program | Sample Size | Program Cost | Percent of Defects |
|---|---|---|---|
| A | .50% | $13,000 | 6.0% |
| B | .65% | 21,000 | 4.7% |
| C | .85% | 36,000 | 1.5% |

**Exhibit 5.16  Quarterly Automaton Maintenance Requirements (in U.S. Dollars)**

| Automaton | Budget |
|---|---|
| Auto1 | $50.00 |
| Auto2 | 105.00 |

# Capital Equipment Changes

As you know from your reading of your company's history in Chapter 2, your company's founders think they have left you in the position of realizing a number of worldwide growth opportunities. Based on their beliefs, they expect the equity value of their company to increase dramatically under your stewardship. If you want to fulfill their expectations, your management group will probably want to reconfigure or expand your company's manufacturing facilities so you can produce more television sets for overseas shipments, increase the absolute size of your initial factory, or create manufacturing facilities and wholesalers in other countries if these options are available. All these strategic moves entail alterations in your company's current manufacturing site or the creation or transfer of capital from one country to another.

# Automaton Additions and Transfers

Through the use of automatons, you can make your company more productive or more efficient, given a similarly valued fixed investment without automatons. This can be done by three methods, either singly or in combination. Your current plant's configuration can be changed by (1) purchasing new automatons, (2) purchasing used automatons from other companies in your industry, or (3) transferring your own automatons from your Home Country factory to one of your own manufacturing facilities in another country.

Regardless whether you purchase new or used equipment or transfer your own Auto1s and Auto2s between factory sites, two quarters of time are required. Additionally, for cash-flow purposes, half the monies involved is dispensed or received during the first quarter of the operation and the remaining half will be dispensed or received during the second quarter of the operation.

As a company policy, your previous management group decided that all automatons would be purchased from the same supplier. This exclusive purchasing arrangement was employed to get the best quoted prices possible and to standardize throughout the corporation the spare parts inventories and maintenance and training procedures associated with the automatons.

After investigating a number of machine-tool manufacturers in Switzerland, Germany, France, Japan, and the United States, your company decided on the family of automatons manufactured by a prominent company in Turin, Italy. As part of the negotiations for the sale of its automatons, your Italian machine-tool manufacturer included as part of its price the costs of installing the automatons and the initial training of the Automaton Technicians who would program them. The shipping costs from Turin to your possible factories, however, are borne by your company, per the schedule in Exhibit 5.17. These shipping costs are amortized as part of the original capital investment.

The automaton purchase prices negotiated by your company's previous management group are presented in your Home Country's currency in Exhibit 5.18. When plant purchases are made in Spain or Germany, the transactions are paid in euros. If they are made in Mexico, Taiwan, or Thailand, they are made in their local currency equivalents according to the exchange rates in effect at the time of sale. Your company at the Corporate level must insure that the receiving country unit has adequate actual and anticipated funds to cover all cash-flow needs associated with the equipment purchase. If not, it is possible that an Overdraft may be forced on your company at its Corporate level.

Another way your company can reconfigure a factory is to transfer automatons from one country's factory to a factory you own in another country. The movement of Auto1s and Auto2s from one country to another is accomplished by entering the Type and number of automatons to be transferred "From" and "To" in your Quarterly Decision Log's section labeled IntraFirm Automaton Transfers. The average depreciated value of the automatons by unit and type will be used when determining the new depreciation charges subsequently incurred by the receiving country's factory and for both country's Plant and Equipment Balance Sheet adjustments.

The transfer of automatons is subject to the shipping charges and dismantling fees listed in Exhibit 5.19. These fees, plus the remaining depreciated Book Value of the automatons being transferred, are paid by the receiving unit's operation. They become part of that unit's Plant and Equipment and will be amortized along with the unit's other depreciable assets. The receiving unit's Cash Account will be debited during the quarter of transfer, and the automatons will be available for production one quarter later. The selling unit's Cash account is credited at the beginning of the transferring quarter, with an appropriate reduction in its Plant and Equipment account for the value of the automaton assets that have been transferred.

### Exhibit 5.17    Automaton Shipping Costs from Turin, Italy (in U.S. Dollars)

**Unit Shipping Costs to:**

| | |
|---|---|
| North America | $45,000 |
| Western Europe | $13,000 |
| Asia | $52,750 |

### Exhibit 5.18    Automaton Price Schedule (in U.S. Dollars)

| Automaton | Purchase Price |
|---|---|
| Auto1 | $250,000 |
| Auto2 | $400,000 |

### Exhibit 5.19    Combined Automaton Shipping Charges and Dismantling Fees (in U. S. Dollars)

| To: | U.S. | Mexico | Germany | Spain | Taiwan | Thailand |
|---|---|---|---|---|---|---|
| **From:** | | | | | | |
| United States | $2,500 | $20,000 | $38,000 | $32,000 | $45,000 | $50,000 |
| Mexico | $5,000 | $2,000 | $12,000 | $9,000 | $17,000 | $19,000 |
| Germany | $21,000 | $22,000 | $1,500 | $16,500 | $31,000 | $22,250 |
| Spain | $17,000 | $11,000 | $4,500 | $1,250 | $34,000 | $36,500 |
| Taiwan | $12,500 | $12,000 | $13,000 | $12,250 | $1,000 | $2,000 |
| Thailand | $7,000 | $6,500 | $6,000 | $5,500 | $1,500 | $750 |

As an example of this type of transaction, assume that you want to send five Auto1s and four Auto2s to a plant you have already established in Spain. The example also assumes that the automatons you are dismantling and shipping to Spain were purchased and installed in your plant in Pennsylvania five and one-half years ago. Accordingly, the combined original book value of

| | Unit Purchase Price | |
|---|---|---|
| Automaton | Original | Residual |
| Auto1 | $250,000 | $112,500 |
| Auto2 | $400,000 | $270,000 |

US$3,650,000 for the automatons you are shipping has fallen to US$1,642,500, given the automaton group's depreciation at US$91,250 per quarter. Broken down by automaton type, each Auto1 is now worth US$112,500 and each Auto2 is worth US$270,000 as shown.

Because a dismantling and shipping charge is required for each automaton amounting to US$32,000 a unit, the entire transaction entails cash and asset flows amounting to US$1,930,500. The U.S. section of your North American Balance Sheet's Cash account would receive a credit in this amount, whereas its Plant and Equipment account would be debited the same amount. An opposite set of actions would occur for the Spanish section of your company's European (EU) Balance Sheet.

## Used Automaton Sales and Purchases

Another method by which you can change your factory's configuration is by purchasing used automatons from other firms in your industry. This process is initiated by entering your intentions in the appropriate Decision Entry window and informing your Game Administrator or instructor that you wish to either buy or sell a number of automatons. The Game Administrator will then post an announcement of your company's wishes on the Bulletin Board of your Global Industry Report. You will also find a summary of all potential and actual automaton sales and purchases as part of the simulation's Asset Sales drop-down menu accessed through your tool bar's Decision Set routine.

Once the announcement has been posted, the forces of the marketplace will determine what happens. You may have responses that range from little or no interest to perhaps a number of lively sessions between your firm and potential buyers or sellers. If an agreement is made, it must be written as a Contract between the two parties. This is done by completing the Automaton Sale and Transfer Agreement in Appendix G and submitting it to the Game Administrator for approval. The Game Administrator will determine whether or not all negotiations have been at arm's length and whether the prices charged and received reflect at least the nominal value of the assets being transferred. If the agreement is approved by the Game Administrator, the number and types of automatons will be transferred from and to the sites referenced in the Automaton Sale and Transfer Agreement.

Any capital gains or losses incurred by the selling company are recorded as "Capital Sales Gains/Losses" under Other Income on the firm's Income Statement. Through this process any gains or losses are taxed or credited at the income tax rate associated with the particular country's operations. No construction supervision costs are associated with these actions as they are easily absorbed by the plant's own supervisory personnel.

## Plant Construction and Outfitting

The simplest and most straightforward way to increase your plant's production capabilities is to increase its base capacity. This is done by increasing the length of your assembly line. Then more workers can be placed along the line's length, in the form of either human workers or automatons.

The beginning size for any plant, whether it was your original plant in Erie or is a new one to be built in a foreign country, must be one that can accommodate at least thirty total workers or fifteen workers per side of the Assembly line. Your current plant can accommodate 140 workers, of which six have already been replaced by three Automatons. Your original plant without Automatons cost US$3,360,000 to build and outfit requiring a capital investment of US$24,000 per worker. Added to this cost are various site-preparation charges and test borings for substrata strength, city, country, and state governmental filings, and various public hearings covering your plant's environmental impact. This component amounted to US$150,000 and must be added to the construction cost of any original plant. This brings your plant's total initial investment up to US$3,510,000 and it is on this amount that depreciation charges are charged. As Automatons are added to a factory, they too will be depreciated on their own schedules.

One method commonly used by firms for reaching foreign markets and for increasing their capacity is to build manufacturing facilities in those markets. If you should do this, your company would avoid restrictive Tariff charges, would benefit from any favorable labor-hour rates, and would eliminate shipping charges to the market in which the new factory was built.

The plant construction and outfitting process is straightforward but time consuming. Before a new plant can be built, site-selection teams from your Home Office inspect a number of potential locations in the country being considered. After a specific site has been selected, land surveys and test borings are taken and legal clearances obtained from local governments. If all goes well, your company can begin construction and outfitting. The entire process encompasses two quarters. Therefore, if a plant's construction began in Quarter 2, the result would be a factory that went on stream in Quarter 4.

The site selection and land surveying involved is conducted by the Home Country's personnel, with local personnel insuring compliance with all local laws, ordinances, and covenants. Because this is a Home Office operation, these costs are about the same regardless of the country being investigated; they amount to $150,000 per plant. As was the case with your original plant, this cost is capitalized along with the factory's construction and outfitting cost. Your company has become very comfortable with the US$24,000 capital per-worker equation, and this is the one that will apply to any new plant construction or expansions initiated by your company.

As an example of the costs and depreciation rates involved in offshore plant construction, assume that you want to build a base 86-worker plant in Mexico, and that you want to replace some of those workers by seven Auto1s and thirteen Auto2s. Exhibit 5.20 shows the costs and depreciation charges resulting from building this new factory. Note that the depreciation charges on Plant and Equipment are on a 20-year amortization schedule, whereas your automatons are on a 10-year depreciation schedule.

When building a factory or expanding its capacity, you must anticipate the cash flows associated with these actions. For cash-flow purposes, half the value of the new plant or expansion must be paid during the first quarter of construction, and the second half must be paid during the second quarter of construction. The quarterly cash needed will be automatically deducted by the simulation, and your firm's Operations Report will indicate "Capacity in Progress" in labor hours. Your firm's relevant Balance Sheet will also indicate "Capital in Progress" during any construction quarter. Once your new plant is on stream or your automatons have been installed, their value will appear as additions to your company's Plant and Equipment. It is at this time depreciation charges will begin on these capacity changes.

**Exhibit 5.20   Building an 86-Worker Base Capacity Factory with Automatons**

| Item | Cost | Depreciation/ Quarter |
|---|---|---|
| Site preparation | $    150,000 | $    1,875 |
| Base plant capacity (86 × $24,000) | 2,064,000 | 25,800 |
| Auto1s (7 × $250,000) | 1,750,000 | 43,750 |
| Auto2s (15 × $400,000) | 6,000,000 | 150,000 |
| Automaton shipping (22 × $45,000) | 990,000 | 24,750 |
| Total | $10,954,000 | $246,175 |

## Almost Everything in Place

By now you and your company have reviewed the overall nature of your industry, have some ideas about how your markets operate, and know how your firm makes its products. The last part about running your company successfully is covered in the next chapter. That chapter deals with company finances and accounting for your company's activities and results.

You can see that many opportunities face your firm and that a number of financial moves may be necessary. Even if you do not do anything dramatic, you will have to monitor the results of your many decisions. This can be done by intelligently using the financial and accounting reports prepared for you by *The Global Business Game*—or others you design for yourself once you more thoroughly understand the strengths and weaknesses of the reports that have already been provided.

## Additional Readings

Cohen, S., and J. Zysman. (1987) Why manufacturing matters: The myth of the post-industrial economy. *California Management Review* 29: 9-26.

Dreyfuss, J. (1988) Victory in the quality crusade. *Fortune,* October 10, 1988, 80-88.

Dunning, J. (1980) Toward an eclectic theory of international production: Some empirical tests. *Journal of International Business Studies* (Spring/Summer): 9-31.

_____ . (1981) *International Production and the Multinational Enterprise.* London: George Allen & Unwin.

Ferdows, K., J. Miller, J. Nakane, and T. Vollmann. (1986) Evolving global manufacturing strategies: Projections into the 1990s. *International Journal of Operations and Production Management* 6: 6-16.

Markides, C., and N. Berg. (1988) Manufacturing offshore is bad business. *Harvard Business Review* (September-October): 113-120.

Schmenner, R. (1984) *Production/Operations Management: Concepts and Situations.* Chicago: Science Research Associates.

Skinner, W. (1985) *Manufacturing: The Formidable Competitive Weapon.* New York: Wiley.

# Chapter 6

# Finance, Financial Markets and Accounting Operations

As a member of your company's management team, you must insure that a steady stream of money flows through all its operations. These flows are both short term and long term in nature. Most importantly, they need to be accurately anticipated if you want to make your company financially efficient. Your short-term needs will probably be filled by using funds received from your current sales, product licenses, and Accounts Receivables. Other short-term funds sources can come from short-term borrowing, currency exchange gains, and interest income coming from Short-Term Investments.

Because your firm might compete in a number of growing markets, you may need to obtain longer-term financing for fixed plant investments and occasional foreign start-up costs. To support these efforts, you can engage in corporate Bond and/or Common Stock sales. If your Game Administrator has set *The Global Business Game* to operate internationally, you will have access to several major international financial markets. Each market's operating patterns, variances, interest rates, and national risks have been incorporated in the GBG's model. In setting this financing challenge, your Game Administrator can choose to (1) use data from the real world's various money markets or (2) supply you with a set of quarterly data that approximates real-world conditions.

If your Game Administrator chooses to use actual money-market data in your simulation, the economic and money-market indicators and data shown in Exhibit 6.1 will be used for each of the simulation's major financial markets of New York City, Frankfurt, and Tokyo. These indicators are commonly available and are listed on a daily basis in such financial sources as Section C of *The Wall Street Journal*, and monthly in the "Monthly Survey of Interest Rates" in the *Business International Money Report*. These indicators will be updated for each quarterly run of your simulation by your Game Administrator, and you should take this information into account as you make your financing decisions.

**Exhibit 6.1   Data Sources for Money Markets and Financial Activities**

| Indicator | New York | Frankfurt | Tokyo |
|---|---|---|---|
| 90-day short-term loan | 3-month Treasury bill | 3-month eurodollar deposit | Money market rate |
| 10-year bonds | U.S. Treasury bond | U.K. government bond | Japanese government bond |
| Stock market activity | Dow-Jones Industrial Average | Frankfurt DAX-30 | Tokyo Nikkei 225 |

You can see from reading this Player's Manual that your company has already created an integrated accounting system and one it feels is adequate for most purposes. Because this has been done, your major accounting task will be to understand the nature of the results reported each quarter and to create *pro forma* income statements and balance sheets of the types presented in Appendices C and D. As you become more familiar with your firm's financial reporting needs, you might consider creating additional spreadsheet-based accounting information systems for yourself.

When your Consolidated or Home Country unit enters the equity market, or any of your local operations enter the debt market, the actual interest rates charged, or the stock issue yield obtained by your firm, will vary depending on the unit's Credit Rating in the current quarter. Accordingly, the debt interest rates associated with the indicators in Exhibit 6.1 present the base upon which your firm will be assessed interest rates on Short-Term loans or its 10-year Bond issues. The range of Credit Ratings employed in the simulation, and their associated interest rates, are presented in Exhibit 6.2.

#### Exhibit 6.2   Credit Ratings and Debt Interest Rates

| Credit Rating | 10-Year Bond Rate | Short-Term Loan |
|---|---|---|
| AAA | Bond Rate + 1.0 point | Short-Term Rate |
| AA | Bond Rate + 1.5 points | Short-Term Rate + 3.0 points |
| A | Bond Rate + 2.5 points | Short-Term Rate + 7.5 points |
| B | Bond Rate + 6.0 points | Short-Term Rate + 15.0 points |
| C | Bond Rate + 8.5 points | Short-Term Rate + 24.0 points |

## Common Stock Issues

One way to finance your company's operations is to issue common stock. This decision is indicated by entering the number of shares you wish to sell. Your firm's initial corporate charter has authorized the sale of up to 10,000,000 shares, of which 2,500,000 shares are already outstanding. This is indicated on the "Paid-In Capital" line of your Income Statement.

Stock issues are a Corporate-level or Home Country decision, so your company's shares are traded on the exchange that is associated with your Home Country's operation. This is the New York Stock Exchange for the simulation's NAFTA countries of Mexico and the United States, the Frankfurt Stock Exchange for the EU countries of Germany and Spain, and the Tokyo Stock Exchange for the APEC countries of Taiwan and Thailand.

Your firm's stock is sold through an underwriter, who insures that all the shares you offered will be sold—although perhaps at a steep discount, if necessary. The underwriter's fee, or commission for underwriting your issue, is a flat $15,000, plus 1.5 percent of the stock issue's total market value. The cash proceeds from the issue, and the share price at which your stock was sold, will vary depending primarily on the issue's size, because the issue temporarily dilutes your shareholders' claims on potential stock dividends. For cash flow purposes, your firm receives the proceeds of the stock sale one month into the issuing quarter.

When setting the initial price for your stock offering, your underwriter takes into consideration the stock's value in the previous quarter. Thereafter the forces of the equity capital marketplace take over. It is almost certain that your stock's price will be discounted, although the exact amount of discounting that will occur cannot be predicted exactly. The net proceeds from the stock sale, after the stock's dilution and the payment of all underwriting fees, are added to Consolidated's Cash account and to Owner's Equity during the quarter of issuance. If your issue sells above its nominal $1.00 par value, the surplus above par is added to your Issues above Par Account. If your stock issue sells for less than its par value, the issue's decrement below par is subtracted from Retained Earnings. Exhibit 6.3 provides an example of the actions and Balance Sheet changes associated with a stock sale of 750,000 shares of Common Stock.

**Exhibit 6.3    A Stock Sale Example**

| | |
|---|---|
| Quarter 1 shares outstanding | 2,500,000 |
| Quarter 1 stock price | $18.50 |
| Market value of shares outstanding (18.50 * 2,500,000) | $46,250,000 |
| Shares issued in Quarter 2 | 750,000 |
| Stock price after dilution effects ($46,250,000/3,250,000) | $    14.23 |
| Issue gross proceeds (14.23 * 750,000) | $10,672,500 |
| Less brokerage fees: | |
|    Flat fee | $    15,000 |
|    Commission | $    160,088 |
| Issue net proceeds | $10,497,413 |
| Proceeds to Paid-In Capital | $    750,000 |
| Proceeds to Issues above Par | $  9,747,413 |

# Treasury Stock Purchases

Your company can purchase its shares on its own account. This action, which is indicated by entering the number of shares you wish to purchase, or "retire," will temporarily increase the value of all remaining outstanding shares, as this operation's temporary effects are the opposite of those associated with a stock issue. To guard against stock price manipulation on your part, your Board of Directors has placed two limitations on your making Treasury Stock actions—the number of shares outstanding cannot fall below 2 million shares at any time, and Retained Earnings must always be positive. The simulation will automatically void any Treasury Stock action whose results would cause either of these conditions to be violated.

When Treasury Stock is purchased, shareholders sell their shares at a premium. This premium is at least 9.0 percent above its most recent quote. Accordingly, a stock that was listed at $24.37 a share on the last day of Quarter 3 would be purchased by your firm in Quarter 4 at a price that would be not less than $26.56. When such a purchase is consummated, your firm's Cash Account is debited the entire cost of the stock purchases with your Paid-In Capital account debited the par value of the shares retired and any excess above par deducted from your Issues Above Par account. Exhibit 6.4 provides an example of these Treasury Stock actions.

**Exhibit 6.4    A Treasury Stock Purchase Example**

| | |
|---|---|
| Quarter 3 shares outstanding | 4,730,000 |
| Quarter 3 stock price | $24.37 |
| Shares purchased in Quarter 4 | 500,000 |
| Estimated Treasury Stock price | $26.56 |
| Stock purchase cost<br>$26.56 × 500,000) | $ 13,280,000 |
| Cost from Paid-In Capital | $    500,000 |
| Cost from Retained Earnings | $ 12,780,000 |

# Dividends

Your shareholders are vitally interested in your company's stock performance, as well as the dividend payout policies you have created for yourself. Thus, you may wish to periodically issue stock dividends, given other financial considerations your company faces. All dividends are issued on a per share basis.

The total value of any quarterly dividend should not exceed your firm's projected Total Retained Earnings for the dividend quarter. Declarations that are greater than Retained Earnings are basically liquidating dividends and will be voided by the simulation. This type of dividend is also frowned upon by your stockholders, who wish to see their company continue as a viable enterprise for many years to come.

# Debt Issues

Your firm can also cover its cash requirements through various combinations of debt financing. This is in the form of short-term debt, long-term debt, and cash transfers from the proceeds of any debt action. These debt instruments come as (1) 90-day, short-term loans obtained from commercial banks in each marketing area's major commercial market and (2) the issuing of 10-year bonds. Should your overall consolidated operations experience a cash shortfall during any operating quarter, the simulation will automatically issue an Overdraft, which is unplanned debt financing of a very expensive and undesirable form.

# Overdrafts

This is basically a distress loan. It is the least attractive and most costly way to finance your company's business. During any particular quarter, an area operation of yours might become technically insolvent. Should this occur, the simulation will first attempt to cover the cash shortfall from idle cash available at your company's Consolidated level. If cash is available, Consolidated will automatically transfer the necessary funds to the deficient local operation without a penalty to the technically bankrupt operation. If cash is insufficient at the Consolidated level, an Overdraft loan will be obtained by Consolidated for each affected local operation, with cash disbursements automatically made to them during the quarter to cover any shortfall.

Because you exhausted all your firm's internal capital sources to arrive at the point that requires an Overdraft, and your company has been unable to accurately forecast its cash flow needs, the cost of an Overdraft is very high. The rates for Consolidated's Overdraft borrowings are about 24.0 percentage points above the prevailing 90-day Short-Term Loan rate available in its Home financial market. In most applications of this simulation, your company's Home Market financial center is New York City.

The simulation will automatically pay off your company's Overdraft during the following quarter. It does this by deducting from your firm's following quarter's cash flow the total amount of the Overdraft plus the Overdraft's interest payment for the quarter. Consequently, to maintain your company's solvency in the payoff quarter, you must plan for this "payment." While your Overdraft loan is outstanding, both the principal and its interest due appear as liabilities on your Consolidated and Country/Market Balance Sheets.

As an example, assuming a cash flow shortfall of US\$147,913 and the Short-Term Rate for the United States, the current quarter would incur a liability of US\$162,150 (147,913 * ((8.50 + 30.0)/4)). This amount would be taken from your company's cash flow in the following quarter, with the interest charge of US\$14,237 appearing on that quarter's Consolidated and Country/Market Income Statements.

# 90-Day Short-Term Loans

Short-term debt may be obtained by any one of your local operations. Given the local operation's Credit Rating, its Short-Term rate is calculated, as shown in Exhibit 6.2, as related to its particular money market. The entire amount being borrowed arrives during the borrowing quarter, with the entire loan being repaid, plus its interest charge, the following quarter. The repayment of this loan does not have to be entered, as the simulation automatically pays off the loan and its associated interest in the following quarter out of your company's operating cash flow. You must, of course, plan for this cash removal when making your financial plans for the quarter.

# 10-Year Bonds

Your company can issue callable 10-year Bonds in multiples of \$1,000. The interest rate on your Bonds depends on (1) the yield rates on comparable 10-year bonds in the world's major money markets, (2) your firm's Credit Rating, and (3) your company's debt-to-equity ratio.

When entering the Bond market, your company enters the dollar amount of the Bonds to be sold in even \$1,000s. You will receive the Bond issue proceeds during the issuing quarter, with the Bond's first interest payment due in the same quarter. Any number of Bonds, or the value of Bonds, can be outstanding at any given time—your firm needs only to services, them, i.e., pay the interest on them, each quarter.

When Bonds are outstanding, their total face value is listed as a liability, and the interest expense for that quarter appears as an Interest charge on your Income Statement. Exhibit 6.5 provides an example of a Bond issue of US$450,000 placed in the New York City money market, when a company has an "A" Credit Rating and U.S. Treasury Bonds have a 5.67% yield. It is very likely any Bond proceeds will be less than their face value. This amount of discounting occurs naturally and is charged as a one-time cost to your interest expenses. In subsequent quarters the only interest charges you incur are those needed to service the Bonds that are outstanding.

**Exhibit 6.5    A Bond Offering Example**

| | |
|---|---|
| U.S. Treasury Bond Rate | 5.67% |
| Unit's Credit Rating | A |
| Bond Interest Rate | 8.17% |
| Bond Issue Amount | US$450,000 |
| Bond Liability | US$450,000 |
| Quarterly Interest Payment | US$9,191 |
| Annual Cash Outflow | US$36,765 |

There is no restriction on the amount of total outstanding Bonds your firm can possess at any time. No new issue, however, can be larger than a unit's Current Assets, less the total of its Current Liabilities and Owner's Equity. Should these restrictions not be met, the Bond issue will fail. It is also very likely that a Bond offering would fail in any quarter where the country unit's preceding quarter's credit rating was a "C".

## Call Option

Your Bonds feature a Call option by which you can retire all or any part of their total value at any time. This option is exercised by entering the monetary value of the Bond amount to be called or retired. When making this retirement, a Call premium of 7.5 percent is levied on the amount being called, and this premium is charged to your firm's Interest account for the quarter's call. Thus, if US$150,000 of a US$400,000 outstanding amount of Bonds were called, your Balance Sheet's Cash account would be debited US$161,250, your Income Statement's Interest account would be debited US$11,250, and your total Bond liability would fall to US$250,000.

## Cash Transfers

Because of the borrowing power of different company units, and variances in interest rates associated with your firm's major money markets, you may wish to transfer cash between your local operations if you have them. This can be done to handle temporary cash flow needs, allow a local operation to make short-term investments in its own money market, or pay for plant construction and equipment transfers.

These transactions are entered as Cash "From" and Cash "To" amounts from "donor" units and "receiving" unit(s). The country operation providing the funds is the transfer*er* or "donor" and the country operation receiving the funds is the transfer*ee* or "receiver." The total value of the Cash Out-Transfers must naturally equal the total value of the Cash In-Transfers.

## Income Taxes

Because you are an international corporation, your earnings are subject to the varying whims and taxation policies of the federal and local governments within which your units operate. All countries impose general taxes on a unit's total income, and Value-Added Taxes may apply to varying degrees from country to country.

Exhibit 6.6 presents the Income Tax rates applicable within each country at the beginning of your simulation. These rates combine federal taxes with any local taxes. These taxes are paid on a quarterly basis and the simulation automatically collects them from your firm's cash flow. Should an operating unit experience losses during a quarter, the amount of those losses is carried for a three-year period and will be used to offset, or act as a tax credit against, profits or earnings made in subsequent quarters.

**Exhibit 6.6    Simplified Income, Value-Added and Dividend Tax Rates**

| Tax | Country | | | | | |
| | Germany | Mexico | Spain | Taiwan | Thailand | U.S. |
|---|---|---|---|---|---|---|
| Income | 73.4% | 50.0% | 35.0% | 25.0% | 35.0% | 47.0% |
| VAT | 15.0% | 15.0% | 12.0% | 6.5% | 20.0% | 0.0% |
| Dividend | 30.0% | 35.0% | 10.0% | 20.0% | 20.0% | 0.0% |

# Value-Added Taxes

Many countries, as a hidden and additional source of easily collected revenue, levy value-added taxes (VATs) on products manufactured within their borders. These taxes can be somewhat complex and confusing. *The Global Business Game* simplifies the assessment and collection of VATs by applying the country's particular VAT rate to the country unit's product sales less the value of all Subassemblies found in the units sold in the quarter. All VATs are automatically collected from each country unit's cash flow and gross revenues to result in the net revenues actually generated by the country unit.

# Dividend Taxes

Many countries tax the dividends or excess capital foreign subsidiaries remit to their overseas owners. The politics of this action are to encourage foreign investors to keep their capital in the country for reinvestment purposes rather than remitting it at a heavy discount to the company's home country. Exhibit 6.6 displays the Dividend Tax rates being used by various nations within the simulation to accomplish this purpose.

When an overseas country unit forwards all or any portion of its Retained Earnings to its Home Country headquarters, that amount will be taxed according to the applicable Dividend Tax rate. As an example, if your German unit had Retained Earnings of DM205,147 and wanted to send DM100,000 of that to Consolidated's Retained Earnings for its own dividend declaration needs, DM30,000 would be taxed away, with the remaining DM70,000 going to the Home Country's Retained Earnings.

# The Euro and "Euroland"

A major step in accomplishing the long-held dream of turning Western Europe into a single economic entity occurred on January 1, 1999. On that date, eleven European countries locked their national currencies to the new euro. Henceforth the exchange rates between Austria, Belgium, Finland, France, Germany, Ireland, Italy, Luxembourg, the Netherlands, Portugal, and Spain were irrevocably fixed against each other and against the euro. These countries, known as "Euroland," can use both their national currencies and the euro internally until January 1, 2002. Thereafter the only currency in circulation throughout Euroland will be the euro itself, which comes in notes of 5, 20, 50, and 100 euros and coins of 1, 2, 5, 20, and 50 euro cents.

All major European corporations began converting their accounting systems and financial portfolios well before January 1, 1999. Strong signals from the February 7, 1992, Treaty of Maastricht and the Madrid Summit of December 15–16, 1995, indicated that the European Monetary Union would be a reality. *The Global Business Game* assumes a complete conversion to the euro and states the currency values between and within Spain and Germany in euros rather than in marks or pesetas. Thus, you should think in euros when setting prices and determining costs for Spain and Germany, although the citizens of those countries will still be buying goods and receiving wages in pesetas and D-marks until 2002. Because the exchange rates between Spain and Germany are now frozen, no exchange-rate gains and losses can occur due to business transactions between those two nations. Exchange-rate gains and losses *can* occur, however, between business done in euros versus American dollars, Mexican pesos, New Taiwanese dollars, and Thai baht. At the beginning of 1999, the euro was valued at about $1.18 to the American dollar.

# Exchange Rate Gains and Losses

Your company's previous management group has required that all local profits and losses be converted into the Home Office's currency. This allows for standardized financial comparisons. Your Game Administrator will determine your company's Home Country before the simulation begins as this establishes the base currency employed. Assuming your company's Home Office is in the United States, the relevant currency would be the U.S. dollar.

Any time a nation's currency changes in value relative to that of other nations, gains and losses on the exchange or conversion of those currencies will occur. If the U.S. dollar falls in value relative to another currency, the American Home Country company realizes exchange-rate losses. If the U.S. dollar rises in its relative value, the American company receives exchange-rate gains. These effects can be substantial if one of the currencies is especially volatile and a large volume of sales is made in that currency. The sum of all currency gains and losses are considered additions or subtractions from your reported profits and Corporate-level Retained Earnings, therefore affecting your firm's Owner's Equity and the amount of dividends you can pay your shareholders.

To illustrate the effects of currency fluctuations on profits and intercompany comparisons, assume that the currency and exchange values shown in Exhibit 6.7 were in effect for Quarters 3 and 4 between the United States, Mexico, and Taiwan. Between the two periods shown US dollars rose in relation to Mexican pesos 0.0204, or 2.04 percent ((8.7850 - 8.6096) 8.6096). US dollars in relation to Taiwanese dollars fell 0.0031, or .31 percent ((33.961 - 33.856) 33.961) in value.

Now, let us assume that the following Operating Profits and Losses were obtained by your company's operations in Quarter 4 in the United States, Mexico, and Taiwan.

**Exhibit 6.7    A Sample of Currency Rates by Country**

| | Country and Currency | | |
| Quarter | United States Dollars | Mexico Pesos | Taiwan NTDollars |
| --- | --- | --- | --- |
| 3 | 1.00 | 8.6096 | 33.961 |
| 4 | 1.00 | 8.7850 | 33.856 |

## Proxy Income Statement in Local Currencies

Global Industry A Firm 1 MagnaArgus Corporation Quarter 4

| | United States (US$) | Mexico (Mex$) | Taiwan (NT$) |
| --- | --- | --- | --- |
| TOTAL REVENUE | 105,437 | 75,656 | 1,376,647 |
| EXPENSES | 102,001 | 68,546 | 1,174,692 |
| OPERATING PROFIT | 3,436 | 7,110 | 201,955 |

Converting Mexico's and Taiwan's local currencies into American dollars at the Quarter 4's exchange rates produces the following Consolidated and country-related exchange-rate gains and losses:

## Proxy Income Statement in Home Office Currency (000)

Global Industry A Firm 1 MagnaArgus Corporation Quarter 4

|  | United States (US$) | Mexico (US$) | Taiwan (US$) | Consolidated (US$) |
|---|---|---|---|---|
| TOTAL REVENUE | 105,437.0 | 8,612.0 | 40,662.0 | 154,711.0 |
| EXPENSES | 102,001.0 | 7,803.0 | 34,697.0 | 144,501.0 |
| OPERATING PROFIT | 3,436.0 | 809.0 | 5,965.0 | 10,210.0 |
| Exchange Gain/Loss |  | + 17 | - 18 | - 1 |

Exchange-rate gains were recorded between Quarters 3 and 4 because the value of the American dollar rose in relation to the Mexican peso. This gain was US$17,000 after rounding, as it took 17 fewer American dollars to convert Mexico's Quarter 4 earnings into dollars. Because the value of the American dollar fell in relation to the New Taiwanese dollar between the two quarters, exchange-rate losses amounted to about US$18,000 after rounding.

## Short-Term Investments

Your company has two other nonoperating revenue sources in addition to selling automatons to other firms in your industry. These sources are revenues from the sale of Patent rights and their accompanying royalty payments and the proceeds from locally placed Short-Term Investments.

To make a Short-Term Investment for an operating quarter, you designate the monetary value that is to be placed in each country's respective 3-month, short-term money market. This amount is immediately withdrawn from your company unit's cash flow at the beginning of the quarter but will return to your unit's Cash account at the end of the quarter, plus its interest income, which appears as Investment Income on your unit's Income Statement. The interest rate or yield on this investment will be that of the 90-day Short-Term money rate found in the money markets of New York City, Frankfurt, and Tokyo.

## Money Circles and Hedging

In prior years in the world of international commerce, firms often either capitalized on the slow pace of international currency transactions or attempted to protect themselves from wild currency fluctuations. In the former case, various firms could create money circles. These circles took advantage of the "float" or long time it took banks to reconcile their international currency accounts. In the latter case, firms felt it was useful to hedge their currency activities.

Through the advent of electronic reporting and electronic money transfers, the delay or lack of information that made these activities possible or lucrative in the past no longer exist. Thus your firm cannot create a money circle, nor would it be useful to engage in hedging operations.

# Accounting and Cash Flow Operations

The accounting system created by your company a number of years ago planned on having multiple revenue and cost sources from both its own country's operations and from those overseas. In this regard the accounting statements consist, in their most elaborate form, of three separate Global Area Reports, whose results are gathered and summarized in a Consolidated Report. The Global Area Reports present the results from the two countries where business can be conducted.

In this manual, we have previously described the nature of every item on the simulation's Income Statements, Balance Sheets, Industry Report, and Operating Statements. The present section describes various accounting procedures instituted by the simulation, starting with your company's Income Statement. The many Income Statement entries that are budgeted only by the firm—such as Advertising, Training and Development, and Research and Development—or that must be forecasted but are subject to forecasting errors, are not described in this section but have already been covered in earlier chapters. By way of summarizing this section, the more abstract cash flow implications of various entries and accounts are presented in Exhibit 6.8.

### Exhibit 6.8  Summary of Cash Flow Operations

| | |
|---|---|
| Accounts Receivable | 20.0% of Net Sales and Operating Revenue. All revenues associated with "Other" non-operating Income is collected during the quarter |
| Accounts Payable | 10.0% of factory worker wages for the quarter |
| | 25.0% of Subassembly purchases |
| | 30.0% of General Administration expenses |
| | 30.0% of Sales Representatives' Base Salaries and Commissions |

# Gross Receipts

This account summarizes all revenue associated with the sale of television sets. Included in these receipts are any VATs assessed by a federal government. You must rebate this VAT to each country's tax collector. Thus the value of the VAT is subtracted from Gross Receipts to produce the Net Sales or Operating Revenue produced by your company. Approximately 80.0 percent of Net Sales are collected during the current quarter with the remaining amount going to Accounts Receivables for collection in the following quarter.

# Other Income

Because your company has been defined as a manufacturer and seller of television sets, income from any other source or sources must be considered as nonoperating or exceptional income. The three items in this account category are pure cash in-flow by the end of the quarter, although your firm *could* take a bookkeeping loss on the sale of Equipment, which would be charged against current earnings.

# Cost of Goods Sold

Your company operates under the standard weighted cost inventory method. The unit value of each of your company's three products is the weighted value per unit of the pool of (1) units drawn from any Finished Goods held over in Inventory from previous quarters and (2) the current quarter's unit production costs and volumes. No LIFO or FIFO option is available to your company. The value of the raw materials or Subassembly portion of each product's valuation is determined by the weighted average cost of the pool of raw materials from which your television sets are assembled. About 90.0 percent of your firm's production costs associated with worker wages are current quarter cash out-flows, with the remaining 10.0 percent portion becoming an Accounts Payable item, due the following quarter.

If tariffs are being levied on the sale of imported products by a particular host nation, these charges would be added to the Country unit's Cost of Goods Sold at this time. These tariffs act to increase the cost of any products you sell in the host country, which are not produced locally, and you should consider these tariffs when setting the prices of your television sets.

# General Administration

This is a collection of executive compensation, Supervisors' wages, Technician salaries, and an overhead assessment based on plant size. Approximately 70.0 percent of this expense is a current cash outflow, with the remaining portion an Accounts Payable.

# Depreciation

This is a noncash expense, with general Plant and Equipment being depreciated on a 20-year, straight-line schedule. Automatons are a special category of equipment subject to high economic obsolescence and are accordingly depreciated on a 10-year, straight-line schedule. These assets begin their depreciation once they have been installed and are listed as Capital in Progress while going through the installation and construction process.

# Interest Charges

Any Short-Term Loans or Bonds held by your company were contracted for in a previous quarter. Accordingly, the interest charges associated with them are current quarter cash outflows. Your Short-Term Loans, plus their interest charge, are automatically paid off by the simulation, so you should accordingly anticipate this cash flow requirement.

Overdrafts incurred by firms are not anticipated but are forced on a company that is technically insolvent during the operating quarter. In this regard the amount of the Overdraft, plus its interest charge, is a cash outflow element that must be planned on by the company for the following quarter.

# Income Tax

Income Taxes are assessed at the simplified and combined federal and local rates presented in Exhibit 6.6. These taxes are collected quarterly and therefore are a current cash flow item. If your firm has negative profits for the quarter, a negative Income Tax amount will appear on your firm's Income Statement, and your Retained Earnings will be debited by the entire amount of the quarter's loss. This negative Tax is a tax credit, which will be held in your company's records to act as a deduction from any profits your firm earns within the next three years.

# Capital in Progress

This account sums the value of all monies contracted for the construction of new Plant and Equipment, the expansion of current plant capacity and the Interfirm and Intrafirm transfer of automatons. The values recorded here for Interfirm and Intrafirm automaton transfers will be the amounts agreed upon between the parties involved and duly recorded and approved by the Game Administrator on the appropriate Automaton Sale and Transfer Agreement form found in Appendix G of this Manual. The amount for new automaton purchases by automaton type is at the rates posted in Exhibit 5.17, Automaton Price Schedule. New plant construction, or plant line expansion, will be at the rate of US$24,000 per worker. Thus, if you wanted to build a plant that could be staffed by 20 line assemblers, you would have to spend US$480,000 on that facility.

Any set-up or transportation charges associated with capacity expansions or automaton transfers are immediately included in the cost, and the entire amount, from the quarter in which expansions are contracted, is depreciated at the rate applicable to the technology being depreciated. One-half of the cash flow cost of such an operation would be taken from your Cash account or any other concurrent source of cash. The full amount of the action would appear on your Balance Sheet as Capital in Progress and that Capital would start being depreciated once it has been completely installed. The other half of the action's required cash flow would come from cash sources you provide during the following quarter's activities.

## Total to Retained Earnings

This residual item can be used for internal funding purposes or can be the source of dividend declarations. For offshore units it is an amount that is subject to transfer to your firm's Home Country for use at that site. If any of these Retained Earnings are sent to your Home Country, they are subject to any existing Dividend Taxes. This tax is a current cash flow item and must be anticipated by your operating unit before the Retained Earnings transfer is made.

## Accounting and Cash Flow Operations

The Income Statements, Balance Sheets, and Operations Reports generated by *The Global Business Game* summarize the results produced by the many decisions you will make over the game's duration. To help you understand these reports, and to help you see how the results presented in the game's reports are created, a number of sample forms and print-outs have been prepared. The materials presented in this section are only for illustrative purposes. The decisions that produced these results, and the scenarios being presented, do not necessarily represent the best strategies that could have been pursued. They also do not represent how the industry you will be playing in will operate given the way your Game Administrator may set up the competition.

In this example we are examining the activities of Firm 1, MagnaArgus Corporation. The overall results of its decisions for Quarter 4, 1999 are on pages 101-103. The Decision Logs, where the company recorded its decisions for the quarter, precede the game's company reports.

Firm 1 has remained a fairly simple operation and appears to be implementing a Grand Strategy of Market Concentration and a Generic Strategy of Narrow Focus. It has expanded factory operations in the United States without engaging in either marketing or manufacturing in various foreign countries. After four quarters of play the company is solidly in first place although long-term events may jeopardize its profitability.

### Income Statement Results

MagnaArgus had net sales at the Consolidated level of $14,695,317. No value-added taxes were collected as it did not have foreign country operations. It had no other income sources such as the sale of plant and equipment, product licenses or short-term investments. Its costs appear to be well-controlled and it is completely debt-free. Its greatest expense is its cost-of-goods sold which *could* be reduced through the introduction of greater levels of plant automation. A review of MagnaArgus' Balance Sheet indicates it has adequate internal funds for such an endeavor.

### Balance Sheet Results

Firm 1's Balance Sheets are presented on page 115. At this point the firm is actually too liquid despite paying out $2.6 million in dividends in the quarter. This liquidity has actually lessened its ability to be financially productive although ample monies are available for either automating its American factory or expanding overseas with either marketing and/or manufacturing operations.

### Cash Flow Operations

Cash flow operations for your company in *The Global Business Game* can become somewhat complicated because of the large number of transactions involved. The cash inflow and outflow work sheets supplied to you in Appendix

B may help you in this regard. After working with them for awhile many teams in the game create spread-sheet versions of them to eliminate much of the quarterly, repetitive mathematics involved.

To help you better understand your company's cash flow operations, Exhibit 6.9 summarizes Firm 1's cash flow operations. As can be seen in the exhibit, a cash inflow of US$19,199,728 was associated with its Quarter 4, 1999 results. Its cash outflows of $11,508,552 for the same period resulted in an overall cash surplus of $7,691,176.

# Entering Decisions

The Player's Manual has now taken you through the basic mechanics of *The Global Business Game*, as well as providing you with exercises in Chapter 3 designed to help you form a dynamic, flexible, and productive top-management group. The next and final chapter will deal with inputting your decisions to the simulation, obtaining your quarterly results, downloading files that you might use to create spreadsheet programs for your company, answering commonly asked questions about the game, and responding to any Critical Incidents.

### Additional Readings

Bower, J. (1986) *Managing the Resource Allocation Process*. Boston: Harvard Business School Press.

Choi, F., and I. Czechowicz. (1983) Assessing foreign subsidiary performance: A multinational comparison. *Management International Review* 23: 14–25.

Ernst and Young International. (1995) *Worldwide Corporate Tax Guide*. New York: Ernst & Young.

Hood, N., and S. Young. (1979) *The Economics of Multinational Enterprise*. New York: Longman.

Lessard, D. (1985) Transfer prices, taxes and financial markets: Implications of international financial transfers within the multinational corporation. In D. R. Lessard (ed.), *International Financial Management: Theory and Application*. New York: Wiley.

Naumann-Etienne, R. (1974) A framework for financial decisions in multinational corporations: A summary of recent research. *Journal of Financial and Quantitative Analysis*, November: 859–874.

Scholes, M. S., and M. A. Wolfeson. (1992) *Taxes and Business Strategy: A Planning Approach*. Englewood Cliffs, N.J.: Prentice-Hall.

Shapiro, A. (1978) Capital budgeting for the multinational corporation. *Financial Management*, Spring: 7–16.

Srinivasan, V., and Y. Kim. (1986) Payments netting in international cash management: A network optimization approach. *Journal of International Business Studies* 17: 1–20.

Tilles, S. (1966) Strategies for allocating funds. *Harvard Business Review* 44: 72–80.

# Global Industry A Report
Year 1999 Quarter 4

| | US$ U.S. | MEX$ Mexico | DM Germany | Pta. Spain | NT$ Taiwan | B Thailand |
|---|---|---|---|---|---|---|
| Wage Rates: | | | | | | |
| 25" TV | 17.56 | 11.25 | 46.84 | 1,674.50 | 158.27 | 137.75 |
| 27" TV | 17.74 | 11.60 | 47.80 | 1,715.00 | 162.81 | 141.71 |
| Short-Term Rate | 4.73% | 7.80% | 4.30% | 8.40% | 5.61% | 10.45% |
| Bond Rate | 7.95% | 9.50% | 7.20% | 11.40% | 9.78% | 13.07% |
| Stock Market Index | 10537.05 | 8936.57 | 5490.64 | 5490.64 | 15664.29 | 15664.29 |
| GDP Q4 1999 | 100.00 | 100.00 | 100.00 | 100.00 | 100.00 | 100.00 |
| GDP Q1 2000 | 100.00 | 103.25 | 102.00 | 100.00 | 103.00 | 107.00 |
| GDP Q4 2000 | 100.23 | 113.65 | 108.24 | 100.23 | 112.55 | 131.08 |

| Subassemblies | Grade A | Grade B | Grade C |
|---|---|---|---|
| Group 1 | 168.96 | 128.80 | 115.00 |
| Group 2 | 579.31 | 463.45 | 403.00 |

## Bulletin

It is rumored that Firm 3, Home Electronics, Inc., is engaged in feasibility studies for construction of a moderately-sized plant in Thailand.

Industry experts believe subassembly component costs in the electronics industry will remain fairly steady for the next few quarters.

United States - No contract bids for 27" TVs were successful this quarter.

United States - No contract bids for 25" TVs were successful this quarter.

United States - Firm1 issued dividends in the amount of US$ 1.00 per share.

United States - Firm2 sold 200,000 shares at US$ 13.75 per share during the quarter.

United States - Firm3 sold 500,000 shares at US$ 35.94 per share during the quarter.

United States - Firm4 sold 121,000 shares at US$ 45.10 per share during the quarter.

The Home Electronics King retail chain is soliciting private-label bids for its Kingston brand of television sets for delivery next quarter. The winning bidder will supply the following with a Quality Index at or above 7.56:

25" TVs   2,050

27" TVs   4,000

Critical Incident(s) 3, 5 must be responded to next quarter.

# Global Industry A Report
Year 1999 Quarter 4
## Firm Summaries
### Firm 1 - MagnaArgus Corporation

|  | US$ U.S. | MEX$ Mexico | DM Germany | Pta. Spain | NT$ Taiwan | B Thailand |
|---|---|---|---|---|---|---|
| 25" TV: | | | | | | |
|   List Price | 125.00 | 0.00 | 0.00 | 0.00 | 0.00 | 0.00 |
|   Actual Price | 122.00 | 0.00 | 0.00 | 0.00 | 0.00 | 0.00 |
| 27" TV: | | | | | | |
|   List Price | 145.00 | 0.00 | 0.00 | 0.00 | 0.00 | 0.00 |
|   Actual Price | 135.00 | 0.00 | 0.00 | 0.00 | 0.00 | 0.00 |
| Contract Bid | | | | | | |
|   25" TV | 0.00 | 0.00 | 0.00 | 0.00 | 0.00 | 0.00 |
|   27" TV | 0.00 | 0.00 | 0.00 | 0.00 | 0.00 | 0.00 |
| Sales Offices | 4 | 0 | 0 | 0 | 0 | 0 |
| Distribution Centers | 2 | 0 | 0 | 0 | 0 | 0 |
| C-Wholesaler | 3 | 0 | 0 | 0 | 0 | 0 |
| I-Wholesaler | 0 | 0 | 0 | 0 | 0 | 0 |
| Salesreps | 6 | 0 | 0 | 0 | 0 | 0 |

### Firm 2 - Global Megapolis, Corp.

|  | US$ U.S. | MEX$ Mexico | DM Germany | Pta. Spain | NT$ Taiwan | B Thailand |
|---|---|---|---|---|---|---|
| 25" TV: | | | | | | |
|   List Price | 105.00 | 0.00 | 171.00 | 14725.00 | 3040.00 | 3705.00 |
|   Actual Price | 102.83 | 0.00 | 165.00 | 14500.00 | 3000.00 | 3700.00 |
| 27" TV: | | | | | | |
|   List Price | 123.00 | 0.00 | 188.00 | 14900.00 | 3210.00 | 3900.00 |
|   Actual Price | 122.40 | 0.00 | 185.00 | 14800.00 | 3150.00 | 3850.00 |
| Contract Bid | | | | | | |
|   25" TV | 0.00 | 0.00 | 0.00 | 0.00 | 0.00 | 0.00 |
|   27" TV | 0.00 | 0.00 | 0.00 | 0.00 | 0.00 | 0.00 |
| Sales Offices | 3 | 0 | 1 | 1 | 1 | 1 |
| Distribution Centers | 1 | 0 | 1 | 1 | 1 | 1 |
| C-Wholesaler | 0 | 0 | 0 | 0 | 0 | 0 |
| I-Wholesaler | 4 | 0 | 1 | 1 | 1 | 1 |
| Salesreps | 6 | 0 | 3 | 3 | 2 | 2 |

### Firm 3 - Home Electronics, Inc.

|  | US$ U.S. | MEX$ Mexico | DM Germany | Pta. Spain | NT$ Taiwan | B Thailand |
|---|---|---|---|---|---|---|
| 25" TV: | | | | | | |
|   List Price | 110.00 | 893.00 | 181.80 | 15190.00 | 0.00 | 0.00 |
|   Actual Price | 109.00 | 890.00 | 181.00 | 15000.00 | 0.00 | 0.00 |
| 27" TV: | | | | | | |
|   List Price | 134.00 | 940.00 | 185.00 | 17000.00 | 0.00 | 0.00 |
|   Actual Price | 133.00 | 930.00 | 184.50 | 16000.00 | 0.00 | 0.00 |
| Contract Bid | | | | | | |
|   25" TV | 0.00 | 0.00 | 0.00 | 0.00 | 0.00 | 0.00 |
|   27" TV | 0.00 | 0.00 | 0.00 | 0.00 | 0.00 | 0.00 |
| Sales Offices | 5 | 1 | 2 | 1 | 0 | 0 |
| Distribution Centers | 2 | 1 | 1 | 1 | 0 | 0 |
| C-Wholesaler | 4 | 0 | 0 | 1 | 0 | 0 |
| I-Wholesaler | 0 | 2 | 2 | 0 | 0 | 0 |
| Salesreps | 5 | 3 | 3 | 2 | 0 | 0 |

# Global Industry A Report
Year 1999 Quarter4
## Firm Summaries
### Firm 4 - Voltavision Company

| | US$ U.S. | MEX$ Mexico | DM Germany | Pta. Spain | NT$ Taiwan | B Thailand |
|---|---|---|---|---|---|---|
| 25" TV: | | | | | | |
|   List Price | 125.00 | 1200.00 | 0.00 | 0.00 | 0.00 | 0.00 |
|   Actual Price | 123.00 | 1195.00 | 0.00 | 0.00 | 0.00 | 0.00 |
| 27" TV: | | | | | | |
|   List Price | 147.00 | 1345.00 | 0.00 | 0.00 | 0.00 | 0.00 |
|   Actual Price | 146.00 | 1341.00 | 0.00 | 0.00 | 0.00 | 0.00 |
| Contract Bid | | | | | | |
|   25" TV | 0.00 | 0.00 | 0.00 | 0.00 | 0.00 | 0.00 |
|   27" TV | 0.00 | 0.00 | 0.00 | 0.00 | 0.00 | 0.00 |
| Sales Offices | 3 | 2 | 0 | 0 | 0 | 0 |
| Distribution Centers | 1 | 1 | 0 | 0 | 0 | 0 |
| C-Wholesaler | 2 | 1 | 0 | 0 | 0 | 0 |
| I-Wholesaler | 4 | 0 | 0 | 0 | 0 | 0 |
| Salesreps | 8 | 3 | 0 | 0 | 0 | 0 |

# Global Industry A Report
Year 1998 Quarter 4
## Consolidated Performance Indicators

| Firm | US$ Profit | ROA | E.P.S | ROE | US$ Stock Price | Perform. Index |
|---|---|---|---|---|---|---|
| Firm 1 - MagnaArgus Corporation | 2,772,132 | 17.82% | 1.066 | 16.42% | 55.47 | 0.98 |
| Firm 2 - Global Megapolis, Corp. | 274,328 | 0.60% | 0.070 | 0.57% | 16.36 | 0.10 |
| Firm 3 - Home Electronics, Inc. | 778,258 | 1.05% | 0.201 | 0.92% | 44.75 | 0.26 |
| Firm 4 - Voltavision Company | 1,830,678 | 6.77% | 0.628 | 4.69% | 61.55 | 0.58 |

## Game-To-Date Consolidated Performance Indicators

| Firm | US$ Profit | ROA | E.P.S | ROE | US$ Stock Price | Perform. Index |
|---|---|---|---|---|---|---|
| Firm 1 - MagnaArgus Corporation | 7,562,565 | 13.25% | 0.727 | 12.06% | 47.28 | 1.00 |
| Firm 2 - Global Megapolis, Corp. | 98,739 | 0.09% | 0.007 | 0.09% | 16.16 | 0.08 |
| Firm 3 - Home Electronics, Inc. | 3,188,096 | 2.15% | 0.240 | 2.15% | 39.69 | 0.39 |
| Firm 4 - Voltavision Company | 4,430,970 | 5.74% | 0.396 | 4.56% | 42.78 | 0.57 |

## Decision Log

Industry __A__    Firm __1__    Quarter __4__    Year _1999_

## Marketing

| Decision | United States | Mexico | Germany | Spain | Taiwan | Thailand |
|---|---|---|---|---|---|---|
| 25" TV List Price | 125.00 | | | | | |
| 25" TV Actual Price | 122.00 | | | | | |
| 27" TV List Price | 145.00 | | | | | |
| 27" TV Actual Price | 143.00 | | | | | |
| 25" TV Contract Bid | 0 | | | | | |
| 27" TV Contract Bid | 0 | | | | | |
| 25" TV Advertising | 4,000 | | | | | |
| 27" TV Advertising | 9,000 | | | | | |
| Sales Offices | 4 | | | | | |
| Distribution Centers | 2 | | | | | |
| Independent Wholesalers | 0 | | | | | |
| Company-Owned Wholesalers | 3 | | | | | |
| Sales Representatives | 6 | | | | | |
| Trainees | 0 | | | | | |
| Sales Rep Base Salary | 6,500 | | | | | |
| 25" TV Commission | 1.00% | | | | | |
| 27" TV Commission | 1.00% | | | | | |
| Sales Rep Training | 5,000 | | | | | |
| Product R&D | 5,000 | | | | | |

## Decision Log

Industry __A__    Firm __1__    Quarter __4__    Year _1999_

### Marketing Logistics

| Decision | United States | Mexico | Germany | Spain | Taiwan | Thailand |
|---|---|---|---|---|---|---|
| 25" TV Distribution from: | 0 | | | | | |
| 25" TV Distribution to: | 0 | | | | | |
| 27" TV Distribution from: | 0 | | | | | |
| 27" TV Distribution to: | 0 | | | | | |
| 25" TV Contract Distribution | 0 | | | | | |
| 27" TV Contract Distribution | 0 | | | | | |
| Surface Shipping | 0 | | | | | |
| ExAir Shipping | 0 | | | | | |

### Subassembly Purchases

| Decision | United States | Mexico | Germany | Spain | Taiwan | Thailand |
|---|---|---|---|---|---|---|
| Group 1 Grade A | 3,474 | | | | | |
| Group 1 Grade B | 3,474 | | | | | |
| Group 1 Grade C | 0 | | | | | |
| Group 2 Grade A | 2,796 | | | | | |
| Group 2 Grade B | 2,796 | | | | | |
| Group 2 Grade C | 0 | | | | | |

## Decision Log

Industry __A__    Firm __1__    Quarter __4__    Year _1999_

## Production and Operations Management

| Decision | United States | Mexico | Germany | Spain | Taiwan | Thailand |
|---|---|---|---|---|---|---|
| Shift 1 25" TVs | 24,140 | | | | | |
| Shift 2 25" TVs | 21,726 | | | | | |
| Shift 1 27" TVs | 21,726 | | | | | |
| Shift 2 27" TVs | 19,554 | | | | | |
| Line Supervisors | 3 | | | | | |
| Shift 1 25" TV Workers | 83 | | | | | |
| Shift 2 25" TV Workers | 93 | | | | | |
| Shift 1 27" TV Workers | 83 | | | | | |
| Shift 2 27" TV Workers | 83 | | | | | |
| Automaton Technicians | 3 | | | | | |
| Line Worker Training | 4,000 | | | | | |
| Automaton Technician Training | 4,000 | | | | | |
| Quality Control Training | 13,000 | | | | | |
| Quality Control Program | C | | | | | |

## Decision Log

Industry __A__     Firm __1__     Quarter __4__     Year __1999__

## Financial Management

| Decision | United States | Mexico | Germany | Spain | Taiwan | Thailand |
|---|---|---|---|---|---|---|
| Stock Issue | 0 | | | | | |
| Stock Purchase | 0 | | | | | |
| Stock Dividend | 1.00 | | | | | |
| Short-Term Investment | 0 | | | | | |
| Short-Term Loan | 0 | | | | | |
| Bond Issue | 0 | | | | | |
| Bond Call | 0 | | | | | |
| Cash Distribution to: | 0 | | | | | |
| Cash Distribution from: | 0 | | | | | |
| To Retained Earnings | 0 | | | | | |

## Decision Log

Industry __A__    Firm __1__    Quarter __4__    Year _1998_

## Plant Capacity and Plant Maintenance

| Decision | United States | Mexico | Germany | Spain | Taiwan | Thailand |
|---|---|---|---|---|---|---|
| Base Capacity | 0 | | | | | |
| Automaton Type 1 | 0 | | | | | |
| Automaton Type 2 | 0 | | | | | |
| General Maintenance | 5,5000 | | | | | |
| Auto 1 Maintenance | 110 | | | | | |
| Auto 2 Maintenance | 250 | | | | | |

## Marketing Research Request

| Question | Charge | Choice |
|---|---|---|
| 1 | $1,500 | |
| 2 | $1,500 | |
| 3 | $500 | |
| 4 | $500 | |
| 5 | $1,000 | |
| 6 | $2,000 | |
| 7 | $2,000 | |
| 8 | $750 | |
| 9 | $250 | |
| 10 | $250 | |
| 11 | $300 | |
| 12 | $300 | |
| Total | | |

## Critical Incident Response

| Incident | Response |
|---|---|
| 3 | 3 |
| 5 | 1 |
| | |

## Intrafirm Automaton Transfers

| From: | U.S. | Mexico | Germany | Spain | Taiwan | Thailand |
|---|---|---|---|---|---|---|
| United States<br>Auto 1<br>Auto 2 | XX<br>XX | | | | | |
| Mexico<br>Auto 1<br>Auto 2 | | XX<br>XX | | | | |
| Germany<br>Auto 1<br>Auto 2 | | | XX<br>XX | | | |
| Spain<br>Auto 1<br>Auto 2 | | | | XX<br>XX | | |
| Taiwan<br>Auto 1<br>Auto 2 | | | | | XX<br>XX | |
| Thailand<br>Auto 1<br>Auto 2 | | | | | | XX<br>XX |

# Operations Report
Year 1999 Quarter 4

## Firm 1 - MagnaArgus Corporation

|  | U.S. | Mexico | Germany | Spain | Taiwan | Thailand |
|---|---|---|---|---|---|---|
| Credit Rating | AAA | AAA | AAA | AAA | AAA | AAA |
| Bond Rate | 8.95% | 10.50% | 8.20% | 12.40% | 10.78% | 14.07% |
| Short-Term Rate | 4.73% | 7.80 | 4.30 | 8.40% | 5.61% | 10.45% |
| 25" TV Sales: | | | | | | |
|    C-Wholesaler | 42658 | 0 | 0 | 0 | 0 | 0 |
|    I-Wholesaler | 0 | 0 | 0 | 0 | 0 | 0 |
| 27" TV Sales: | | | | | | |
|    C-Wholesaler | 37837 | 0 | 0 | 0 | 0 | 0 |
|    I-Wholesaler | 0 | 0 | 0 | 0 | 0 | 0 |
| Contract Sales: | | | | | | |
|    25" TV | 0 | 0 | 0 | 0 | 0 | 0 |
|    27" TV | 0 | 0 | 0 | 0 | 0 | 0 |
| Market Share: | | | | | | |
|    25" TV | 30.1% | 0.0% | 0.0% | 0.0% | 0.0% | 0.0% |
|    27" TV | 26.6% | 0.0% | 0.0% | 0.0% | 0.0% | 0.0% |
| Backorders: | | | | | | |
|    25" TV | 0 | 0 | 0 | 0 | 0 | 0 |
|    27" TV | 6725 | 0 | 0 | 0 | 0 | 0 |
| Production: | | | | | | |
|    Shift 1 25" TV | 23920 | 0 | 0 | 0 | 0 | 0 |
|    Shift 1 27" TV | 20068 | 0 | 0 | 0 | 0 | 0 |
|    Shift 2 25" TV | 21726 | 0 | 0 | 0 | 0 | 0 |
|    Shift 2 27" TV | 18094 | 0 | 0 | 0 | 0 | 0 |
|    Overtime 25" TV | 220 | 0 | 0 | 0 | 0 | 0 |
|    Overtime 27" TV | 0 | 0 | 0 | 0 | 0 | 0 |
| Plant Supervisors | 3 | 0 | 0 | 0 | 0 | 0 |
| Workers: | | | | | | |
|    Shift 1 25" TV | 74 | 0 | 0 | 0 | 0 | 0 |
|    Shift 1 27" TV | 74 | 0 | 0 | 0 | 0 | 0 |
|    Shift 2 25" TV | 83 | 0 | 0 | 0 | 0 | 0 |
|    Shift 2 27" TV | 74 | 0 | 0 | 0 | 0 | 0 |
| Hours Delivered: | | | | | | |
|    Shift 1 25" TV | 43056.0 | 0.00 | 0.00 | 0.00 | 0.00 | 0.00 |
|    Shift 1 27" TV | 40136.0 | 0.00 | 0.00 | 0.00 | 0.00 | 0.00 |
|    Shift 2 25" TV | 39106.8 | 0.00 | 0.00 | 0.00 | 0.00 | 0.00 |
|    Shift 2 27" TV | 36188.0 | 0.00 | 0.00 | 0.00 | 0.00 | 0.00 |
|    Overtime 25" TV | 396.0 | 0.00 | 0.00 | 0.00 | 0.00 | 0.00 |
|    Overtime 27" TV | 0.0 | 0.00 | 0.00 | 0.00 | 0.00 | 0.00 |
| Warranty Work: | | | | | | |
|    25" TV | 588 | 0 | 0 | 0 | 0 | 0 |
|    27" TV | 346 | 0 | 0 | 0 | 0 | 0 |
| Goods In Transit: | | | | | | |
|    25" TV | 0 | 0 | 0 | 0 | 0 | 0 |
|    27" TV | 0 | 0 | 0 | 0 | 0 | 0 |
|    Contract 25" TV | 0 | 0 | 0 | 0 | 0 | 0 |
|    Contract 27" TV | 0 | 0 | 0 | 0 | 0 | 0 |

| Finished Goods Inventory: | | | | | | |
|---|---|---|---|---|---|---|
| 25" TV | 2818 | 0 | 0 | 0 | 0 | 0 |
| 27" TV | 0 | 0 | 0 | 0 | 0 | 0 |
| Unit Cost: | | | | | | |
| 25" TV | 79.675 | 0.000 | 0.000 | 0.000 | 0.000 | 0.000 |
| 27" TV | 91.356 | 0.000 | 0.000 | 0.000 | 0.000 | 0.000 |
| Quality Index: | | | | | | |
| 25" TV | 7.74 | 0.00 | 0.00 | 0.00 | 0.00 | 0.00 |
| 27" TV | 7.74 | 0.00 | 0.00 | 0.00 | 0.00 | 0.00 |
| Contract | 0.00 | 0.00 | 0.00 | 0.00 | 0.00 | 0.00 |
| Subassembly Inventory: | | | | | | |
| Group 1 Grade A | 382821 | 0 | 0 | 0 | 0 | 0 |
| Group 1 Grade B | 377304 | 0 | 0 | 0 | 0 | 0 |
| Group 1 Grade C | 14 | 0 | 0 | 0 | 0 | 0 |
| Group 2 Grade A | 291159 | 0 | 0 | 0 | 0 | 0 |
| Group 2 Grade B | 289677 | 0 | 0 | 0 | 0 | 0 |
| Group 2 Grade C | 3 | 0 | 0 | 0 | 0 | 0 |
| Plant Configuration: | | | | | | |
| Base Capacity | 160 | 0 | 0 | 0 | 0 | 0 |
| Automaton 1 Machines | 2 | 0 | 0 | 0 | 0 | 0 |
| Automaton 2 Machines | 1 | 0 | 0 | 0 | 0 | 0 |
| Labor Hours | 86905 | 0 | 0 | 0 | 0 | 0 |
| New Capacity In Progress: | | | | | | |
| Base Capacity | 0 | 0 | 0 | 0 | 0 | 0 |
| Automaton 1 Machines | 0 | 0 | 0 | 0 | 0 | 0 |
| Automaton 2 Machines | 0 | 0 | 0 | 0 | 0 | 0 |
| Product Distribution From: | | | | | | |
| 25" TV | 0 | 0 | 0 | 0 | 0 | 0 |
| 27" TV | 0 | 0 | 0 | 0 | 0 | 0 |
| Contract | 0 | 0 | 0 | 0 | 0 | 0 |
| Product Distribution To: | | | | | | |
| 25" TV | 0 | 0 | 0 | 0 | 0 | 0 |
| 27" TV | 0 | 0 | 0 | 0 | 0 | 0 |
| Contract | 0 | 0 | 0 | 0 | 0 | 0 |
| Shipping Method: | | | | | | |
| Surface | 55541 | 0 | 0 | 0 | 0 | 0 |
| Express Air | 0 | 0 | 0 | 0 | 0 | 0 |
| Automaton Distribution: | | | | | | |
| Automaton 1 Machines | 0 | 0 | 0 | 0 | 0 | 0 |
| Automaton 2 Machines | 0 | 0 | 0 | 0 | 0 | 0 |
| Maintenance Effect | 1.46 | 0.00 | 0.00 | 0.00 | 0.00 | 0.00 |
| Cash: | | | | | | |
| From | 0 | 0 | 0 | 0 | 0 | 0 |
| To | 0 | 0 | 0 | 0 | 0 | 0 |
| Retained Earnings From | 0 | 0 | 0 | 0 | 0 | 0 |

# NAFTA Consolidated Income Statement
Year 1999 Quarter 4

## Firm 1 - MagnaArgus Corporation

| | US$ Consolidated | US$ U.S. | MEX$ Mexico |
|---|---|---|---|
| **Revenues:** | | | |
| Gross Revenues | 14,695,317 | 14,695,317 | 0 |
| Value-Added Tax | 0 | 0 | 0 |
| Net Sales | 14,695,317 | 14,695,317 | 0 |
| | | | |
| Other Income: | | | |
| Capital Sales Gains/Losses | 0 | 0 | 0 |
| Investment Income | 0 | 0 | 0 |
| Licenses | 0 | 0 | 0 |
| Non-Operating Income | 0 | 0 | 0 |
| **Total Revenue** | 14,695,317 | 14,695,317 | 0 |
| | | | |
| **Expenses:** | | | |
| Cost of Goods Sold | 6,916,185 | 6,916,185 | 0 |
| Advertising | 13,000 | 13,000 | 0 |
| General Administration | 188,379 | 188,379 | 0 |
| Sales Offices | 614,000 | 614,000 | 0 |
| Distribution Centers | 240,929 | 240,929 | 0 |
| Wholesale Operations | 662,990 | 662,990 | 0 |
| Sales Force Salaries | 170,843 | 170,843 | 0 |
| Trainees | 0 | 0 | 0 |
| Training and Development | 13,000 | 13,000 | 0 |
| Inventory Charges | 238,358 | 238,358 | 0 |
| Shipping | 210,821 | 210,821 | 0 |
| License Fees | 0 | 0 | 0 |
| Research and Development | 5,000 | 5,000 | 0 |
| Quality Control | 109,764 | 109,764 | 0 |
| Depreciation | 75,750 | 75,750 | 0 |
| Maintenance | 5,860 | 5,860 | 0 |
| Interest Charges: | | | |
| Overdrafts | 0 | 0 | 0 |
| Short-Term Loan | 0 | 0 | 0 |
| Bonds | 0 | 0 | 0 |
| Miscellaneous | 0 | 0 | 0 |
| **Total Expenses** | 9,464,880 | 9,464,880 | 0 |
| | | | |
| Income Before Taxes | 5,230,437 | 5,230,437 | 0 |
| Income Tax | 2,458,305 | 2,458,305 | 0 |
| Dividend Tax | 0 | 0 | 0 |
| **Net Income** | 2,772,132 | 2,772,132 | 0 |

# NAFTA Consolidated Income Statement

Year 1999 Quarter 4

## Firm 1 - MagnaArgus Corporation

| | US$ Consolidated | US$ U.S. | MEX$ Mexico |
|---|---|---|---|
| **Assets:** | | | |
| Cash | 4,634,559 | 4,634,559 | 0 |
| Accounts Receivable | 2,939,063 | 2,939,063 | 0 |
| Tax Credit | 0 | 0 | 0 |
| Short-Term Investments | 0 | 0 | 0 |
| Due From Country Unit(s) | XXX | 0 | XXX |
| Inventories: | | | |
|   Subassemblies | 4,162,031 | 4,162,031 | 0 |
|   Finished Goods | 224,524 | 224,524 | 0 |
| Goods in Transit | 0 | 0 | 0 |
|   Total Current Assets | 11,960,177 | 11,960,177 | 0 |
| Capital in Progress | 0 | 0 | 0 |
| Plant and Equipment | 5,025,000 | 5,025,000 | 0 |
| Less Depreciation | 1,429,500 | 1,429,500 | 0 |
|   Total Fixed Assets | 3,595,500 | 3,595,500 | 0 |
| **Total Assets** | 15,555,677 | 15,555,677 | 0 |
| | | | |
| **Liabilities and Owner's Equity:** | | | |
| Accounts Payable | 1,417,465 | 1,417,465 | 0 |
| Overdraft | 0 | 0 | 0 |
| Due to Home Country | XXX | XXX | 0 |
| Short-Term Loan | 0 | 0 | 0 |
|   Total Current Liabilities | 1,417,465 | 1,417,465 | 0 |
| Bonds | 0 | 0 | 0 |
|   Total Liabilities | 1,417,465 | 1,417,465 | 0 |
| Stockholder's Equity: | | | |
|   Common Stock | 2,600,000 | 2,600,000 | XXX |
|   Paid-In Capital | 2,740,995 | 2,740,995 | XXX |
|   Current Earnings | 2,772,132 | 2,772,132 | 0 |
|   Retained Earnings/Deficit | 6,025,086 | 6,025,086 | 0 |
|   Exchange Gains/Losses | 0 | 0 | XXX |
|   Total Stockholder's Equity | 14,138,213 | 14,138,213 | 0 |
| **Total Liabilities and Owner's Equity** | 15,555,677 | 15,555,677 | 0 |

**Exhibit 6.9 Cash Inflow Operations**

| Cash Inflow Item | Amount | Explanation |
| --- | --- | --- |
| Current Sales | 11,756,254 | 80.0% of the firm's current sales which were 14,695,317. |
| Cash Account | 4,795,060 | Cash available from the last day of Quarter 3, 1999. |
| Accounts Receivable | 2,648,414 | Accounts Receivables from Quarter 3, 1999 collected this quarter. |
| Short Term Investment | 0 | The firm had no Short Term Investments, debt or stock issues or any other income sources. |
| Short Term Loan | 0 | |
| Bond Sale | 0 | |
| Stock Sale | 0 | |
| Patent Income | 0 | |
| Credits | 0 | |
| Cash Transfer | 0 | |
| TOTAL CASH IN | 19,199,728 | The company's operations experienced a cash inflow of this amount. |

**Exhibit 6.10 Cash Outflow Operations**

| Cash Outflow Item | Amount | Explanation |
|---|---|---|
| Factory Wages | 2,281,587 | 90.0% of the firm's factory Wage Bill which amounted to $2,535,096. |
| Subassemblies | 2,962,481 | 75.0% of the firm's cost of $3,949,975 for Subassemblies ordered for Quarter 1, 2000. |
| Advertising | 13,000 | Budgeted by the firm. |
| Administration | 131,865 | 70.0% of the company's Administrative Overhead expenditure of $188,379 for Executive Compensation, Automaton Technicians, Line Supervisors, Plant Superintendency and plant size. |
| Sales Offices | 614,000 | All expenses for the operation of Sales Offices. |
| Distribution Centers | 240,929 | All expenses for the operation of two Distribution Centers and Warranty work on 588 25" TVs and 346 27" sets. |
| Wholesale Operations | 662,990 | All expenses associated with running its own wholesaling operations. |
| Sales Force Salaries | 119,590 | 70.0% of the Base Salaries and Commissions earned by the company's Sales Representatives. |
| Training | 26,000 | Budgeted training and development programs for Automaton Technicians, Assembly Line Workers, Sales Trainees and Sales Representatives. |
| Inventory Charges | 238,358 | Inventory and handling charges for all goods manufactured and handled at the factory level. |
| Shipping | 210,821 | Charges on the lots of Subassemblies purchased for the quarter. |
| License Fees | 0 | Fees for any patents purchased. |
| R & D | 5,000 | Research and Development monies budgeted for the quarter. |
| Quality Control | 109,764 | The company's Quality Control budget. |
| Maintenance | 5,860 | Factory and Automaton maintenance budgets. |
| Accounts Payable | 1,337,560 | The company did not engage in any debt or equity issues. |
| Overdraft | 0 | |
| Short Term Loan | 0 | |
| Bond Interest | 0 | |
| Bond Call | 0 | |
| Stock Dividend | 2,600,000 | The firm issued a $1.00 per share dividend. |
| Treasury Stock | 0 | No Treasury Stock was purchased. |
| Capital In Progress | 0 | No new plants were being built or expanded. |
| Cash Transfer | 0 | No money was transferred into the company. |
| TOTAL CASH OUT | 11,508,552 | The total cash outflows associated with Firm 1's operations. |

**Chapter 7**

# Simulation Operations and Playing Procedures

We have now come to the part of the game where you must transfer all your decisions from your Decision Logs. This is done by your inputting your decisions to the medium used by your Game Administrator or Instructor to access the simulation's various programs. Although you will be installing *The Global Business Game* on your personal computer via a CD-ROM, you will be interacting with your Game Administrator and the game itself with a 3.5" floppy company disk. After every company's decisions have been collected and submitted to the simulation and the quarter has been run successfully, you will be given feedback on your company's performance through the results generated by the game. These results will be handed back to you via your company disk.

This chapter deals with how your game will be typically configured at most locations. There any number of options your Game Administrator could employ for interacting with the game's model, such as a Website, FAXs between you and all parties connected with the industry being simulated or a local area network (LAN). Your Game Administrator will explain to you the procedures in effect at your location.

## General Diskette Operations and Procedures

You have received as part of your Player's Manual a CD-ROM, which contains the Player Application that is needed to run your part of the simulation, and a 1.44MB floppy disc labeled "Decision Disk". This disk is used to enter your firm's quarterly decisions and to retrieve your results after each quarter. To interact with the programs you must first Install the CD-ROM's programs on the computer you are using. Once that application has been installed you can then enter and later access the results from the game.

The initial installation of the GBG, your company Start-Up process and the quarterly Decision Set input and output stages should follow the process diagrammed below. If you have a dedicated laptop or desktop computer you will only have to Install your GBG program once. If you do not have a dedicated personal computer and are perhaps installing and using the GBG Program on a shared computer in your school or business's computer laboratory, the GBG Program will probably be automatically removed from the system after its use. In this case you will have to re-install the GBG each time it is used. If that is your situation the sequence, after Initializing your firm, would follow the dashed path each time you enter your firm's Decision Set.

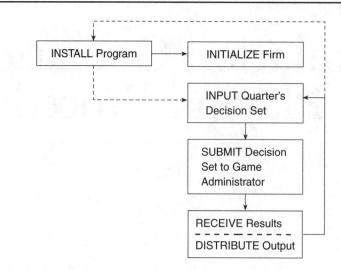

## System Requirements

To run the GBG's applications you will need a personal computer with the following configuration and memory sizes:

| | |
|---|---|
| Computer/Processor | Personal or multi-media computer with an 80486 or higher processor. |
| Operating System | Microsoft Windows 95, Windows 98, or Windows NT 4.0. |
| Memory | In Windows 95 or 98, 8MB of RAM. |
| | In Windows NT, 16MB of RAM. |
| Disk Drives: | |
|   Hard Disk | 12MB of free hard-drive space. |
|   CD-ROM | A standard CD-ROM drive. |
|   Floppy | 1.44MB |
| Monitor | VGA or higher-resolution video adapter. Super VGA, 256-color ideal. |
| Peripherals | Any printer supported by Windows. |
| | Windows-compatible mouse or other pointing device. |

## Using Windows

*The Global Business Game* assumes you have a working familiarity with Windows, its screen layouts and its operating conventions. If this is not the case you may wish to refer to any of the following simply written books for the rudiments required.

Crawford, S., and N. Salkind, *The ABCs of Windows 98.* Alameda, CA: Sybex International, 1998.

Matthews, M., *Microsoft Windows 987 Companion.* Redmond, WA: Microsoft Press 1998.

Rathbone, A. *Windows 98 For Dummies.* Foster City CA: IDG Books International, 1998.

Stinson, C., *Running Microsoft Windows 98.* Redmond, WA: Microsoft Press, 1998.

## Player Application Installation

Do the following to install *The Global Business Game* on your computer:

1. After opening Windows insert the **GBG Program CD-ROM** in your computer's CD-ROM drive. This will normally be your "D" drive.

2. Click on **Browse**, Select the **D drive** and then double Click on **Setup.exe**.

3. Follow the installation wizard instructions that appear on the screen.

After you have completed the installation process, you can launch the **GBG Player** application by choosing **Start, Programs, The Global Business Game**, and then **GBG Player**.

## Running GBG Player

Before you can begin inputting your company's first round of decisions you must first identify your company, the industry in which it is competing and the members of your management team. It is assumed at this point you have been assigned to a company and your Game Administrator has provided you with the Industry letter that applies to your company. These letters can run from "A" to "I" as it is possible to create up to nine separate industries in *The Global Business Game.*

*Initializing Your Company.* Within Windows launch *The Global Business Game* by choosing **Start, Programs, The Global Business Game**, and then **GBG Player**. You will first see a screen that identifies *The Global Business Game* followed shortly by a **Getting Started** screen. Those screens shown in Screen 7.1 have you initialize your company the first time you use the program, and allow you to continue using the program after the game has begun.

**Screen 7.1   Opening Global Business Game Screens**

The **Getting Started** screen makes it possible for you to "Initialize Company" or "Open an Existing Firm". Because you are just starting your operations should Select "Initialize Company". Once the game begins you will subsequently choose "Open an Existing Firm" to retrieve your results and to input your new set of decisions for the quarter to your 1.44MB Decision Disk.

Initialize your company by following the directions found on the screen and by filling-in the appropriate spaces as shown in Screen 7.2. You will be asked to create a name for your firm as well as a Password. Your Decision Disk is Passworded so your competitors cannot engage in "dirty tricks" by intercepting it using its contents for their own purposes. Be sure to write down your Password and insure that all members of your management team know the password. If you forget your Password it cannot be retrieved even by your Game Administrator. In such cases you will have to re-initialize your company after obtaining an updated disk from the Game Administrator.

**Screen 7.2   Initializing Your Company**

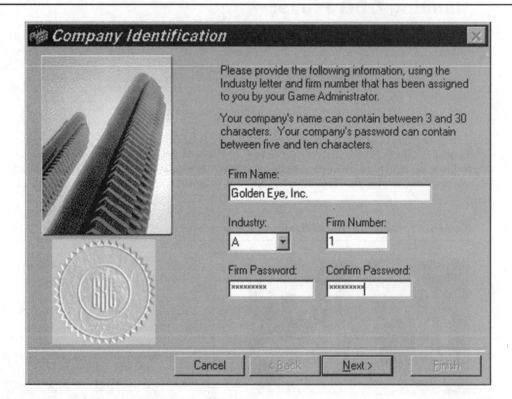

As the next part of the Initializing process you will be asked to list the names, telephone numbers, e-mail addresses and student identification numbers of all those on your management team. As your enter this information on the "Management Group" spreadsheet the columns will widen automatically to provide you with enough space for all entries. See Screen 7.3. This is done so your Game Administrator can contact various members of your firm should any problems occur with your Decision Input or the game's overall processing. The final part of Initializing your company requires you to save in Screen 7-4 this input. You should "Save firm to a diskette" as this disk will have to be turned in to your Game Administrator. It would also be a good idea to save again to a backup floppy if you do not have a dedicated personal computer or to the hard drive of your personal computer if it is under your control.

**Screen 7.3   Company Roster**

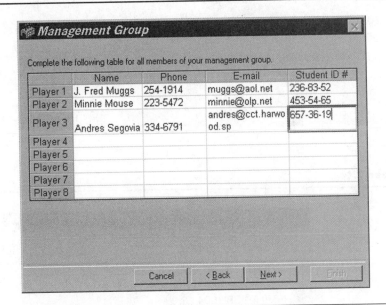

**Screen 7.4a   Saving Company Input**

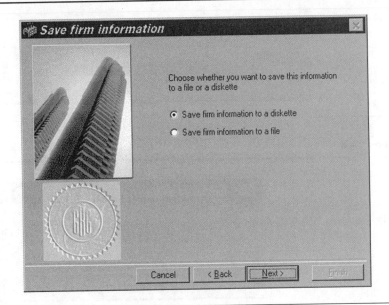

**Screen 7.4b**

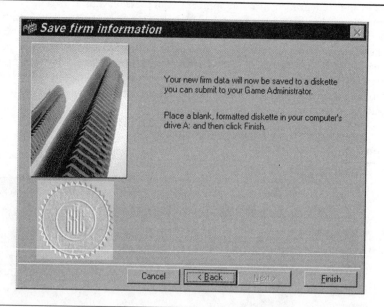

**Screen 7.4c**

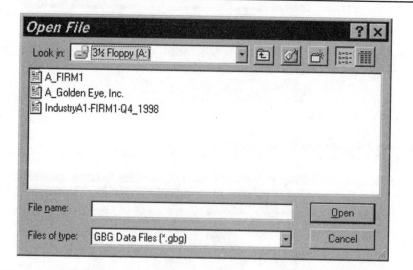

**Screen 7.4d**

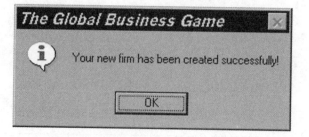

*Entering and Editing Decisions.* You can see by now the GBG has been designed to look and feel like a typical Windows application. It has a Main Menu and a GBG Desktop. Within this desktop you can open as many windows as you like. And as in Windows, these windows can be maximized, minimized or dragged.

To re-enter GBG click on **File** and then **Open**. "Open File" appears as in Screen 7.5. It is assumed here you are using your 1.44MB floppy in Drive A. Use "Look in" dropdown menu to click on to your 3 1/2" Floppy. Your firm's file will appear. In this case it is A_Golden Eye, which indicates Industry A, Firm 1. Click "Open" and you will have to go through the security check shown in Screen 7.6. You have three chances here before striking out.

**Screen 7.5   Open File Open Player Application**

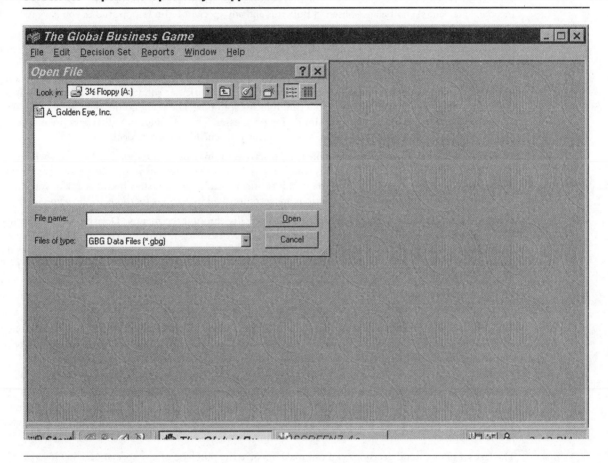

**Screen 7.6   Security Check**

A Main Bar will appear. It has six headings— *File, Edit, Decision Set, Reports, Windows and Help.* You may be familiar with some of these headings such as **File**, **Edit**, **Windows** and **Help**. Others are unique to *The Global Business Game.* The GBG's **File** allows you to enter "New" which is used for creating a new company or "Open" which is used to open your firm's files after you have initialized your company. It is here that you also "Save" your decision sets after making all your decisions "Print" your results after your diskette has been returned to you by the Game Administrator. **Edit** gives you the opportunity to cut, paste and copy entries. The **Windows** menu allows you to arrange how your menus will be displayed while **Help** allows you to search on key topics associated with the game.

The unique items found on your Menu Bar are found in **Reports** and **Decision Set**. The drop down menu associated with **Reports** gives you access to the simulation's Global Industry Report, your company's Operations Report(s), Income Statement(s) and Balance Sheet(s), Bulletins and any special Merlin Group studies you have requested.

You will spend the greatest amount of your time interacting with the game's **Decision Set** section. In this drop down menu, you will find ten sections which conform to the layout of your Decision Logs. Clicking on **Decision Set** produces a drop down menu such as that shown in Screen 7.7. You will find at the screen's bottom six tabs associated with the game's functional areas. If you are playing a game that allows you to compete in a number of countries, these operations are accessed by "spinning on" the particular country in the combination box provided. Only those countries in effect are available through this spin box. The year and quarters shown will automatically update themselves every quarter as the simulation progresses. The "B" column will always present your past period's decisions while the "C" column is reserved for your current quarter's decisions.

Over the game's run you may wish to take special actions, or may have to respond to Critical Incidents invoked by your Game Administrator. These actions entail asset sales to other firms in your industry of either subcontracted television sets, patent licenses or Automatons, intra-firm Automaton transfers between any of your Country Units and bids for private label sales. These actions are accomplished by various methods in the game.

Bidding for private label sales is accomplished unilaterally through the menus "Decision Set, Marketing" and "Decision Set, Logistics". You should first set your bid price as part of your Marketing decisions followed by dedicating the correct number of units requested by Home Electronics King as part of your Logistics decisions. If your company wins the bid the dedicated units will automatically be deducted from your firm's Home Country inventory. If your company does not win the bid the dedicated units become part of your company's regular supply of finished goods.

Intra-firm Automaton transfers are also unilateral actions. To accomplish these transfers you access "Asset Transfers" within "Decision Set". As presented in Screen 7.8 the menu reminds you of the Automatons you have available by Country Unit and the various countries that can receive them. Your company can engage in these activities without notifying the Game Administrator.

Your firm's Critical Incident responses are another set of unilateral actions your company can engage in. If your Game Administrator invokes the need for Critical Incident responses, you must respond to them via "Decision Set, Critical Incidents" as in Screen 7.9. Should you not respond to the Critical Incident(s) your Home Country Unit will automatically be fined $50,000 through its Miscellaneous account. The incidents themselves, and the possible responses available to you, are found in Appendix E.

The last set of unilateral decisions you can make involve the purchase of any special Merlin Group studies. These are purchased via "Decision Set, Merlin Group Report Requests." Screen 7.10 shows you the drop-down menu that allows you to make your requests. As you check off the reports you want their total cost will be summed for you and will appear as a next-quarter Miscellaneous expense to your firm. In this example the company is spending $4,000.00 to get the answers to Questions 1, 3 and 6.

When you have completed your firm's set of decisions for the quarter return to **File** and select **Save**. This action stores the work you have done thus far. If you use the command "Save As" your decision file or Decision Set for the quarter will be saved under a new name you assign to it and possibly to a different location of your choice. You will also have to provide your Game Administrator with your firm's diskette so your decisions can be read into the computer. This is done via the same "Save Firm Information" screen you used to store your firm's initialization input.

As part of the game's "Save" routine, the program will edit your decisions to make sure they are acceptable, or within range for the game's model. This editing will not correct, or make incorrect decisions "correct". It merely edits them so they can be processed by the game's programs. If any of your company's decisions cannot be accepted by the game, and these usually are typographical errors, number transpositions or data in the wrong spreadsheet fields, you will receive a "Bounds" worksheet displaying your errors. By clicking "OK" you signify that you want the "flagged" decision to actually be used by the simulation regardless of its unacceptability during the editing process.

**Screen 7.7    Entering Decisions**

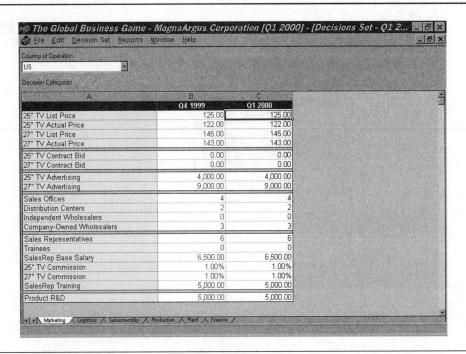

**Screen 7.8    Asset Transfers**

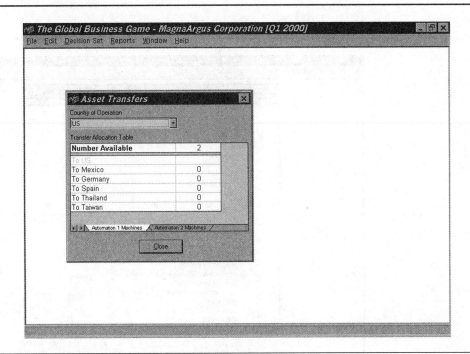

**Screen 7.9    Critical Incident Responses**

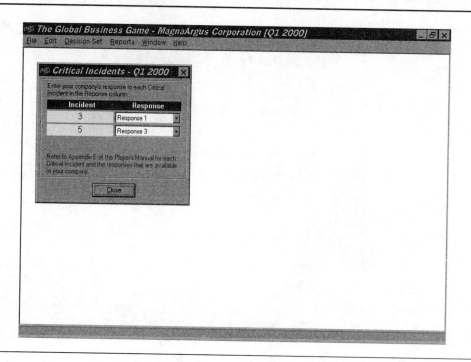

**Screen 7.10    Merlin Reports Requests**

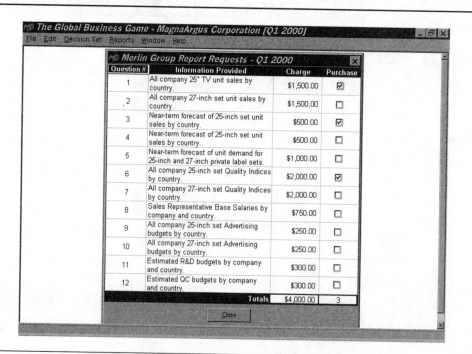

| **Functional Area** | **Answer or Suggested Solution** |
|---|---|

## Marketing

"I haven't been able to get a Patented feature for my TVs, even although I've spent a lot of R&D money on the effort."

The simulation rewards a constant stream of R&D money, so you may have been spending irregular amounts over the past number of quarters. What you think is "a lot of money" may not be very much. You can find out the R&D budgets of various firms in your industry by buying a market research study from The Merlin Group. This would indicate to you what your competitor's are doing and if they are perhaps having the same experience that you are having.

"I'd like to trick my competitors by posting a very high List Price for my TVs while actually selling them for a very low Actual Price. Do you think this is a good idea?"

In doing this you may fool somebody for a while, but your firm's Actual Prices are divulged to your competitors the following quarter. In doing this you are also costing your firm money, as Sales Representative Commissions are paid on your List Prices, although you are collecting revenue only on your Actual Prices.

"I think our company has enough Quality to really get high sales. How do I let my customers know I have high quality?"

The best you can do here is to engage in more total sales promotion efforts than do your competitors. Make sure your Advertising budgets, Sales Representative Base Salaries and unit Commissions are higher, on a per unit basis, than your competition. It would also be wise to get a Market Research study from The Merlin Group to check whether the Quality Ratings on your TVs are really that much better than your competition's. You may be trying to advertise something you actually do not have.

"Can I design "better" advertisements than those being used by my rivals?"

No, you cannot design better advertisements, but you *can* out-advertise your competitors by spending more money than they do.

## Production

"No matter how I figure it, my unit costs are always different than what I forecast."

After things settle down in your plant, you should be able to calculate your unit costs fairly accurately. Some of the reasons why you may be off when forecasting unit costs are associated with down time caused by running out of Subassemblies or worker absenteeism during the quarter, not correctly calculating the weighted cost of the mix of Subassembly Grades used in the production run, and the higher wage rates forced on 25" TVs when you have them assembled by 27" line workers.

"The number of labor hours delivered by my workers never comes up to what I have ordered. What causes this?"

The number of workers who actually come to work each day, week, and quarter is related to your firm's Maintenance budget at each plant and the number of vacation days, sick days, and absenteeism rates associated with each country's labor practices and work ethic. You *can* affect the nondelivery of labor hours by increasing your Maintenance budgets. You *cannot* affect those factors tied to each country's labor practices and work ethic. In this area you must anticipate these realities which are presented in Exhibit 5.7 in your *Player's Manual*.

"I'm getting a lot of returns and high Warranty charges. How can I get rid of them?"

Returns cannot be completely eliminated but you can minimize returns by producing TVs with greater intrinsic quality and/or increasing the level of the Quality Control inspections programs at each factory. You can produce sets with greater intrinsic quality by increasing the number of Supervisors you have per shift, engaging in more Work Crew Training program and using more AUTOMATONs as part of your assembly operations.

| "How do I know if my Maintenance budgets are either too high or too low?" | You will never know if they are too high but you can determine whether they are too low. The best indication that these budgets are too low is when the number of labor hours available in your plant(s) falls. This decrease in available labor hours indicates some of your equipment is unusable due to poor Maintenance and that you should increase this budget so that more equipment is not destroyed. |

## Finance/Accounting

| "How can I 'beef up' my firm's stock price?" | Your company's stock price is largely determined by your firm's earnings, its Retained Earnings and the number of shares you have outstanding. You can "beef up" your firm's stock price by working on these three elements, i.e., have high earnings, a large pool of Retained Earnings from which you can declare dividends and relatively few shares outstanding. The latter element can be improved by purchasing Treasury Stock with reduces the number of shares outstanding thereby increasing your firm's earnings-per-share. |
| "No matter how hard I try I always miscalculate my firm's cash flow needs! What is causing this?" | One of the reasons is your overlooking any one of the large number of items figured into your firm's cash flow needs. You may also not understand the leads and lags of the various flows associated with different operations. If you have all of the above correctly considered, the next major reason cash flows are not what they were projected to be is the fact that revenues, primarily sales, and costs, mostly unit manufacturing costs, were more or less than forecasted. It may be that your sales projections were too high and therefore actual cash from sales was lower than anticipated. It also may have occurred that your firm's unit manufacturing costs were greater than projected therefore reducing the operating profit you had anticipated for the quarter. |

After reviewing your firm's decision inputs it would be a good idea to print-out your decision set for your records and to make sure the decisions you entered on your Decision disk are the same ones you had on your Decision Logs. This is done by clicking on **File** and then onto **Print**. Once you have submitted your Decision Set it is very difficult to correct any decision or data input mistakes you have made.

*Viewing and Printing Results.* After you have submitted your Decision Set to the Game Administrator your firm's results will be returned to you via the same Decision Disk. To get your results under Windows launch *The Global Business Game.* Go through the same security clearance after clicking on "Open" and accessing your company's file found on your floppy. Click on **Reports**. A drop-down menu will appear where you can choose the particular report you would like to view. You can either print out your results from the screen or by going to **Print** within the **File** menu or CTRL F within the screen you are viewing.

*Trouble-Shooting and Commonly-Asked Questions.* Most questions players pose about business games center around "Why did this happen?" or "I don't understand how the game does this!" This section cannot answer every question you may have about the game as, in life, some events or things cannot be explained fully. What *can* be answered, however, are various things you may have over overlooked or not even considered when making a decision. In doing this you may have caused the unanticipated or unexplainable results you and your company have obtained. The following section lists various questions and suggested answers by the game's major functional areas of marketing, production, finance and accounting.

*Getting Help.* While this chapter's previous section dealt with commonly-asked questions about how to work with certain aspects of your company, you can get additional help at any time when you are operating within *The Global Business Game.* This is done by going to **Help** on the game's toolbar. This **Help** routine operates in the same fashion as that found within Windows. **Help** covers all the game's Contents, provides quick definitions for all entries appearing on the game's print-outs as well as providing an Index for searching various topics within **Help**. If you are unfamiliar with how **Help** operates, or how to be efficient with its use, you can click on to "How to use Help" within this menu.

## Appendix A: Decision Log

Industry _____    Firm _____    Quarter _____    Year _____

### Intrafirm Automaton Transfers

| From: | United States | Mexico | Germany | Spain | Taiwan | Thailand |
|---|---|---|---|---|---|---|
| United States<br>Auto 1<br>Auto 2 | XX<br>XX | | | | | |
| Mexico<br>Auto 1<br>Auto 2 | | XX<br>XX | | | | |
| Germany<br>Auto 1<br>Auto 2 | | | XX<br>XX | | | |
| Spain<br>Auto 1<br>Auto 2 | | | | XX<br>XX | | |
| Taiwan<br>Auto 1<br>Auto 2 | | | | | XX<br>XX | |
| Thailand<br>Auto 1<br>Auto 2 | | | | | | XX<br>XX |

## Appendix A: Decision Log

Industry _____    Firm _____    Quarter _____    Year _____

### Marketing

| Decision | United States | Mexico | Germany | Spain | Taiwan | Thailand |
|---|---|---|---|---|---|---|
| 25" TV List Price | | | | | | |
| 25" TV Actual Price | | | | | | |
| 27" TV List Price | | | | | | |
| 27" TV Actual Price | | | | | | |
| 25" TV Contract Bid | | | | | | |
| 27" TV Contract Bid | | | | | | |
| 25" TV Advertising | | | | | | |
| 27" TV Advertising | | | | | | |
| Sales Offices | | | | | | |
| Distribution Centers | | | | | | |
| Independent Wholesalers | | | | | | |
| Company-Owned Wholesalers | | | | | | |
| Sales Representatives | | | | | | |
| Sales Rep Base Salary | | | | | | |
| 25" TV Commission | | | | | | |
| 27" TV Commission | | | | | | |
| Sales Rep Training | | | | | | |
| Product R&D | | | | | | |

## Appendix A: Decision Log

Industry _____   Firm _____   Quarter _____   Year _____

### Marketing Logistics

| Decision | United States | Mexico | Germany | Spain | Taiwan | Thailand |
|---|---|---|---|---|---|---|
| 25" TV Distribution from: | | | | | | |
| 25" TV Distribution to: | | | | | | |
| 27" TV Distribution from: | | | | | | |
| 27" TV Distribution to: | | | | | | |
| 25" TV Contract Distribution | | | | | | |
| 27" TV Contract Distribution | | | | | | |
| Surface Shipping | | | | | | |
| ExAir Shipping | | | | | | |

### Subassembly Purchases

| Decision | United States | Mexico | Germany | Spain | Taiwan | Thailand |
|---|---|---|---|---|---|---|
| Group 1 Grade A | | | | | | |
| Group 1 Grade B | | | | | | |
| Group 1 Grade C | | | | | | |
| Group 2 Grade A | | | | | | |
| Group 2 Grade B | | | | | | |
| Group 2 Grade C | | | | | | |

## Appendix A: Decision Log

Industry _____    Firm _____    Quarter _____    Year _____

## Production and Operations Management

| Decision | United States | Mexico | Germany | Spain | Taiwan | Thailand |
|---|---|---|---|---|---|---|
| Shift 1 25" TVs | | | | | | |
| Shift 2 25" TVs | | | | | | |
| Shift 1 27" TVs | | | | | | |
| Shift 2 27" TVs | | | | | | |
| Line Supervisors | | | | | | |
| Shift 1, 25" TV, Workers | | | | | | |
| Shift 2, 25" TV, Workers | | | | | | |
| Shift 1, 27" TV, Workers | | | | | | |
| Shift 2, 27" TV, Workers | | | | | | |
| Automaton Technicians | | | | | | |
| Line Worker Training | | | | | | |
| Automaton Technician Training | | | | | | |
| Quality Control Training | | | | | | |
| QC Sampling Program | | | | | | |

## Appendix A: Decision Log

Industry _____    Firm _____    Quarter _____    Year _____

### Financial Management

| Decision | United States | Mexico | Germany | Spain | Taiwan | Thailand |
|---|---|---|---|---|---|---|
| Stock Issue | | | | | | |
| Stock Purchase | | | | | | |
| Stock Dividend | | | | | | |
| Short-Term Investment | | | | | | |
| Short-Term Loan | | | | | | |
| Bond Issue | | | | | | |
| Bond Call | | | | | | |
| Cash Distribution to: | | | | | | |
| Cash Distribution from: | | | | | | |
| To Retained Earnings | | | | | | |

## Appendix A: Decision Log

Industry _____    Firm _____    Quarter _____    Year _____

### Plant Capacity and Plant Maintenance

| Decision | United States | Mexico | Germany | Spain | Taiwan | Thailand |
|---|---|---|---|---|---|---|
| Base Capacity | | | | | | |
| Automaton Type 1 | | | | | | |
| Automaton Type 2 | | | | | | |
| Line Maintenance | | | | | | |
| Auto 1 Maintenance | | | | | | |
| Auto 2 Maintenance | | | | | | |

### Marketing Research Request

| Question | Charge | Choice |
|---|---|---|
| 1 | $1,500 | |
| 2 | $1,500 | |
| 3 | $500 | |
| 4 | $500 | |
| 5 | $1,000 | |
| 6 | $2,000 | |
| 7 | $2,000 | |
| 8 | $750 | |
| 9 | $250 | |
| 10 | $250 | |
| 11 | $300 | |
| 12 | $300 | |
| Total | | |

### Critical Incident Response

| Incident | Response |
|---|---|
| | |
| | |
| | |

**Appendix A: Decision Log**

Industry _____    Firm _____    Quarter _____    Year _____

**Intrafirm Automaton Transfers**

| From: | United States | Mexico | Germany | Spain | Taiwan | Thailand |
|---|---|---|---|---|---|---|
| United States<br>Auto 1<br>Auto 2 | XX<br>XX | | | | | |
| Mexico<br>Auto 1<br>Auto 2 | | XX<br>XX | | | | |
| Germany<br>Auto 1<br>Auto 2 | | | XX<br>XX | | | |
| Spain<br>Auto 1<br>Auto 2 | | | | XX<br>XX | | |
| Taiwan<br>Auto 1<br>Auto 2 | | | | | XX<br>XX | |
| Thailand<br>Auto 1<br>Auto 2 | | | | | | XX<br>XX |

## Appendix A: Decision Log

Industry _____    Firm _____    Quarter _____    Year _____

### Marketing

| Decision | United States | Mexico | Germany | Spain | Taiwan | Thailand |
|---|---|---|---|---|---|---|
| 25" TV List Price | | | | | | |
| 25" TV Actual Price | | | | | | |
| 27" TV List Price | | | | | | |
| 27" TV Actual Price | | | | | | |
| 25" TV Contract Bid | | | | | | |
| 27" TV Contract Bid | | | | | | |
| 25" TV Advertising | | | | | | |
| 27" TV Advertising | | | | | | |
| Sales Offices | | | | | | |
| Distribution Centers | | | | | | |
| Independent Wholesalers | | | | | | |
| Company-Owned Wholesalers | | | | | | |
| Sales Representatives | | | | | | |
| Sales Rep Base Salary | | | | | | |
| 25" TV Commission | | | | | | |
| 27" TV Commission | | | | | | |
| Sales Rep Training | | | | | | |
| Product R&D | | | | | | |

## Appendix A: Decision Log

Industry _____   Firm _____   Quarter _____   Year _____

### Marketing Logistics

| Decision | United States | Mexico | Germany | Spain | Taiwan | Thailand |
|---|---|---|---|---|---|---|
| 25" TV Distribution from: | | | | | | |
| 25" TV Distribution to: | | | | | | |
| 27" TV Distribution from: | | | | | | |
| 27" TV Distribution to: | | | | | | |
| 25" TV Contract Distribution | | | | | | |
| 27" TV Contract Distribution | | | | | | |
| Surface Shipping | | | | | | |
| ExAir Shipping | | | | | | |

### Subassembly Purchases

| Decision | United States | Mexico | Germany | Spain | Taiwan | Thailand |
|---|---|---|---|---|---|---|
| Group 1 Grade A | | | | | | |
| Group 1 Grade B | | | | | | |
| Group 1 Grade C | | | | | | |
| Group 2 Grade A | | | | | | |
| Group 2 Grade B | | | | | | |
| Group 2 Grade C | | | | | | |

## Appendix A: Decision Log

Industry _____ Firm _____ Quarter _____ Year _____

## Production and Operations Management

| Decision | United States | Mexico | Germany | Spain | Taiwan | Thailand |
|---|---|---|---|---|---|---|
| Shift 1 25" TVs | | | | | | |
| Shift 2 25" TVs | | | | | | |
| Shift 1 27" TVs | | | | | | |
| Shift 2 27" TVs | | | | | | |
| Line Supervisors | | | | | | |
| Shift 1, 25" TV, Workers | | | | | | |
| Shift 2, 25" TV, Workers | | | | | | |
| Shift 1, 27" TV, Workers | | | | | | |
| Shift 2, 27" TV, Workers | | | | | | |
| Automaton Technicians | | | | | | |
| Line Worker Training | | | | | | |
| Automaton Technician Training | | | | | | |
| Quality Control Training | | | | | | |
| QC Sampling Program | | | | | | |

## Appendix A: Decision Log

Industry _____    Firm _____    Quarter _____    Year _____

## Financial Management

| Decision | United States | Mexico | Germany | Spain | Taiwan | Thailand |
|---|---|---|---|---|---|---|
| Stock Issue | | | | | | |
| Stock Purchase | | | | | | |
| Stock Dividend | | | | | | |
| Short-Term Investment | | | | | | |
| Short-Term Loan | | | | | | |
| Bond Issue | | | | | | |
| Bond Call | | | | | | |
| Cash Distribution to: | | | | | | |
| Cash Distribution from: | | | | | | |
| To Retained Earnings | | | | | | |

## Appendix A: Decision Log

Industry _____    Firm _____    Quarter _____    Year _____

### Plant Capacity and Plant Maintenance

| Decision | United States | Mexico | Germany | Spain | Taiwan | Thailand |
|---|---|---|---|---|---|---|
| Base Capacity | | | | | | |
| Automaton Type 1 | | | | | | |
| Automaton Type 2 | | | | | | |
| Line Maintenance | | | | | | |
| Auto 1 Maintenance | | | | | | |
| Auto 2 Maintenance | | | | | | |

### Marketing Research Request

| Question | Charge | Choice |
|---|---|---|
| 1 | $1,500 | |
| 2 | $1,500 | |
| 3 | $500 | |
| 4 | $500 | |
| 5 | $1,000 | |
| 6 | $2,000 | |
| 7 | $2,000 | |
| 8 | $750 | |
| 9 | $250 | |
| 10 | $250 | |
| 11 | $300 | |
| 12 | $300 | |
| Total | | |

### Critical Incident Response

| Incident | Response |
|---|---|
| | |
| | |
| | |

## Appendix A: Decision Log

Industry _____    Firm _____    Quarter _____    Year _____

## Intrafirm Automaton Transfers

| From: | United States | Mexico | Germany | Spain | Taiwan | Thailand |
|---|---|---|---|---|---|---|
| United States<br>Auto 1<br>Auto 2 | XX<br>XX | | | | | |
| Mexico<br>Auto 1<br>Auto 2 | | XX<br>XX | | | | |
| Germany<br>Auto 1<br>Auto 2 | | | XX<br>XX | | | |
| Spain<br>Auto 1<br>Auto 2 | | | | XX<br>XX | | |
| Taiwan<br>Auto 1<br>Auto 2 | | | | | XX<br>XX | |
| Thailand<br>Auto 1<br>Auto 2 | | | | | | XX<br>XX |

## Appendix A: Decision Log

Industry _____　　Firm _____　　Quarter _____　　Year _____

### Marketing

| Decision | United States | Mexico | Germany | Spain | Taiwan | Thailand |
|---|---|---|---|---|---|---|
| 25" TV List Price | | | | | | |
| 25" TV Actual Price | | | | | | |
| 27" TV List Price | | | | | | |
| 27" TV Actual Price | | | | | | |
| 25" TV Contract Bid | | | | | | |
| 27" TV Contract Bid | | | | | | |
| 25" TV Advertising | | | | | | |
| 27" TV Advertising | | | | | | |
| Sales Offices | | | | | | |
| Distribution Centers | | | | | | |
| Independent Wholesalers | | | | | | |
| Company-Owned Wholesalers | | | | | | |
| Sales Representatives | | | | | | |
| Sales Rep Base Salary | | | | | | |
| 25" TV Commission | | | | | | |
| 27" TV Commission | | | | | | |
| Sales Rep Training | | | | | | |
| Product R&D | | | | | | |

## Appendix A: Decision Log

Industry _____    Firm _____    Quarter _____    Year _____

### Marketing Logistics

| Decision | United States | Mexico | Germany | Spain | Taiwan | Thailand |
|---|---|---|---|---|---|---|
| 25" TV Distribution from: | | | | | | |
| 25" TV Distribution to: | | | | | | |
| 27" TV Distribution from: | | | | | | |
| 27" TV Distribution to: | | | | | | |
| 25" TV Contract Distribution | | | | | | |
| 27" TV Contract Distribution | | | | | | |
| Surface Shipping | | | | | | |
| ExAir Shipping | | | | | | |

### Subassembly Purchases

| Decision | United States | Mexico | Germany | Spain | Taiwan | Thailand |
|---|---|---|---|---|---|---|
| Group 1 Grade A | | | | | | |
| Group 1 Grade B | | | | | | |
| Group 1 Grade C | | | | | | |
| Group 2 Grade A | | | | | | |
| Group 2 Grade B | | | | | | |
| Group 2 Grade C | | | | | | |

## Appendix A: Decision Log

Industry _____ Firm _____ Quarter _____ Year _____

### Production and Operations Management

| Decision | United States | Mexico | Germany | Spain | Taiwan | Thailand |
|---|---|---|---|---|---|---|
| Shift 1 25" TVs | | | | | | |
| Shift 2 25" TVs | | | | | | |
| Shift 1 27" TVs | | | | | | |
| Shift 2 27" TVs | | | | | | |
| Line Supervisors | | | | | | |
| Shift 1, 25" TV, Workers | | | | | | |
| Shift 2, 25" TV, Workers | | | | | | |
| Shift 1, 27" TV, Workers | | | | | | |
| Shift 2, 27" TV, Workers | | | | | | |
| Automaton Technicians | | | | | | |
| Line Worker Training | | | | | | |
| Automaton Technician Training | | | | | | |
| Quality Control Training | | | | | | |
| QC Sampling Program | | | | | | |

## Appendix A: Decision Log

Industry _____    Firm _____    Quarter _____    Year _____

### Financial Management

| Decision | United States | Mexico | Germany | Spain | Taiwan | Thailand |
|---|---|---|---|---|---|---|
| Stock Issue | | | | | | |
| Stock Purchase | | | | | | |
| Stock Dividend | | | | | | |
| Short-Term Investment | | | | | | |
| Short-Term Loan | | | | | | |
| Bond Issue | | | | | | |
| Bond Call | | | | | | |
| Cash Distribution to: | | | | | | |
| Cash Distribution from: | | | | | | |
| To Retained Earnings | | | | | | |

## Appendix A: Decision Log

Industry _____    Firm _____    Quarter _____    Year _____

### Plant Capacity and Plant Maintenance

| Decision | United States | Mexico | Germany | Spain | Taiwan | Thailand |
|---|---|---|---|---|---|---|
| Base Capacity | | | | | | |
| Automaton Type 1 | | | | | | |
| Automaton Type 2 | | | | | | |
| Line Maintenance | | | | | | |
| Auto 1 Maintenance | | | | | | |
| Auto 2 Maintenance | | | | | | |

### Marketing Research Request

| Question | Charge | Choice |
|---|---|---|
| 1 | $1,500 | |
| 2 | $1,500 | |
| 3 | $500 | |
| 4 | $500 | |
| 5 | $1,000 | |
| 6 | $2,000 | |
| 7 | $2,000 | |
| 8 | $750 | |
| 9 | $250 | |
| 10 | $250 | |
| 11 | $300 | |
| 12 | $300 | |
| Total | | |

### Critical Incident Response

| Incident | Response |
|---|---|
| | |
| | |
| | |

## Appendix A: Decision Log

Industry _____ Firm _____ Quarter _____ Year _____

## Intrafirm Automaton Transfers

| From: | United States | Mexico | Germany | Spain | Taiwan | Thailand |
|---|---|---|---|---|---|---|
| United States<br>Auto 1<br>Auto 2 | XX<br>XX | | | | | |
| Mexico<br>Auto 1<br>Auto 2 | | XX<br>XX | | | | |
| Germany<br>Auto 1<br>Auto 2 | | | XX<br>XX | | | |
| Spain<br>Auto 1<br>Auto 2 | | | | XX<br>XX | | |
| Taiwan<br>Auto 1<br>Auto 2 | | | | | XX<br>XX | |
| Thailand<br>Auto 1<br>Auto 2 | | | | | | XX<br>XX |

## Appendix A: Decision Log

Industry _____    Firm _____    Quarter _____    Year _____

### Marketing

| Decision | United States | Mexico | Germany | Spain | Taiwan | Thailand |
|---|---|---|---|---|---|---|
| 25" TV List Price | | | | | | |
| 25" TV Actual Price | | | | | | |
| 27" TV List Price | | | | | | |
| 27" TV Actual Price | | | | | | |
| 25" TV Contract Bid | | | | | | |
| 27" TV Contract Bid | | | | | | |
| 25" TV Advertising | | | | | | |
| 27" TV Advertising | | | | | | |
| Sales Offices | | | | | | |
| Distribution Centers | | | | | | |
| Independent Wholesalers | | | | | | |
| Company-Owned Wholesalers | | | | | | |
| Sales Representatives | | | | | | |
| Sales Rep Base Salary | | | | | | |
| 25" TV Commission | | | | | | |
| 27" TV Commission | | | | | | |
| Sales Rep Training | | | | | | |
| Product R&D | | | | | | |

## Appendix A: Decision Log

Industry _____    Firm _____    Quarter _____    Year _____

**Marketing Logistics**

| Decision | United States | Mexico | Germany | Spain | Taiwan | Thailand |
|---|---|---|---|---|---|---|
| 25" TV Distribution from: | | | | | | |
| 25" TV Distribution to: | | | | | | |
| 27" TV Distribution from: | | | | | | |
| 27" TV Distribution to: | | | | | | |
| 25" TV Contract Distribution | | | | | | |
| 27" TV Contract Distribution | | | | | | |
| Surface Shipping | | | | | | |
| ExAir Shipping | | | | | | |

**Subassembly Purchases**

| Decision | United States | Mexico | Germany | Spain | Taiwan | Thailand |
|---|---|---|---|---|---|---|
| Group 1 Grade A | | | | | | |
| Group 1 Grade B | | | | | | |
| Group 1 Grade C | | | | | | |
| Group 2 Grade A | | | | | | |
| Group 2 Grade B | | | | | | |
| Group 2 Grade C | | | | | | |

## Appendix A: Decision Log

Industry _____    Firm _____    Quarter _____    Year _____

## Production and Operations Management

| Decision | United States | Mexico | Germany | Spain | Taiwan | Thailand |
|---|---|---|---|---|---|---|
| Shift 1 25" TVs | | | | | | |
| Shift 2 25" TVs | | | | | | |
| Shift 1 27" TVs | | | | | | |
| Shift 2 27" TVs | | | | | | |
| Line Supervisors | | | | | | |
| Shift 1, 25" TV, Workers | | | | | | |
| Shift 2, 25" TV, Workers | | | | | | |
| Shift 1, 27" TV, Workers | | | | | | |
| Shift 2, 27" TV, Workers | | | | | | |
| Automaton Technicians | | | | | | |
| Line Worker Training | | | | | | |
| Automaton Technician Training | | | | | | |
| Quality Control Training | | | | | | |
| QC Sampling Program | | | | | | |

## Appendix A: Decision Log

Industry _____    Firm _____    Quarter _____    Year _____

### Financial Management

| Decision | United States | Mexico | Germany | Spain | Taiwan | Thailand |
|---|---|---|---|---|---|---|
| Stock Issue | | | | | | |
| Stock Purchase | | | | | | |
| Stock Dividend | | | | | | |
| Short-Term Investment | | | | | | |
| Short-Term Loan | | | | | | |
| Bond Issue | | | | | | |
| Bond Call | | | | | | |
| Cash Distribution to: | | | | | | |
| Cash Distribution from: | | | | | | |
| To Retained Earnings | | | | | | |

## Appendix A: Decision Log

Industry _____    Firm _____    Quarter _____    Year _____

### Plant Capacity and Plant Maintenance

| Decision | United States | Mexico | Germany | Spain | Taiwan | Thailand |
|---|---|---|---|---|---|---|
| Base Capacity | | | | | | |
| Automaton Type 1 | | | | | | |
| Automaton Type 2 | | | | | | |
| Line Maintenance | | | | | | |
| Auto 1 Maintenance | | | | | | |
| Auto 2 Maintenance | | | | | | |

### Marketing Research Request

| Question | Charge | Choice |
|---|---|---|
| 1 | $1,500 | |
| 2 | $1,500 | |
| 3 | $500 | |
| 4 | $500 | |
| 5 | $1,000 | |
| 6 | $2,000 | |
| 7 | $2,000 | |
| 8 | $750 | |
| 9 | $250 | |
| 10 | $250 | |
| 11 | $300 | |
| 12 | $300 | |
| Total | | |

### Critical Incident Response

| Incident | Response |
|---|---|
| | |
| | |
| | |

## Appendix A: Decision Log

Industry _____    Firm _____    Quarter _____    Year _____

## Intrafirm Automaton Transfers

| From: | United States | Mexico | Germany | Spain | Taiwan | Thailand |
|---|---|---|---|---|---|---|
| United States<br>Auto 1<br>Auto 2 | XX<br>XX | | | | | |
| Mexico<br>Auto 1<br>Auto 2 | | XX<br>XX | | | | |
| Germany<br>Auto 1<br>Auto 2 | | | XX<br>XX | | | |
| Spain<br>Auto 1<br>Auto 2 | | | | XX<br>XX | | |
| Taiwan<br>Auto 1<br>Auto 2 | | | | | XX<br>XX | |
| Thailand<br>Auto 1<br>Auto 2 | | | | | | XX<br>XX |

## Appendix A: Decision Log

Industry _____    Firm _____    Quarter _____    Year _____

### Marketing

| Decision | United States | Mexico | Germany | Spain | Taiwan | Thailand |
|---|---|---|---|---|---|---|
| 25" TV List Price | | | | | | |
| 25" TV Actual Price | | | | | | |
| 27" TV List Price | | | | | | |
| 27" TV Actual Price | | | | | | |
| 25" TV Contract Bid | | | | | | |
| 27" TV Contract Bid | | | | | | |
| 25" TV Advertising | | | | | | |
| 27" TV Advertising | | | | | | |
| Sales Offices | | | | | | |
| Distribution Centers | | | | | | |
| Independent Wholesalers | | | | | | |
| Company-Owned Wholesalers | | | | | | |
| Sales Representatives | | | | | | |
| Sales Rep Base Salary | | | | | | |
| 25" TV Commission | | | | | | |
| 27" TV Commission | | | | | | |
| Sales Rep Training | | | | | | |
| Product R&D | | | | | | |

## Appendix A: Decision Log

Industry _____    Firm _____    Quarter _____    Year _____

### Marketing Logistics

| Decision | United States | Mexico | Germany | Spain | Taiwan | Thailand |
|---|---|---|---|---|---|---|
| 25" TV Distribution from: | | | | | | |
| 25" TV Distribution to: | | | | | | |
| 27" TV Distribution from: | | | | | | |
| 27" TV Distribution to: | | | | | | |
| 25" TV Contract Distribution | | | | | | |
| 27" TV Contract Distribution | | | | | | |
| Surface Shipping | | | | | | |
| ExAir Shipping | | | | | | |

### Subassembly Purchases

| Decision | United States | Mexico | Germany | Spain | Taiwan | Thailand |
|---|---|---|---|---|---|---|
| Group 1 Grade A | | | | | | |
| Group 1 Grade B | | | | | | |
| Group 1 Grade C | | | | | | |
| Group 2 Grade A | | | | | | |
| Group 2 Grade B | | | | | | |
| Group 2 Grade C | | | | | | |

**Appendix A: Decision Log**

Industry _____    Firm _____    Quarter _____    Year _____

**Production and Operations Management**

| Decision | United States | Mexico | Germany | Spain | Taiwan | Thailand |
|---|---|---|---|---|---|---|
| Shift 1 25" TVs | | | | | | |
| Shift 2 25" TVs | | | | | | |
| Shift 1 27" TVs | | | | | | |
| Shift 2 27" TVs | | | | | | |
| Line Supervisors | | | | | | |
| Shift 1, 25" TV, Workers | | | | | | |
| Shift 2, 25" TV, Workers | | | | | | |
| Shift 1, 27" TV, Workers | | | | | | |
| Shift 2, 27" TV, Workers | | | | | | |
| Automaton Technicians | | | | | | |
| Line Worker Training | | | | | | |
| Automaton Technician Training | | | | | | |
| Quality Control Training | | | | | | |
| QC Sampling Program | | | | | | |

## Appendix A: Decision Log

Industry _____    Firm _____    Quarter _____    Year _____

### Financial Management

| Decision | United States | Mexico | Germany | Spain | Taiwan | Thailand |
|---|---|---|---|---|---|---|
| Stock Issue | | | | | | |
| Stock Purchase | | | | | | |
| Stock Dividend | | | | | | |
| Short-Term Investment | | | | | | |
| Short-Term Loan | | | | | | |
| Bond Issue | | | | | | |
| Bond Call | | | | | | |
| Cash Distribution to: | | | | | | |
| Cash Distribution from: | | | | | | |
| To Retained Earnings | | | | | | |

## Appendix A: Decision Log

Industry _____    Firm _____    Quarter _____    Year _____

### Plant Capacity and Plant Maintenance

| Decision | United States | Mexico | Germany | Spain | Taiwan | Thailand |
|---|---|---|---|---|---|---|
| Base Capacity | | | | | | |
| Automaton Type 1 | | | | | | |
| Automaton Type 2 | | | | | | |
| Line Maintenance | | | | | | |
| Auto 1 Maintenance | | | | | | |
| Auto 2 Maintenance | | | | | | |

### Marketing Research Request

| Question | Charge | Choice |
|---|---|---|
| 1 | $1,500 | |
| 2 | $1,500 | |
| 3 | $500 | |
| 4 | $500 | |
| 5 | $1,000 | |
| 6 | $2,000 | |
| 7 | $2,000 | |
| 8 | $750 | |
| 9 | $250 | |
| 10 | $250 | |
| 11 | $300 | |
| 12 | $300 | |
| Total | | |

### Critical Incident Response

| Incident | Response |
|---|---|
| | |
| | |
| | |

## Appendix A: Decision Log

Industry _____   Firm _____   Quarter _____   Year _____

### Intrafirm Automaton Transfers

| From: | United States | Mexico | Germany | Spain | Taiwan | Thailand |
|---|---|---|---|---|---|---|
| United States<br>Auto 1<br>Auto 2 | XX<br>XX | | | | | |
| Mexico<br>Auto 1<br>Auto 2 | | XX<br>XX | | | | |
| Germany<br>Auto 1<br>Auto 2 | | | XX<br>XX | | | |
| Spain<br>Auto 1<br>Auto 2 | | | | XX<br>XX | | |
| Taiwan<br>Auto 1<br>Auto 2 | | | | | XX<br>XX | |
| Thailand<br>Auto 1<br>Auto 2 | | | | | | XX<br>XX |

## Appendix A: Decision Log

Industry _____    Firm _____    Quarter _____    Year _____

## Marketing

| Decision | United States | Mexico | Germany | Spain | Taiwan | Thailand |
|---|---|---|---|---|---|---|
| 25" TV List Price | | | | | | |
| 25" TV Actual Price | | | | | | |
| 27" TV List Price | | | | | | |
| 27" TV Actual Price | | | | | | |
| 25" TV Contract Bid | | | | | | |
| 27" TV Contract Bid | | | | | | |
| 25" TV Advertising | | | | | | |
| 27" TV Advertising | | | | | | |
| Sales Offices | | | | | | |
| Distribution Centers | | | | | | |
| Independent Wholesalers | | | | | | |
| Company-Owned Wholesalers | | | | | | |
| Sales Representatives | | | | | | |
| Sales Rep Base Salary | | | | | | |
| 25" TV Commission | | | | | | |
| 27" TV Commission | | | | | | |
| Sales Rep Training | | | | | | |
| Product R&D | | | | | | |

## Appendix A: Decision Log

Industry _____    Firm _____    Quarter _____    Year _____

## Marketing Logistics

| Decision | United States | Mexico | Germany | Spain | Taiwan | Thailand |
|---|---|---|---|---|---|---|
| 25" TV Distribution from: | | | | | | |
| 25" TV Distribution to: | | | | | | |
| 27" TV Distribution from: | | | | | | |
| 27" TV Distribution to: | | | | | | |
| 25" TV Contract Distribution | | | | | | |
| 27" TV Contract Distribution | | | | | | |
| Surface Shipping | | | | | | |
| ExAir Shipping | | | | | | |

## Subassembly Purchases

| Decision | United States | Mexico | Germany | Spain | Taiwan | Thailand |
|---|---|---|---|---|---|---|
| Group 1 Grade A | | | | | | |
| Group 1 Grade B | | | | | | |
| Group 1 Grade C | | | | | | |
| Group 2 Grade A | | | | | | |
| Group 2 Grade B | | | | | | |
| Group 2 Grade C | | | | | | |

## Appendix A: Decision Log

Industry _____    Firm _____    Quarter _____    Year _____

### Production and Operations Management

| Decision | United States | Mexico | Germany | Spain | Taiwan | Thailand |
|---|---|---|---|---|---|---|
| Shift 1 25" TVs | | | | | | |
| Shift 2 25" TVs | | | | | | |
| Shift 1 27" TVs | | | | | | |
| Shift 2 27" TVs | | | | | | |
| Line Supervisors | | | | | | |
| Shift 1, 25" TV, Workers | | | | | | |
| Shift 2, 25" TV, Workers | | | | | | |
| Shift 1, 27" TV, Workers | | | | | | |
| Shift 2, 27" TV, Workers | | | | | | |
| Automaton Technicians | | | | | | |
| Line Worker Training | | | | | | |
| Automaton Technician Training | | | | | | |
| Quality Control Training | | | | | | |
| QC Sampling Program | | | | | | |

## Appendix A: Decision Log

Industry _____    Firm _____    Quarter _____    Year _____

### Financial Management

| Decision | United States | Mexico | Germany | Spain | Taiwan | Thailand |
|---|---|---|---|---|---|---|
| Stock Issue | | | | | | |
| Stock Purchase | | | | | | |
| Stock Dividend | | | | | | |
| Short-Term Investment | | | | | | |
| Short-Term Loan | | | | | | |
| Bond Issue | | | | | | |
| Bond Call | | | | | | |
| Cash Distribution to: | | | | | | |
| Cash Distribution from: | | | | | | |
| To Retained Earnings | | | | | | |

## Appendix A: Decision Log

Industry _____    Firm _____    Quarter _____    Year _____

### Plant Capacity and Plant Maintenance

| Decision | United States | Mexico | Germany | Spain | Taiwan | Thailand |
|---|---|---|---|---|---|---|
| Base Capacity | | | | | | |
| Automaton Type 1 | | | | | | |
| Automaton Type 2 | | | | | | |
| Line Maintenance | | | | | | |
| Auto 1 Maintenance | | | | | | |
| Auto 2 Maintenance | | | | | | |

### Marketing Research Request

| Question | Charge | Choice |
|---|---|---|
| 1 | $1,500 | |
| 2 | $1,500 | |
| 3 | $500 | |
| 4 | $500 | |
| 5 | $1,000 | |
| 6 | $2,000 | |
| 7 | $2,000 | |
| 8 | $750 | |
| 9 | $250 | |
| 10 | $250 | |
| 11 | $300 | |
| 12 | $300 | |
| Total | | |

### Critical Incident Response

| Incident | Response |
|---|---|
| | |
| | |
| | |

## Appendix B: Cash Inflow Work Sheet

| Cash Inflow | U.S. | Mexico | Germany | Spain | Taiwan | Thailand |
|---|---|---|---|---|---|---|
| Current Sales | | | | | | |
| Cash Account | | | | | | |
| Accounts Receivable | | | | | | |
| Short-Term Investment Income | | | | | | |
| Short-Term Loan | | | | | | |
| Bond Sale | | | | | | |
| Stock Sale | | | | | | |
| Patents/Licensing Income | | | | | | |
| Miscellaneous: Credits | | | | | | |
| Capital Sales | | | | | | |
| Cash Transfer | | | | | | |
| Total Cash In | | | | | | |

## Appendix B: Cash Inflow Work Sheet

| Cash Inflow | U.S. | Mexico | Germany | Spain | Taiwan | Thailand |
|---|---|---|---|---|---|---|
| Current Sales | | | | | | |
| Cash Account | | | | | | |
| Accounts Receivable | | | | | | |
| Short-Term Investment Income | | | | | | |
| Short-Term Loan | | | | | | |
| Bond Sale | | | | | | |
| Stock Sale | | | | | | |
| Patents/Licensing Income | | | | | | |
| Miscellaneous: Credits | | | | | | |
| Capital Sales | | | | | | |
| Cash Transfer | | | | | | |
| Total Cash In | | | | | | |

## Appendix B: Cash Inflow Work Sheet

| Cash Inflow | U.S. | Mexico | Germany | Spain | Taiwan | Thailand |
|---|---|---|---|---|---|---|
| Current Sales | | | | | | |
| Cash Account | | | | | | |
| Accounts Receivable | | | | | | |
| Short-Term Investment Income | | | | | | |
| Short-Term Loan | | | | | | |
| Bond Sale | | | | | | |
| Stock Sale | | | | | | |
| Patents/Licensing Income | | | | | | |
| Miscellaneous: Credits | | | | | | |
| Capital Sales | | | | | | |
| Cash Transfer | | | | | | |
| Total Cash In | | | | | | |

## Appendix B: Cash Outflow Work Sheet

| Cash Outflow | U.S. | Mexico | Germany | Spain | Taiwan | Thailand |
|---|---|---|---|---|---|---|
| Factory Wages | | | | | | |
| Subassemblies | | | | | | |
| Advertising | | | | | | |
| Administrative | | | | | | |
| Sales Offices | | | | | | |
| District Centers | | | | | | |
| Wholesaling | | | | | | |
| Sales Force | | | | | | |
| Training | | | | | | |
| Inventory Charges | | | | | | |
| Shipping | | | | | | |
| Patent/Licensing Fees | | | | | | |
| Research & Development | | | | | | |
| Quality Circles | | | | | | |
| Maintenance | | | | | | |
| Miscellaneous | | | | | | |
| Accounts Payable | | | | | | |
| Overdraft | | | | | | |
| Short-Term Loans | | | | | | |
| Bond Interest | | | | | | |
| Bond Call | | | | | | |
| Short-Term Dividends | | | | | | |
| Treasury Stock | | | | | | |
| Capital in Progress | | | | | | |
| Cash Transfer | | | | | | |
| Total Cash Out | | | | | | |

## Appendix B: Cash Outflow Work Sheet

| Cash Outflow | U.S. | Mexico | Germany | Spain | Taiwan | Thailand |
|---|---|---|---|---|---|---|
| Factory Wages | | | | | | |
| Subassemblies | | | | | | |
| Advertising | | | | | | |
| Administrative | | | | | | |
| Sales Offices | | | | | | |
| Distribution Centers | | | | | | |
| Wholesaling | | | | | | |
| Sales Force | | | | | | |
| Training | | | | | | |
| Inventory Charges | | | | | | |
| Shipping | | | | | | |
| Patent/Licensing Fees | | | | | | |
| Research & Development | | | | | | |
| Quality Circles | | | | | | |
| Maintenance | | | | | | |
| Miscellaneous | | | | | | |
| Accounts Payable | | | | | | |
| Overdraft | | | | | | |
| Short-Term Loans | | | | | | |
| Bond Interest | | | | | | |
| Bond Call | | | | | | |
| Short-Term Dividends | | | | | | |
| Treasury Stock | | | | | | |
| Capital in Progress | | | | | | |
| Cash Transfer | | | | | | |
| Total Cash Out | | | | | | |

**Appendix B: Cash Outflow Work Sheet**

| Cash Outflow | U.S. | Mexico | Germany | Spain | Taiwan | Thailand |
|---|---|---|---|---|---|---|
| Factory Wages | | | | | | |
| Subassemblies | | | | | | |
| Advertising | | | | | | |
| Administrative | | | | | | |
| Sales Offices | | | | | | |
| Distribution Centers | | | | | | |
| Wholesaling | | | | | | |
| Sales Force | | | | | | |
| Training | | | | | | |
| Inventory Charges | | | | | | |
| Shipping | | | | | | |
| Patent/Licensing Fees | | | | | | |
| Research & Development | | | | | | |
| Quality Circles | | | | | | |
| Maintenance | | | | | | |
| Miscellaneous | | | | | | |
| Accounts Payable | | | | | | |
| Overdraft | | | | | | |
| Short-Term Loans | | | | | | |
| Bond Interest | | | | | | |
| Bond Call | | | | | | |
| Stock Dividends | | | | | | |
| Treasury Stock | | | | | | |
| Capital in Progress | | | | | | |
| Cash Transfer | | | | | | |
| Total Cash Out | | | | | | |

## Appendix C: Revenue *Pro Forma* Income Statement

Firm _____    Quarter _____ , 19 _____    Country Unit _____

### Revenues

|  | Forecast | Actual |
|---|---|---|
| Gross Revenues | | |
| Less: Value-Added Tax | | |
| Net Sales and Operating Revenue | | |
| **Other Income** | | |
| Plant/Equipment Sales | | |
| Investment Income | | |
| Licensing Income | | |
| Total Revenue | | |

## Appendix C: Expenses *Pro Forma* Income Statement

Firm _____    Quarter _____ ,    19 _____    Country Unit _____

### Expenses

|  | Forecast | Actual |
|---|---|---|
| Cost of Goods Sold |  |  |
| Advertising |  |  |
| General Administration |  |  |
| Sales Offices |  |  |
| Distribution Centers |  |  |
| Wholesale Operations |  |  |
| Sales Force Salaries |  |  |
| Training and Development |  |  |
| Trainees |  |  |
| Inventory Charges |  |  |
| Shipping |  |  |
| License Fees |  |  |
| Research and Development |  |  |
| Quality Control |  |  |
| Depreciation |  |  |
| Maintenance |  |  |
| Interest Charges:<br>    Overdrafts |  |  |
|     Short-Term Loan |  |  |
|     Bonds |  |  |
| Miscellaneous |  |  |
|     Total Expenses |  |  |
| Income Before Taxes |  |  |
| Income Tax |  |  |
| Dividend Tax |  |  |
|     Net Income |  |  |

## Appendix D: Assets *Pro Forma* Balance Sheet

Firm _____    Quarter _____,    19 _____    Country Unit _____

## Assets

|  | Forecast | Actual |
|---|---|---|
| Cash |  |  |
| Accounts Receivable |  |  |
| Tax Credit |  |  |
| Short-Term Investments |  |  |
| Due From Country Unit(s) |  |  |
| Inventories:<br>  Subassemblies |  |  |
|   Finished Goods |  |  |
| Goods in Transit |  |  |
|     Total Current Assets |  |  |
| Capital in Progress |  |  |
| Plant and Equipment |  |  |
| Less: Depreciation |  |  |
|   Total Fixed Assets |  |  |
| Total Assets |  |  |

## Appendix D: Liabilities and Owner's Equity *Pro Forma* Balance Sheet

Firm _____    Quarter _____ ,    19 _____    Country Unit _____

### Liabilities and owner's equity

|  | Forecast | Actual |
|---|---|---|
| Accounts Payable |  |  |
| Overdraft |  |  |
| Due to Home Country |  |  |
| Short-Term Loan |  |  |
| Total Current Liabilities |  |  |
| Bonds |  |  |
| Total Liabilities |  |  |
| Common Stock |  |  |
| Paid-in-Capital Current Earnings |  |  |
| Retained Earnings/Deficit |  |  |
| Exchange Gains/Losses |  |  |
| Total Stockholder's Equity |  |  |
| Total Liabilities and Owner's Equity |  |  |

# Appendix E

## Critical Incident 1    Bill Fisher's New Salary Bonus System

After serving in your company's Chicago Sales Office as the area's top sales representative for five years, Bill Fisher was moved to your South Jersey District Sales Office in Trenton, N.J., four months ago to improve its below-average performance. After looking over his salesmen's records and getting to know each better by going on calls with them, he was concerned that some were not as productive as he felt they could be. He also sensed that many, especially the district's senior reps, had fallen into old patterns, weren't looking for new business, and needed to improve their selling techniques.

Bill felt the crux of the problem came from how the company's sales bonuses were calculated. As he explained, "The system we have now is the traditional one. I sit down with the rep at the beginning of the year and we set what we agree are reasonable sales goals. If a rep beats the goal, they get the bonus. If they don't . . . no bonus. While this all sounds straightforward, it's much more complicated than that. We spend a lot of time arguing over what's a reasonable goal. Even worse, most reps meet the goal, but I think they could do even more."

To fix the situation, Bill has devised what he calls the "Market Share Gain Plan." Under this system, each sale rep is ranked against all the other districts' reps regarding the market shares of the company's television sets they produce in their sales area. Bill reasoned, "We live and die on market share, and we have to increase our market penetration. What I'm doing is rewarding those who produce what we need. Those who increase their market shares the most get the biggest bonuses, and those who lose market share get closer supervision from me. That way they'll be able to do better next season. If they ultimately don't improve after all my help, I'm afraid I'd have to let them go."

Before implementing his system, Fisher paid a "courtesy call" to the Human Resources Management Department because of his plan's payroll ramifications. Despite his enthusiasm, the HRM Department cautioned him about certain potential problems.

Those who receive Bill's "help" after not getting their bonuses might consider this a form of punishment or a way of singling them out for ridicule among their peers. The ability of a single sales rep to produce market share gains was also thought to be problematical. To some degree, your company's market share in any sales area is a function of the quality and prices of the sets being offered by your competitors. A sales representative has no control over this. More importantly, some in the HRM Department felt Bill's system might discriminate against older sales reps, as they had established market shares, whereas new sales reps started out from low market shares, which might be more easily increased.

RESPONSES:

1. Let Bill Fisher implement his "Market Share Gain Plan." He believes most reps will get some type of bonus and that those who don't "make bonus" might get one the following year after getting help from him. It is believed this option would generate additional profits of $250,000 and would appear as a Credit to your Miscellaneous Account for the quarter.

2. Let Bill Fisher implement his "Market Share Gain Plan" on a trial basis in two separate New Jersey sales areas, with one area under the control of one of your senior sales reps and the other under the control of a junior sales representative. This option would cost your firm $15,000 and would appear as an additional one-quarter Sales Force expense.

3. Step back and have Bill present his "Market Share Gain Plan" at a district meeting of all sales representatives to get their feedback. It is believed strong objections would be heard from your older sales reps but they make up only 25 percent of the district's selling staff. The cost of this option would be $110,000, which is the value Bill puts on the lost margins he thinks his plan would produce if implemented immediately.

4. Don't implement the plan and concentrate on improving the selling techniques of all sales representatives. This option requires you to spend at least $10,000 per country on Salesrep Training for the next four consecutive quarters.

## Critical Incident 2   "You Have to Get Their Attention"

John Englehart threw off his jacket, loosened his tie, and said to no one in particular, "Trying to sell our sets cold canvas is really frustrating. What we need is something that will get our foot in the door so we can make our pitch."

Englehart's complaint received a sympathetic response from the Sales Office's other sales reps. They all had spent many idle hours trying to see the retail buyers who might buy your TVs. As John asserted, "To make a sale you have to get their attention. If we can just do that, we can sell more goods, and make it easier to get our commissions, and we'll stop wasting time cooling our heels in waiting rooms. Let's all try to brainstorm this thing. I'm sure we can come up with some good ideas."

On that note a number of notions were bandied about. Helen Fernandez suggested putting together a mailing list of the market's major retailers who were not stocking your company's sets. Mike Hardaway tagged onto that idea but suggested that some type of gift with the letter might really get the buyers' attention. "Why not offer everyone on the list $35 for an appointment? I've heard some other companies have done this with pretty good results." "I don't know about that idea, Mike," Helen responded. "That sort of sounds like a bribe to me or that we're really desperate." "Well, maybe we can tone it down a bit, or be more subtle, but I think we're on the right track. Any more good ideas?" John asked. "What do you think we should do?"

RESPONSES:

1. Send out a mailing offering a straight $30 cash gift to no more than 400 retail buyers whose stores do not stock your sets. The entire charge of $14,000 will be billed to your firm's Sales Force expense for the quarter.

2. Combine the above mailing list with a list of all retailers presently stocking your sets. Offer all recipients an appropriate "Seasons Greetings" gift valued at about $20. In a form letter, thank all those who are stocking your sets for their business with wishes for a successful New Year. For those not stocking your TVs, indicate you will be contacting them soon to show them how to have an even more successful coming year by stocking your sets. The entire cost of $55,000 for this mailing will be billed to your firm's Sales Force expense for the quarter.

3. Send a letter offering to all retailers not stocking your sets a $50 rebate on the first order they place with your company. On this order only they will also receive an additional $2 special allowance for each set purchased. You estimate about 100 retailers will respond with an appointment and that the average order will be for 12 sets. The entire cost of this option will be added to your firm's Sales Office expense in the current quarter.

4. Increase the space of your company's booth at the upcoming Home Electronics Trade Show in New York City's Javits Trade Center. Invite every retailer in all your markets to visit your "Hospitality Center" when they are at the trade show. The cost of this response will add $35,000 to your firm's Advertising expense for the quarter.

## Critical Incident 3   The New Automaton Technician

One of your brightest, up-and-coming younger workers is having some on-the-job problems. Consuelo Hernandez came to your company as a secretary right after graduating with a community college degree in secretarial science. She had real hands-on knowledge of every piece of equipment and all software associated with the modern business office. Consuelo quickly fitted in because of her cheerful personality and willingness to learn.

From the very start of her employment she had made it clear, but in a very nice manner, that she was ambitious and was willing to try anything that would promote her career and give her a well-rounded view of your firm's operations. Because of her skills and energy level, after three years Consuelo had grown beyond her job requirements but could not assume Executive Secretary or Office Manager status because very competent people with greater seniority already occupied those positions.

Rather than losing her to some other company, and because it was believed her knowledge of programmable software and practical computer savvy would transfer to the skill requirement side of an Automaton Technician's job, Consuelo was offered such a position. As you had expected, Consuelo gladly accepted the challenge, as it gave her exposure to the factory side of your operations, a totally new line of advancement, and a pay raise.

As Consuelo had done in your office, she quickly caught onto the job's requirements after going through a short technical training program conducted off-site by your Automaton manufacturer. *That* was not the problem. What *was* the problem were complaints she has brought to you about the hazing she was subjected to, much of it which was verbally and graphically sexually suggestive. When probed about the comments and cat-calls yelled out by line workers as she passed through the factory, Consuelo broke down crying and handed you a sheaf of crudely scrawled notes and cardboard signs that made all sorts of sexual propositions to her.

Before taking any action in this regard, you and your Plant Superintendent toured your Erie, Pennsylvania, factory to follow up on Consuelo's view of the situation. An inspection of the factory's walls and girder columns found them to be clean, freshly painted and free of graffiti. The walls and stalls in the men's toilet facilities, however, were covered with felt-tipped pornographic messages and pictures, a few of which listed Consuelo's home telephone number and a list of the "services" she would provide.

As your tour continued later in the day, the Plant Superintendent observed, "Boys will be boys," and said that the male line workers were just having a little fun to break up the monotony of their jobs. As far as he was concerned, they did not mean any harm and "Consuelo should learn how to take it." When asked what should be done about the situation your Superintendent replied, "Look, I can talk to the guys and tell them to knock it off. I don't know if it will do any good, though. She sort of causes the problem herself. You know, it's those tight T-shirts she wears. It's okay for guys to wear them in here because of all the heat, but for her to wear one . . . that's just asking for trouble. What I want to know from you is why did you have to put such a good-looking gal in here in the first place!"

Based on this information, what do you believe is your best course of action? You are aware of the recent U.S. Supreme Court ruling that employers must insure their general work environments are free of sexual harassment and that class action suits by the government are appropriate when such conditions are not being met in the victims' eyes. You are also aware that your female assembly-line workers, who make up about 25 percent of these workers, are following Consuelo's case with great interest.

RESPONSES:

1. Have your Plant Superintendent hold a meeting of all line workers to remind them that sexual comments, and the display of pornography, violate your company's standing policies intended to insure that a sexual harassment–free environment exists in all work spaces. This option, taken for one-half hour on company time, results in a nonsignificant cost to your firm.

2. Hold a mandatory three-part weekly series of workshops and plant conferences on sexual harassment. These one-hour meetings would be held on company time at the beginning of Wednesday's plant operations and would cost your Home Country plant. This would cost your company US$140,000 for training and estimated lost-productivity costs for the current quarter. The charge would be processed through your Miscellaneous account.

3. Advise Consuelo that you understand the pressure under which she has been placed. Caution her, however, that there are always "two sides to every story" and that she may be partially the cause of her trouble. Suggest to her that she be more circumspect about her attire in the factory and offer to return her to her former secretarial position. This action causes your firm no out-of-pocket expense.

4. Fire your Plant Superintendent as a demonstration "that you mean business" about sexual harassment and that he has failed to enforce your company's harassment-free policy. This response will cost your firm US$120,000 through your current quarter's Miscellaneous account for the "early retirement" of this superintendent.

## Critical Incident 4   How to Implement a Structural Change

"Look, we're going to have to change who pays these Warranty costs we're getting sooner or later, so I say let's do it now and get it over as fast as possible." With these words Tim Martinko, your company's Marketing Director, summarized how he would go about changing who is really responsible for minimizing Warranty work and their costs.

Almost the opposite tack was being suggested by your Operations Manager, Joe Graham, and your Quality Control Supervisor, David Hubanks. "It took a long time for this problem to develop, so it'll take a long time for it to be resolved," David observed. "I think we should go about this slowly, so everybody feels comfortable about what has to be done."

After much wrangling over who was accountable for the Warranty charges currently being absorbed by your Distribution Centers, the argument has finally come down to these polar positions. In its desire to be fast in its response to problems over defective sets, your company set up repair facilities as close to your customers as possible. It was felt this would be at the Distribution Center level as opposed to the Wholesaler level where control over repairs would be stronger. Once these repair facilities had been established in your Distribution Centers, it was logical to have the Centers pay for the Warranty repairs, as they were doing the work. Also, by having them bear these expenses, they would be encouraged to minimize these costs as much as possible.

Over the years, however, your Distribution Centers have started to feel they are bearing the brunt of having to fix TV's they think your plants should have made right in the first place. They also have reasoned that by having the Distribution Centers fix whatever is wrong with the sets, the plants have no incentive to minimize assembly errors.

So far no decision has been made about how to solve this problem. As the person in charge of implementing whatever change is ultimately decided upon, however, which of the following do you think would be the best course of action for you to take?

RESPONSES:

1. Rather than changing who pays for the Warranty repairs, take action to minimize any off-quality TVs coming out of your factories. Demonstrate to your Distribution Centers your good faith in this regard by guaranteeing that every plant's Quality Control program will be at the maximum level from this quarter forward. This response will cost your firm the price of the standard "C" Sample Size Quality Control Program in addition to the Quality Control Supervisor's regular US$10,000 quarterly salary.

2. Rather than changing who pays for the Warranty repairs, have all defective television sets shipped ExAir, for the fastest customer service possible, to their factories of origin. All shipping charges, inventory and handling charges, and Warranty repair costs will be borne by the factory involved and this procedure would continue for the remainder of the simulation.

3. Have each Distribution Center continue to repair all sets under Warranty, but have the repair charges paid by each factory of origin. This option merely switches who pays for the repairs. Accordingly, all Warranty repair costs would be charged to your firm's General Administration expense for the remainder of the game.

4. Delay determining who pays for the Warranty work costs for one quarter. Create a Warranty Work Task Force made of relevant personnel from your Distribution Centers, your Quality Control Department, and Line Supervisors. Their task would be to create in one quarter a mutually agreeable payment method, the only constraint being that the solution must result in optimal service to customers who have brought their sets in for repairs. It is assumed this option will not produce new out-of-pocket costs to your firm.

# Critical Incident 5   Ferdie Milano Fights Back

At the beginning of the 1999 selling year, Bill Fisher implemented his new "Market Share Gain Plan." This system rated sales reps on the market shares they produced in each of their sales areas. Many of the younger reps liked the system and reaped sizeable bonuses. Ferdinand ("Ferdie") Milano, however, was struggling. Once the district's top salesman, he was now ranked at the bottom, and this was vexing to both him and Bill Fisher. Ferdie was mad because he was no longer getting bonuses, and Bill was frustrated because he had spent many fruitless hours trying to turn Ferdie around.

Bill had made a number of dual calls with Ferdie and had worked with him on his sales presentations. He also mailed him technical literature describing advances in electronics technology and how those advances made the company's sets more competitive. Ferdie didn't respond well to these suggestions and said to others that he was "in Bill's doghouse" and might lose his job.

The breaking point between them came when Bill happened to be in Ferdie's Lawrenceville, N.J., neighborhood at about 9:30 a.m. on other business. As he drove by, he saw the company's grey car in the driveway even though all sales reps were supposed to be "on territory" by that time. Because he suspected something was wrong, and Ferdie had been submitting Territory Activity Reports showing he was making calls every morning by 8 a.m., Bill started to make regular check-ups. More often than not, the company car was in the driveway.

This was enough for Bill. Over coffee and donuts at their favorite diner on a Thursday morning, he handed Ferdie a dismissal notice effective immediately. Bill then followed Ferdie home where he told him to hand over the company car keys as well as the company's sales literature. Ferdie was broken-hearted and humiliated and stated in no uncertain terms that he "was not going to take this lying down" and that his "life had been ruined".

The Newark, N.J., law firm of McDuff & Rice has just served your company with notice that its client Ferdinand Milano is threatening a lawsuit. The terms of the settlement would be reinstatement of his position, three months' back wages and $750,000 for pain and suffering, the payment of all associated legal fees filed by McDuff & Rice, a written apology from Bill Fisher, and the revocation of your company's Market Share Gain Plan. If these terms were not met, McDuff & Rice would file on Milano's behalf a 13-count age discrimination complaint. Under N.J.S.A. 10:51-2(d), the New Jersey Law against Discrimination, it would be claimed that your company created a motivation system that was prejudiced against its senior sales representatives and that you fired Ferdie in retaliation for not accepting your firm's "Voluntary Enhanced Retirement Program" offered earlier in the year.

RESPONSES:

1. Settle out of court by accepting all of Ferdie Milano's terms. This option would cost your firm $771,450, which would appear as a Miscellaneous expense for the current quarter.

2. Negotiate with the law firm, assuming their terms are just "talking points." You can assume the negotiations would last six months, during which back wages would mount but Ferdie might ultimately settle for $350,000 and no job reinstatement. This amount would show as an expense of $350,000 for the present quarter.

3. Allow the lawsuit to go to a jury trial in the State of New Jersey. Your company lawyers believe they would win the case, based on Ferdie's lack of response to Bill's efforts to rehabilitate him and the fact that many sales reps have done well under the new bonus system. Should you lose the case, which your lawyers believe is unlikely, they believe a jury's award for this case might range from $1.5 to $2.5 million. An amount comparable to awards given for such cases would appear as an expense item in the current quarter's Miscellaneous account.

4. Launch a countersuit for $500,000 plus court costs against Ferdie Milano and the law firm of McDuff & Rice. In your lawsuit, you are claiming (a) the filing of inappropriate and exorbitant lawyers' fees by McDuff & Rice as part of the possible out-of-court settlement and (b) defamation of Bill Fisher's character by Ferdie in public statements he has made about his former boss and your company. If successful, this response would result in a net credit of $500,000 to your firm's Miscellaneous account in the current quarter.

# Critical Incident 6   "Hell No to This *Baksheesh* Stuff!"

You have recently sent Robert Frazier, one of your Country Liaison executives, around the world with your Operations Manager, Joseph Graham, to scout possible new plant locations. They are now summarizing for you their estimation of the prospects for building new plants overseas.

"As far as I can see, we have a large number of choices, especially in Asia, which is also closest to our Hong Kong supplier." Bob Frazier continued, "Our labor costs would be very low and the infrastructures available to us would be adequate for an assembly operation like ours."

"I have to agree with you on that," Joe Graham responded. "But I have a real problem with some other things, especially with the ethics some of those foreign businessmen showed me. And I thought it was even worse in the case of some of the government people we met."

"Well, you'll just have to get used to that . . . they've operated this way for years and that's how it's done over there." Bob leaned across the table to emphasize his point. "Even more, it's good to get on their good side, and a little bit of *baksheesh* can save you a whole lot of time and money in the long run."

This comment seemed to trigger an anger that had been boiling inside Joe all during the trip. "I don't care if you call it *blat, baksheesh*, or *grease*! It's all illegal, and I don't think we should have any part of it. It just galls me that we have to line the pocket of some puny little bureaucrat just to process some papers that he's supposed to do in the first place! I know there has to be a law somewhere against this."

On that note a rambling discussion ensued. It was pointed out that the U.S. Foreign Corrupt Practices Act of 1977 allows for personal payments to foreign government and company officials as gratuities for performing "nondiscretionary" services or engaging in activities that are appropriately within the scope of their job descriptions. In this case, a small payment is not illegal. It was pointed out, however, that problems arise over what are considered "small" versus "large" payments, and what are "nondiscretionary" versus "discretionary" actions or are actions outside the scope of the official's strict job duties.

Given that your company may eventually build a plant in a country where you will face this problem, what position do you think your company should take?

RESPONSES:

1. Avoid building any new plants in Asia, where the practice of *baksheesh* is widespread.

2. Avoid breaking any American laws by conducting all negotiations on plant sites in a "neutral" nation such as Liechtenstein, Vanuatu, the Netherlands Antilles, or the Cayman Islands, where such activities are not illegal or are not monitored closely. This option would add the equivalent of US$250,000 to the cost of constructing your next plant in either Taiwan or Thailand and would be amortized along with the original investment expense.

3. Be practical and follow the "rules of the road" and deal with the problem on a plant-by-plant and country-by-country basis. This response would cause your Miscellaneous account to be debited the equivalent of US$75,000 for each plant subsequently built in Thailand or Taiwan.

4. Hire local middlemen to represent your company in all negotiations with government officials and relevant businessmen. This option would add US$80,000 to the cost of building any APEC factory.

## Critical Incident 7    Jumping the Gun or Fast to Market?

After seeing all your company's R&D monies for the past three quarters being pumped into developing a new comb filter circuit for your TV sets, your Marketing Director, Helen Monroe, wants the feature installed in all new units starting next quarter. While the technology itself is proven, has worked exceptionally well in prototype sets, and would be a real, marketable breakthrough for your line of TVs, a few assembly-related problems exist. The circuit itself, while on a smaller board, must be protected from heat and therefore requires the tricky insertion of a heat shield next to the unit on the TV's chassis. Therein lies the heated argument that is going on between Helen and Joe Graham, your Operations Management Director.

Helen was summarizing her position for the group that had witnessed the debate. "I read in the *Wall Street Journal* that Japan's carmakers take only 26–30 months to take their cars from concept to production with Mazda doing it in only 21 months. In the United States we take 29 to 46 months. Gillette introduces its products on a two-year cycle instead of every three years as they did before . . . and because Bell Helicopter reduced its product-to-market time from 24 to 12 months it got a new $113.0 million contract for Army training helicopters. You know the early bird gets the worm. We can't sit on this feature even if we have a few little problems putting the set together. Let me propose this . . . We can 'up' our Quality Control budget to catch any sets that don't work, and we can rebate to our Distribution Centers the unit repair costs of any sets above the norm that come back for Warranty work. This way we'll beat the competition to market with something big and we've covered any assembly problems that might crop up."

Joe Graham responded, "I don't care what you read in the *Journal* or about getting worms. All that speed to market hasn't kept Mazda from losing money year after year and losing market share to boot. Rushing products to market is really dangerous to your firm's quality image. Remember IBM had to recall the Warp version of its OS/2 after it came out? And what about all the bugs in first release of Windows 95? I think we should wait another quarter to design some type of 'snap' assembly that combines the new comb filter circuit with the shield that is needed. Let's make haste slowly on this."

Given the need to get a payback on your R&D expenses, as well as the potential increases in sales that might accompany the introduction of your set's superior comb filter, which of the following alternatives do you want to implement?

RESPONSES:

1. Bring the product to market immediately. This option presents no out-of-pocket expenses to your firm.

2. Delay the introduction of the new feature for at least one quarter during which any actual assembly problems associated with the installation of the new comb filter are worked out completely. This option costs your firm $85,000 for production-related R&D, which is charged to your company's General Administration expense for one quarter.

3. Bring the product to market immediately, and also contract for a "C" Sample Size Quality Control Program, which would allow only 1.5 percent of all defective products to reach the market. The US$36,000 charge for a study of this size would be processed in the normal manner.

4. Bring the product to market immediately and budget a "C" Sample Size Quality Control Program, and also rebate to your Distribution Centers Warranty repair costs for half of all sets returned for the next two quarters.

## Critical Incident 8   Making Our Quality Circle Program Work

Your Quality Control Supervisor, David Hubanks, has just summarized for you the results of one quarter's worth of Quality Circle meetings he's held. "I think the ideas that have come out of these meetings are pretty good and I think we can implement some of them. Although I think we can get even more participation in the future, what's most important now is getting our line workers thinking 'quality' and involved in the quality process. Unfortunately, even though we've paid our line people to attend our Quality Circle meetings after work Wednesday, our attendance has been uneven, and I don't think we have much momentum going for us."

When you asked him if he had any ideas about getting momentum and better meeting attendance, Hubanks responded, "A simple solution would be to hold our meetings during regular factory working hours at full pay. They're already here and we wouldn't be infringing on their leisure time, kid pick-up obligations, and supper time. I think this solution would deal with the problem of getting good attendance. On the other hand, I don't think it gets to the core issue of getting our workers to want to do things better or to realize that we *have* to do better to be competitive in this business."

"Well, then," you responded, "what are your thoughts about dealing with that?"

David Hubanks then provided you with four ways to motivate your assembly line workers to get involved in a company-wide Total Quality Management program. Which one of the following would you select?

RESPONSES:

1. Conduct all future Quality Circle meetings on company time, thereby demonstrating that you are serious about quality. Have the first four meetings chaired by a motivational-type speaker from the Crosby College of Quality. This response would cost you US$20,000 for the speaker and an estimated US$180,000 in lost productivity. All expenses would be charged to your firm's Miscellaneous account.

2. Create a number of benchmarking groups who would visit other factories in the area using similar manufacturing and assembly techniques. These groups would report back in your Quality Circle meetings what they have discovered. This response would cost you US$65,000 for two quarters and would be part of your firm's Miscellaneous costs.

3. Have an independent consultant do a Survey Feedback study to determine what your factory workers feel about job satisfaction, their attitudes, performance, organizational climate, and the quality of work relationships. The consultant would use the information to stimulate discussions during Quality Circle meetings on company time about organizational problems while ultimately generating a plan for organizational change. This alternative would cost your company US$35,000 for one quarter for the consultant, over and above estimated lost productivity costs of US$180,000 to your Miscellaneous account for the rest of the simulation.

4. Demonstrate the need for change to your workers by bringing to your factory a panel of customers who have had repeated Warranty work problems with sets. Use this customer feedback to promote discussions during subsequent Quality Circle meetings on company time on the need for change and the need for customer satisfaction. This response would cost your company US$4,000 for one quarter, in addition to US$180,000 in lost productivity per quarter for the remaining quarters of the game. These expenses would be charged to your Miscellaneous account.

# Critical Incident 9   Getting a Better Grasp of the Market

Because your company's previous management group felt that international operations might be in its future, a well-regarded consulting firm had been retained to make recommendations as to how to go about "internationalizing" your company. The prime focus of their effort was to give your company, which has always had a strong domestic product structure, the ability to understand foreign markets.

The consulting firm's basic recommendation was to create an International Division, which would consolidate in one unit the Country Liaison executives now part of your company's General Administration expense. By housing these executives together, it was reasoned, they could more easily share general information while retaining the unique knowledge they possess about their particular country's business practices and culture. They would also be given new power to influence product development priorities within your firm's R&D operation. The new International Division would be headed by a vice president who would report directly to your company's CEO and would have veto power over international capital appropriations and the rationing of television sets between domestic customers and any offshore operations.

Given that your company might create an International Division, four ways have been suggested to increase its internal effectiveness after it has been created. Each one has its pros and cons.

RESPONSES:

1. Have the division grow in influence by doubling the number of liaison specialists per country. This decision will add to your General Administration expense the equivalent of US$25,000 per quarter for each offshore Country/Market for the rest of the simulation.

2. Increase the division's influence by stationing your country specialists in the R&D Department, with a dual reporting relationship to the heads of the R&D Department and the International Division. This decision does not result in an out-of-pocket cost to your company.

3. Increase the division's influence by stationing your country specialists in the Marketing Department, with a dual reporting relationship to the heads of the Marketing Department and the International Division. This decision does not result in an out-of-pocket cost to your company.

4. Create cross-functional marketing and product development teams with it being mandatory that your Country Liaison Specialists serve on those teams. Because of the time involved with these activities, one additional Country Liaison executive would have to be hired at the equivalent of US$25,000 per quarter. This expense would be added to your General Administration expense.

# Critical Incident 10   "Are Our TVs Really Global?"

The discussion about how to advertise your television sets overseas between your Marketing Director, Helen Monroe, and one of your Country Liaison executives, Corinna del Greco, was getting heated.

Helen, trying to drive home her essential arguments, explained, "We're competing in a global industry. That basically means the same TV set can be sold around the world regardless of the country's nature. If you agree with me on that point it means we should have a standard logotype and a universal advertising campaign for all our sets. Nowadays all TV sets are like commodities. They're basically the same on the outside and fundamentally the same inside. If there *is* a difference between the various brands, most consumers wouldn't know the difference or don't care to know. Even more important for us, we grind our TVs out like cookies, which drives down their costs because of the economies of scale we get by doing this. We should apply the same principle to our advertising campaign. By using the same ad campaign over and over again from country to country, we get our own economies of scale."

Corinna replied a bit more coolly but just as emphatically, "Are our TVs really as global as you seem to think they are? The TVs might be the same but the world's markets aren't that simple. These might all be the same sets, but they mean different things to those living in different countries. Also, some features that are important in one country are not that important in other countries. For example, the remote controls that are so important to German and American consumers are not that important to those in Taiwan and Thailand. In fact, for those in Taiwan and Thailand a remote control is a liability, because it's expensive to replace their batteries all the time.

I urge you to reconsider your position and let me help you design ad campaigns and themes that are uniquely identified with the needs of each of the foreign markets we hope to enter."

On that note, a number of graduated alternatives were jointly developed by Helen and Corinna over the next few weeks. Choose one of the following from the set they have presented to you.

RESPONSES:

1. Follow Helen's basic idea and use the same advertising theme in all markets. This suggestion entails a one-time advertising design cost of US$25,000, which is processed through your firm's Miscellaneous account this quarter.

2. Create an advertising program that emphasizes the same logotype in all advertisements, with slight variations in pictorial layouts and body copy from country to country. This alternative entails a one-time advertising design cost of US$25,000, processed through your firm's Miscellaneous account this quarter plus an additional US$4,000 charge for the number of foreign countries your Game Administrator has allowed your firm to consider for entry.

3. Develop an advertising program that employs a basic image and logotype but is differentiated by the major markets of NAFTA, EC, and ASEAN. This response costs your company US$25,000 for creating the campaign's basic image and logotype and US$7,000 for each of the major markets your Game Administrator has allowed your firm to consider for entry.

4. Follow Corinna's basic idea and create a different advertising theme for each market based on consumer research conducted in each country. This suggestion costs your company, for each country where your products are sold, the equivalent of US$7,000 for a consumer research study and an amount equal to US$25,000 for each unique advertisement required. A total charge of US$32,000 will be processed for each country currently being commercialized in the current quarter with the same amount being charged whenever a new country is entered.

## Appendix F: Patent Licensing Sale and Transfer Agreement

TO:   GBG Game Administrator

FROM:   Firm _____

SUBJECT:   Patent Licensing Sale and Transfer Agreement

DATE:   _____

Our company would like to inform you that an agreement has been reached between our firm and Firm _____ to transfer our new patent to them beginning in Quarter _____, 19 _____, for the sum of $_____. The following are each company's authorized signatories to this contract, with a summary of the terms we have agreed upon.

_____
(For the "Selling" firm)

_____
(For the "Purchasing" firm)

Implementation Date:

Quarter _____

Year 19 _____

Cash Value:

$_____

Game Administrator Approval:

_____

**Appendix G: Automaton Sale and Transfer Agreement**

TO:    GBG Game Administrator

FROM:    Firm _____

SUBJECT:    Automaton Sale and Transfer Agreement

DATE:    _____


Our company would like to inform you that an agreement has been reached between our firm and Firm _____ to transfer a quantity of automatons to them in Quarter _____, 19 _____, for the total sum of $_____. The following are each company's authorized signatories to this contract, with a summary of the terms we have agreed upon.


_____
(For the "Selling" firm)


_____
(For the "Purchasing" firm)


Transferals

Country _____ Auto1s _____ Auto2s _____

Country _____ Auto1s _____ Auto2s _____

Country _____ Auto1s _____ Auto2s _____

Country _____ Auto1s _____ Auto2s _____


Implementation Date:

Quarter _____

Year 19 _____


Total Cash Value:

$_____

Game Administrator Approval:

_____

## Appendix H: Product Sale and Transfer Agreement

TO:    GBG Game Administrator

FROM:    Firm _____

SUBJECT:    Automaton Sale and Transfer Agreement

DATE:    _____

Our company would like to inform you that an agreement has been reached between our firm and Firm _____ to transfer to them a quantity of our television sets with a Quality Grade Level at or above _____ in Quarter _____, 19 _____, for the total sum of $_____. The following are each company's authorized signatories to this contract, with a summary of the terms we have agreed upon.

_____
(For the "Selling" firm)

_____
(For the "Purchasing" firm)

Transfers

Country _____ 25" sets _____ 27" sets _____

Country _____ 25" sets _____ 27" sets _____

Country _____ 25" sets _____ 27" sets _____

Country _____ 25" sets _____ 27" sets _____

Minimum Quality Grade Level: _____

Implementation Date:

Quarter _____

Year 19 _____

Total Cash Value:

$ _____

Game Administrator Approval:

_____

**Appendix I: Private Brand Bid**

TO:    GBG Game Administrator

FROM:    Firm _____

SUBJECT:    Private Brand Bid

DATE: _____

We would like to inform you that we would like to respond to Home Electronics King's bid solicitation for television sets to arrive at their distribution centers in Quarter _____ , 19 _____ . The following summarizes the unit price, quantity and set sizes that we would like to offer at or above Quality Grade Level specified in the retailer's solicitation.

_____
(For the "Selling" firm)

Offer

Country _____ :

    Quantity 25" sets _____ Unit price _____

    Quantity 27" sets _____ Unit price _____

Country _____ :

    Quantity 25" sets _____ Unit price _____

    Quantity 27" sets _____ Unit price _____

Country _____ :

    Quantity 25" sets _____ Unit price _____

    Quantity 27" sets _____ Unit price _____

Implementation Date:

Quarter _____

Year 19 _____

Game Administrator Approval:

_____

**Appendix J: Game Debriefing Form**

Industry: _____

Firm: _____


Please complete the following form to help you gain additional insight into the strategic management issues with which you were involved when you played the *Global Management Game.* Your instructor or Game Administrator may use this form to conduct a class discussion of the business game.

A.  As a group, write a short statement as to the goals and Grand Strategy your company pursued in the simulation. Do this without looking at any of the materials you created for your management team when you began the game.

_____

_____

_____

_____

_____


B.  Now look back at your company's original goals and Grand Strategy. Did they change over the course of the game? Why or why not?

_____

_____

_____

_____

_____


C.  Characterize the organization structure your company actually used on a day-by-day decision-making basis. What were the pros and cons of the organization structure you used?

Pros: _____

_____

_____

_____

Cons: _____

_____

_____

_____

**Appendix J: Game Debriefing Form (continued)**

D. From your experience with the *Global Business Game,* what do you believe are the Key Success Factors for a firm in your simulated industry? What hints for success would you pass on to anyone who played this game in the future—or what specific behaviors do you think they should avoid?

_____

_____

_____

_____

_____

Key Success Factors:

_____

_____

_____

_____

_____

E. Assuming another group of students will take over your company soon, review your firm's original Mission Statement and revise it if necessary, based on your experience with the game and the nature of the competitive forces at work in your particular industry.

End-Game Mission Statement

_____

_____

_____

_____

_____

_____